YOU HAD TO BE THERE

An Odyssey Through Noughties London,
One Night at a Time

———

JODIE HARSH

faber

First published in 2025
by Faber & Faber Limited
The Bindery, 51 Hatton Garden
London ECIN 8HN

Typeset by Sam Matthews
Printed and bound in the UK by CPI Group (UK) Ltd, Croydon CRO 4YY

A CIP record for this book
is available from the British Library

ISBN 978-0-571-39241-4

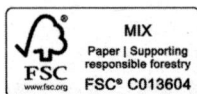

MIX
Paper | Supporting
responsible forestry
FSC
www.fsc.org
FSC® C013604

Printed and bound in the UK on FSC® certified paper in line with our continuing
commitment to ethical business practices, sustainability and the environment.
For further information see faber.co.uk/environmental-policy

Our authorised representative in the EU for product safety is
Easy Access System Europe, Mustamäe tee 50, 10621 Tallinn, Estonia
gpsr.requests@easproject.com

2 4 6 8 10 9 7 5 3 1

This book is dedicated to
those who danced before me,
those who dance with me,
and those who are yet to dance.

CONTENTS

CONTENTS

PRE-PARTY

F or a decade, I barely slept. I frantically jumped from club to club in a London that is lost, but not forgotten. At fifteen years old I discovered the dance floor, and I never left.

Every night of the week, a subterranean escapade awaited. The lights were low, the music was loud, and there was no weather or bad news.

These places gave me and my friends somewhere to unite and let go in a wash of lasers, sound and motion. Whether it was a run-down warehouse, a railway arch, a bougie discotheque or a Soho sleaze pit, important things happened to us.

We shared pleasure. We felt something.

From sunset to sunrise, and beyond, we never stopped. Even when the music did.

————

In the fabled noughties, London was an extraordinary place. But there's always been magic in its clubs. Throughout every decade you'll find hidden rooms that were catalysts of change, incubators of culture, focal points for collectiveness. The time-travelling spell of a tune can bring you right back there, to the dance floor.

Something special happened in this era. Scenes collided, exploded, were reborn and reshaped, *all across town*, at rapid speed. New music, new fashion, new art . . . it all came together in a mad heady rush before a huge crash. Every corner of the city was a messy, beating, slick and sordid stew of adventure.

I ran across cultural gulfs and club scenes. I became intimate with pop stars, heiresses and hustlers. We had something very precious, and I want to share it. I want to immortalise the hot flames that burned brightly and fizzled out, and I want to show that often, behind the worst stories, were the very best people.

You see *everything* at parties. And I was an expert at watching. The most interesting things happen when people think they can't be seen; the raw truth of people doing *exactly* what they want, under the cloak of twilight. That is, essentially, what a nightclub is for.

The further away I travel from that time, the more I realise how special it was. A quick flash of absolute excess. The rules didn't exist in the way we had been told they did. Whenever those of us who lived through it see each other now, we talk about a particular place, or the wildest person, the strangest evening. We remember the people we've lost along the way.

So, come with me, to the clubs that wove through London. These little islands shaped my life; and in some ways, they saved my life. I want us to go dancing in them one last time.

It's easy to forget the beginning of a story, especially when you've tumbled into so many basements and been under the influence of so many sense-altering substances. But I remember it all. Well, most of it.

This is my story, my decade in clubland.

1

THE ASTORIA

There's always a first night. The moment you drop into a mess of lights, movement and bodies, while all around you the world sleeps. You fall in love, connect, disappear into pure feeling. Immediately, I became intoxicated by the dance floor, never to look back. At times it was something of a solace, all those flashing beams cutting through the blackness. At others it was a darker place, one that sucked me in as the strobes and smoke blinded me.

So, let's start from the beginning. They say you always remember your first, and mine was at the Astoria in 2001.

On Saturday, I arrived in London and armed myself with an excellent fake ID forged by the artisans of Oxford Street. For five pounds, this piece of laminated card became my access to possibilities, a photoshopped pass to the promised land.

From there I headed a few streets down into Soho, trundling around bars with rainbow flags strung outside, entering any that would let me in. I wore a pair of sunglasses big enough to conceal my youth, a crop top spelling out the word BITCH in diamanté, and enough pimple-concealing foundation to tarmac a road. I wandered the streets nomadically. I soaked it all in forensically. I discovered a discarded whistle on the toilet floor at the Village. It glowed in the dark, and I claimed it as my own.

This is pre-Jodie Harsh, pre-DJ, pre-anything. It's just J, a little gay boy from Canterbury stepping into the big city alone for the first time. Anticipation churned in my tummy; I was nervous at the unknown. A lump formed in my throat, dreading interactions I'd have to navigate if I made it on to a dance floor at all.

By the evening, I was clamped to a new ensemble. We'd bonded on some shallow level outside a nearby Soho bar called Manto's, connected for life by a cigarette lighter and the hopeful promise of getting into a club with our fake ID. I cannot for the life of me recall anyone's names now; they were so fair-weather I can barely remember their faces. But I can remember feeling they connected me to something I'd been lacking – a sense of community, a clear message of 'you belong here'. London drew kids like me from the towns and villages of isolation that lay beyond it, like some great migration, enticing us with the thought that we might not be alone.

Promises kept, we marched up Charing Cross Road to the London Astoria, the venue that hosted a world-famous weekly party. My new comrades had breathlessly told me about it within minutes of meeting. The club night, G-A-Y, was *full of people like us*. The Astoria was about to become the Eden that housed everything, and everyone, that mattered to me.

I didn't know any of that at the time, of course. I was just pulled along on a whisper and a prayer. We were waifs and strays, looking for a place to feel seen and express our sexuality, a place to be free and dance. Our dads were miles away at home, tutting when adverts for *Queer as Folk* came on the telly, passing unfriendly comment at Stephen Gately being dragged out of the closet on to the front pages, telling us to man up and 'stop acting like a poof'. Homophobia, transphobia and the fear of AIDS rippled through so many homes in the country.

The West End streets offered a refuge. They were literally paved with rainbows – colourful printed flyers advertising the evening's celebrations were handed out by twinks and discarded en route.

THIS SATURDAY: G-A-Y . . . GOOD AS YOU. The club blasted its siren call and, oh, was I ready to respond . . .

And there it was: the Astoria. It stood four storeys tall, an imposing white facade like some American temple. Silver barricades separated the passer-by from the entrance – and me from my dreams. Behind that door was the unknown. Behind that door was adulthood.

I clutched the fake ID tight, repeating my newly invented date of birth in my head as if writing lines in detention. A false backstory memorised, a new life within reach. And then . . .

We got in. Relief. I was a tenner lighter, my pocket half-empty but my hopes filled. As we climbed the foyer's sweeping staircase, I stared at the stamp on my wrist – *G-A-Y* was branded on to my skin. I smiled, knowing I'd been recognised and accepted, if only by Dolly Rocket, the voluptuous woman in drag whose job it was to welcome me and the 1,999 other people attending that night. The mission of scrubbing this ink off my wrist before I arrived home in Kent was still a whole twelve-hour problem away.

At the top of the stairs a set of double doors opened, and a thick, cloying scent hit me like a backhander. Marlboro Lights, poppers, body odour, stale beer, toilet bleach and Jean Paul Gaultier Le Male mixed together like some kind of celebratory birthday cake, one that tasted so buttery, so appealing and so . . . *moreish*. If you could bottle this up and sell it as a scented candle, you could transport tired millennials right back there. You'd make a fortune.

I took in the panorama. It was a room of colossal height, like Canterbury Cathedral, where I was forced to endure long Christmas carol concerts and fables of Jesus. But this place was different – it was filled with *people like me*. There was dancing, and there was kissing. It was airless, furnace-hot; a baptism of fire. Everyone's skin glistened with a film of shimmery sweat. Serotonin flushed into my brain, and my eyes widened. The room felt limitless.

There was an energy in the building that was fresh to my palate. It tasted like unadulterated freedom, a spirit of adventure, and sex . . . dangerous sex.

There were bars along the circumference that sold cheap drinks, and the theatre-like space in the middle was packed, moving as if a single organism. I stood soaking it up from the Outer Hebrides of the room, self-conscious but ready to join the throng and be absorbed into the cavernous, sexy pit of joy. Like a jolt of electric charge, the trance banger 'Who Do You Love Now?' by Dannii Minogue blasted from the giant wall-mounted speakers. I knew the routine – I'd videoed her performance of it on *CD:UK* – and I had just about enough Smirnoff Ice inside me to hit the floor and show it off. Fresh meat, baby – all eyes on me.

My new group of friends loved drugs. Couldn't get enough. I'd never tried anything more than a couple of tokes on a spliff at the park behind school. But, on a night of change and newness, I was easily persuaded, and accepted an offer of a pill. It wasn't quite white, and it was slightly bigger than an aspirin. I took half.

This being the first time I'd enhanced my brain with high levels of mind-altering chemicals, I was beyond nervous. I carried my father's adventurous streak, which often curdled with my mother's neurotic worry. A constant battle.

Instantly, as I swallowed the tablet, a vision of being buried by my grieving family in my BITCH top after a tragic death on the dance floor filled me with pre-emptive regret. I washed the pill down with a glug of tepid Bacardi Breezer and puffed furiously on a cigarette.

The chemicals were in me, working their way through my system.

I blinked and I was stuck in the tar of the packed dance floor: I submitted to its grip. My little spot felt private and intimate, despite it being among thousands of bodies. My motions were restricted, but I felt free.

The club would book all sorts of live music to entertain the crowd at exactly 1.30 a.m. every Saturday night – it was the thing they were famous for. Sometimes it would be a pop star creating a viral moment ready to have splattered over the Monday-morning press, like Geri Halliwell writhing around on stage in a sea of naked dancers, or a boy band like A1 making their all-important gay-club stop on a promotional tour. Sometimes it would be an eighties act singing their Stock Aitken Waterman classics – a Rick Astley or a Bananarama. Back in the nineties, when the club night first began, the Spice Girls and Take That had made their live debuts here. Occasionally there'd be a global music icon – Kylie in the flesh, for example. As she lit my cigarette, a nameless new friend gushed through a story where Mariah Carey wafted through the dance floor, carried on a chaise longue by shirtless men, and pointed out the exact place she had emerged. G-A-Y had mastered the passion and promo balance of live shows, launching some careers into the stratosphere and giving others a late-stage flourish.

The main focus, though, was on the wild gratification of the audience, who blew their shrieking whistles in the direction of the stage. Because of its unrepentant pop pleasure, G-A-Y became a gateway club for so many queer people, the starting line for a noc-turnal journey. It was also a cheap night out in every sense – a spirit-and-mixer combo would only set you back a couple of quid. It was seeing the pop stars that soundtracked our lives that turned this place into sticky flypaper for people like me. And there I was, on my first ever proper night out – bar the school disco – ecstatically and apprehensively awaiting the arrival of both my E high and kitsch pop band Vengaboys.

I felt . . . nothing. The pill hadn't really had any effect. I was a little woozy perhaps, but that was surely just the alcohol and sugar in the four bottles of Smirnoff Ice I'd consumed before arriving at the Astoria. The opening strains of 'Better the Devil You Know' by Kylie rang out, and balloons fell from the sky, a rainstorm of popping pink rubber. The vibration of delight swelled. One of my new friends shouted in my ear, explaining this happened every week at twelve thirty. That exact song, enhanced by the bursting of said balloons and blowing of whistles, signalled one hour until showtime. *So much to take in.*

A voice of God announced that we were sixty minutes from the big live performance. Tensions ran high, but my brain didn't. I asked for another half a pill, suddenly full of bravado. *I'm clearly a tank,* I thought. *Or perhaps it had been a placebo.* I gobbled back the second half, inserted a communal Vicks inhaler into my nose to help initiate the climb, and continued singing along to Kylie.

Within minutes I was dancing, grinding, perspiring. I felt the rub of bodies, the intimacy of strangers, the love of humans I barely knew yet. I fumbled for my whistle and held it in my mouth, my teeth chattering, my loose clench dropping it back to my chest repeatedly.

Up, up, up.

Lights down. Showtime. A cheer erupted. Was I going to faint, or fly up to the ceiling, or both? Fuck. A cowboy, a sailor and their two girl pals appeared on stage under four spotlights like a modern-day Village People. My eyes couldn't focus – they rolled back in their sockets until I caught it happening and blinked it away. My pulse was spiking at a rapid 150 beats per minute. My skin felt like liquid.

'Whoa . . . It's hit me,' I mumbled, as I tried to grasp a reality outside of my own little world. Someone I didn't know asked if I was OK – 'You're as white as a sheet,' he said. But I'd never felt better. My jaw was literally vibrating, which was an alien sensation. I spun on the tightly cramped spot as if I was being sucked into a whirlpool, and as my rotation slowed, my new friends were nowhere to be seen. That should have felt like a bad omen, but I was unbothered. Alone on the dance floor, I was enveloped in the rush. Red and purple lights kissed the heads in front of me, sweaty necks glittered in the flashes. As cheesy as it sounds, in that room of strangers, we were one.

The Vengaboys launched into a huge chorus of those iconic lines 'The Vengabus is coming . . . and everybody's jumping' as euphoria engulfed my entire body, from my toes up to the very end of each hair on my head. The intense currents racing through me felt almost too much for a mere human being to handle. My feet felt like they were lifting off the floor. It was as though I were floating a metre above everyone else. I was taller. I was ascending.

Without wishing to sound snobbish, the Vengaboys hadn't exactly been my taste in music, previously. I'd been listening to Fatboy Slim and Ministry of Sound CDs at home in the lead-up to my admission into club world – but this night and this pill opened a door into a new appreciation of pop music. In my absolute highest moment, as the four performers continued to lip-sync along, I could have sworn my eardrums had actual orgasms. The Vengabus drove through me like the most heavenly chariot. God had reversed into the Astoria to take me to heaven. Every colour appeared brighter, every person in the room was a beautiful angel. Every sound was a present. I was high as fuck. I loved this feeling.

At cruising altitude, I ventured off on a solo wander around my new nirvana. In between the dance floor and balcony was the Keith Moon Bar, a run-down art deco space, with murals on the wall. The mixture of interior design cues was what really gave the Astoria its, let's say, charm: it was a patchwork of visual personalities, and looking back, a bit of an aesthetic mess. But to me, that night, it was a paradise.

Into the toilet. 'This place will be gone soon,' I overheard at the urinal. 'The Crossrail thing is happening, this'll be the first building to get bulldozed,' said the man to his mate as I tried to wee. An ominous warning, and not the last time a sacred space would be under threat of being taken away from us in this ever-evolving city. Change is something you have to get used to in London. Many more playgrounds were to disappear during my decade of decadence. That is the way things work here – places are born and places die, much like the people in them. But I didn't know that yet.

I'd never kissed a boy before, but that night I kissed several. They were encounters that no longer mattered moments after they happened, and now I was kissing another guy by the metallic trough, serenaded by the song of the automatic hand drier. The icy tang of the man's Airwave gum barely concealed his club breath, but I relished his physical, adult connection. My eyes remained open as we locked lips. A name would have been pointless, because there would be more.

Fuck, I was young. Somewhere between fifteen and sixteen years old. Looking back, I can't believe I managed to sneak in that night, considering how tough the Astoria security could be. In retrospect, I was living beyond my years, but I didn't see anything wrong with it back then – my girl pals at school all said they were getting fingered behind the science block at lunchtime. This was *my* personal journey of discovery.

Deep into my ecstasy trip, I was experiencing what's called 'pilly willy' so there wasn't too much action happening other than a snog. 'I'm nineteen,' I lied, 'studying at uni.' In truth, I was a child, but I didn't feel like one. This was no longer playtime.

Alone, I explored the Astoria's steeply tiered dress circle, a memento from its life as a cinema in the 1920s. The tilted floor was sticky, as if covered in treacle. It was littered with discarded plastic cups, making the ascent seem more mission-like during my ecstasy melt. The reward for reaching its summit was an array of dark corners, little cubbyholes of privacy kept intimate by the shun of the disco lights. Near 4 a.m., I reconvened with my friends up there. We swapped stories about what we'd seen, who we'd met.

Before long, I came down with a thud. Holy fuck. I glanced out over the room feeling like Pinocchio at Pleasure Island, my dehydrated brain insisting it was time to leave this sinister place. Faces started to morph vividly, and I couldn't comprehend the half-sentences tumbling out of my friends' mouths. *Get me off this balcony. Get me out of here.*

Heading towards the exit, we were handed a flyer that told us to expect Sophie Ellis-Bextor next Saturday, singing her new song,

'Murder on the Dancefloor'. These were the days of hunting down little printed creations to find out what was happening next in clubland. I'd take the flyers home and keep them under my bed, sneaking looks at them every evening as the school week slowly dragged along.

The light pollution of Charing Cross Road hit hard, and I could no longer feel the hug of a sub-bass or protective blanket of dark space. We'd stayed at the Astoria until the cusp of the bitter end – just us, some stragglers, the slow-moving bar staff and the poised cleaners. Paranoia hit as a security guard eyed me up – *Does he know I'm underage?* I needed to be allowed to return. I belonged there. My eyes darted away, my head down, securing my shades back on to my face, out into the unstirred air.

I was still so high that Soho felt radioactive. Dawn was threatening to crack open and the sky's inkiness began to dilute. The streets were empty aside from the troublemakers and the all-nighters and the binmen. To this day the sound of a truck collecting bottles from a bar sends me to the edge, that shrill fast rattle of glass as I'm coming down. Must be PTSD.

We walked like pirates of the night under the Pillars of Hercules Pub, which formed a rave tunnel and connected Manette Street to Greek Street. Over on Bateman Street, a scraggly fox ravaged the remnants of a kebab from an overflowing bin bag, first ignoring our approaching rowdiness, then turning to smile. Was I hallucinating? A huge rat the size of a terrier scuttled past, ignoring both us and the fox. Like them, we were part of nocturnal nature in this technicoloured square mile now.

Soho was still seedy, dangerous and illicit. Sex shops, brothels, massage parlours and clubs sold encounters, simulated or otherwise.

And I loved it. I'd wanted to be a part of its sleazy grasp since I walked through it with my family on the way to a West End show at the Palladium. I was twelve – their eyes averted from the neon signs of sex and sin, mine drawn to them. A more recent outing to SegaWorld at the Trocadero was almost too much of a tease. Amid the beeping noises and flashing lights, I shot lasers with my dad and sister, and I could feel Soho edging towards me beyond the boundary of Shaftesbury Avenue. That night, from the containment of the child-friendly Rainforest Cafe windows, I could see apparitions of red light from the Windmill and make out signs saying GIRLS GIRLS GIRLS. I was so close, I could smell it. And now, I'd stepped over the threshold.

————

At 5 a.m. we arrived at Old Compton Street, the nerve centre of the Soho scene. By that hour, it was hardly London's most dignified thoroughfare. Compton Cafe was a twenty-four-hour meeting point for the post-clubbers, the homeless, the sex workers and the minicab drivers. It was a shelter as the night wound down, or a pit stop as it continued. This was Soho before it was truly cleaned up and turned into a giant Pret A Manger. We entered with a flourish, and, under the harsh strip lighting, I immediately recognised some faces from the dance floor earlier.

My new tongue piercing was playing my teeth like an instrument in an uncontrollable response to the bump of speed I'd inhaled behind a parked lorry on Soho Square. My skin felt clammy all over as the E worked its way out of my pores. A lukewarm tea burned the inside of my mouth, which I'd well and truly chewed to blisters in my ecstasy trip. A BLT of cardboard consistency was shared between us to secure the indoor table, squeezed next to the slimmest set of stairs in London, which led to a single toilet cubicle and sink.

I had a long journey ahead of me to get back home. If all went to plan, I figured I'd be able to come right down from these drugs and sober up in time to walk through the front door, deflecting questions about where I'd been all night. I garbled a goodbye to my new friends, tossing departing *love yous* about with little depth or meaning, making vague plans to do it again the following weekend. I'd see them several more times, before I found other people who would travel with me through different chapters of my story.

Like the club spaces I fell in love with, friends would also represent a feeling of home. Some would come to stay longer, and others would leave early.

Time crawled slowly as I relocated to Easy Everything, the behemoth internet cafe next to Victoria Station, where rows of computers lined up like soldiers. One pound got me an hour of surfing, another got me an unenthusiastic cup of dirt-water spat from a self-service coffee machine. It was enough to sustain me until the first train home to Canterbury – an 8 a.m. departure. I dreaded the thought of a sneaky rail replacement bus service that could often be sprung on ravers. Engineering works could play havoc with a comedown.

I checked MSN Messenger: none of my friends appeared to be online. Funny, that. I set up an account on Faceparty, some website I'd heard about where you could make new connections and message with people. Boring. I logged into my Gaydar account and chatted to some random guys looking to hook up. I could barely read the messages. My eyes were like saucers, a shell-shocked look across my face in the overhead mirror, my senses well and truly thrown through the wringer. I'd run out of credit and didn't have enough cash left for a £5 Orange phone top-up card, my only possession of value being the train ticket home. But I didn't care. I'd been shown a brand-new world. It felt like I'd been hit by a Tube train but, as I continued to learn, the dildo of consequences rarely arrives lubed.

That night marked the very start of my secret weekends, which quickly became my entire reason to live. Episode one of the soap opera of my life had begun. I'd found my new place of worship, London. Its clubs would become my churches. I was obsessed with the idea of going back there. *You won't be able to keep me away,* I thought.

I'd been told what I was since the primary-school playground – the gay was always shining out of me, the weight of secret queerness burdening my shoulders under the shadow of Section 28. Finally, I was safe to embrace it and fully own it in my own way, with thousands of other people who were like me. Thousands of people who wanted to dance. *Just like me.*

———

A couple of weeks went by, which felt like for ever. I returned for round two. Same train, same places, same faces. We snuck into the KU Bar on Charing Cross Road, where pitchers of Sex on the Beach sold for £5 and Steps played on the speakers. We performed the dance routines at our high-top tables – I knew every move, and we really thought we were 'it'. Each new twink that walked through the door was judged. 'Who's *she*?' Only recently, that would have been me. From the bar, we marched on our path to the Astoria, pounding the pavement brazenly, pills and poppers deep in our pockets, discount wristbands sourced and secured. We were there to dance to sticky pop remixes, until we were thrown back out into the abandoned cityscape.

That Saturday though, my new world was taken away from me, my new lifeline cut short.

There was no live entertainment this time around – presumably all the pop stars were having a weekend off. Instead, it was Slag Tags night, and the club was to become a giant game. Each person would be given a sticker to wear with a number on, and if someone was into you, they'd leave a message on a big noticeboard on the stage that everyone would check. '107, you're cute, can I buy you a drink?', for example. It sounded fun – I couldn't wait to play.

We arrived at the Astoria so close to opening time, we were virtually licking the locks. Under the brutal glare of Centre Point, a problem arose immediately. 'Got any ID?' challenged the bouncer, standing in front of me like an enemy combatant, threatening my journey onwards. I handed him the trusted piece of plastic with the grainy picture of me that I'd paid a few quid for.

'This won't work – got a driver's licence?' The reality was, I wasn't old enough to sit behind a wheel let alone be let in. *Entry: denied.* 'But my flatmate is inside with our door keys,' I pleaded, unconvincingly. 'I really need to get in.' There was no negotiating, and I was going beetroot. The hostile doorman chuckled, and turned away, casting a shadow of doom across my fifteen-year-old face. The gig was up. I was left standing with the sizzling hot-dog vendors outside, my dreams broken.

Just for a moment, I felt stubbed out like a cigarette. But luckily, my new friends were loyal and stuck with me. Plan B.

We found ourselves back at some guy's house down the road, a friend of a friend of a friend. He was in his thirties with a good job in marketing and a pad in the West End – the dream! I was handed a glass of champagne on arrival – I'd never tried it before. *So fancy*, I thought, wincing at its dry, metallic aftertaste.

I was still a few months away from turning sixteen, but I continued to twist the truth and claimed to be nineteen . . . twenty . . . My story wouldn't stay straight, but I remained in character. There was a pile of drugs on the table, and there was house music on the stereo. 'Where are you from?' someone asked. 'London,' I said, untruthfully. I was fearless, naive, delighted, method acting.

The new plan was to go to Trade, an after-hours club that opened early on Sunday mornings and went right on through. Its venue, Turnmills, crouched in the heart of Clerkenwell, which was conveniently a ghost town at the weekends, and therefore kept the club away from prying eyes.

'That place has had its day,' protested one jaded queen as we trailed the men out of the flat and loaded into a cab, squashed together for the short journey through Holborn. Turnmills could have been any other office building, until you saw the snake of bare-limbed bodies queuing outside. It didn't look like it was past its prime to me. As I walked into the subterranean space and felt the pulsating throb of house music, my body ascended once again. Vengaboys this was not.

Upstairs on the ground floor was a Gaudí-inspired coffee shop, all gothic features and exposed industrial pipes. There was a corner table we claimed as our own, a place to gossip once we lost the older guys we'd arrived with, never to be seen again. We passed little bags of pills and powders to each other underneath it. The cafe actually served cakes and breakfast, and presumably helped the club maintain its daytime licence, but we wouldn't order anything – just repeatedly asked for tap water.

While the music at G-A-Y was catchy and shiny, the music at Trade was strictly four-to-the-floor. In the main room there was hard house, a little too banging for me, but down through 'muscle alley' you'd be drawn in to 'Trade Lite', where the soundtrack took a more soulful turn. There you'd be serenaded by diva vocals to take you to church while other people went to *actual* church down the road.

Where you hung out in that club said a lot about you – a personality test, if you will. I spent most of the morning in Trade Lite. The music had more of a groove in there, and I was attracted to its rhythmical patterns much more than the thump of the hard house next door. I heard 'Right On, Right On' by Silicone Soul for the first time, and Frankie Knuckles, Ultra Naté and Louie Vega. Their lush, layered productions wrapped around me like a duvet. I heard Chicago house and Detroit techno. It was a history lesson in the Black, Latin and queer roots of house music. I soaked it all up and I danced, breaking only to enjoy an occasional commitment-free dalliance in an underlit corner.

God, I loved that blissful Saturday night, that Sunday morning. There were lasers, Smokin Jo was DJing, the sound system was great, the floor was packed and I was, without doubt, the youngest person in the building.

I'd managed to slip, once again, through the net into a secret, unusual world. I was a newcomer but definitely not an outsider.

I was indulging my appetite for danger. I was tasting some of the magic yet to come. I wanted to devour as much as possible.

Fuck the Astoria. I had really arrived now, and I was ready to torch the house down.

2

TURNMILLS HEAVEN

Every Saturday, I lied my way into London. So many different fabrications, but always the same destination. Canterbury East Station was my escape hatch, and it was always the 17.37 express train to Victoria that came to my rescue. As it hurtled through villages and greenery, leaving provincial life behind temporarily, I felt relief; as it stopped in the Medway towns of Chatham and Rochester, I'd begin to feel excitement. And as we made our final descent through Bromley South and into the outskirts of London, I felt ready for anything.

I'd stomp through the carriages in search of the least rancid toilet cubicle, where I'd change into a tiny top, clean my infected navel piercing, gel my frosted-tipped hair upwards and sketch on a whisper of eyeliner. As the train rocked violently through tunnels, this metamorphosis was a survival strategy. In Canterbury I was hiding in plain sight, a kid so obviously suppressing queerness to anyone who had working eyes and ears. There, I tried to avoid drawing attention, but in London I felt free to emphasise and embellish and thrive. The shadow self gave way to the true self as the train shot through Beckenham Junction, past Battersea Power Station, and over the final bridge.

I don't want to give the impression I led a Dickensian childhood. Canterbury was a wonderful city to grow up in, but it felt claustrophobic and temporary. My family was loving, and there was certainly no element of neglect – my youth was filled with happiness.

I painted outside of the lines, asked a lot of questions, and had an unruly passion for things like butterflies and dancing – anything on the fringes of what was *cool* for a little boy to like. I obsessed over music and books, and imagination was my primary ingredient. Home was a place of nourishment and care, but as I began to grow, and as my inquisitive mind fixated on more adult interests, my London fact-finding excursions felt essential. My father hated the city – he believed it was expensive and dangerous, which made me want to visit even more. 'If you want to be around prostitutes, poofs and transvestites, that's where they all are,' he warned, oblivious to how appealing that sounded.

———

A combustible energy that was pent up inside me was well and truly detonated at the Astoria. Then, the subterranean paradise of Turnmills had become my sacred stomping ground, my Sunday sabbath. The latter was still off limits after I'd been caught red-handed trying to get in when underage, a fact I managed to keep pretty low-key for my reputation's sake. *ID'd at G-A-Y? God, that's embarrassing . . .* But I didn't care – I was accumulating older friends, and the house music at Trade had matured my palate. 'Are we going down to "Grab a Youngster" after this?' a non-committal pal asked, at the KU Bar. 'Nah, it's shit. They've got A1 on again tonight . . . I'm all right thanks!' I'd reply, saving face.

As often as possible, I'd come up to town in the early afternoon, because I had what I imagined were showbiz things to do before heading out. Sometimes I'd go to Harrods to mooch around the perfume counters, asking for samples. I'd splash out on a bread roll in the Food Halls purely for the green-and-white plastic bag, which would carry serious cachet at school. I'd march up and down Bond Street, hoping to spot Victoria Beckham spilling out of Gucci amid a mountain of couture. I never saw her.

I'd circulate Soho – down Wardour Street, turn left on to Old Compton Street, back up Dean Street and loop round again via Soho Square. While on this circuit I'd spot the same characters – the old lady in a black lace veil walking her tiny dog, the bald man with an eyepatch smoking a cigar, and the portly fellow in a suit always chatting to passers-by outside L'Escargot, who I later learned was the owner. These faces captivated me, their character arcs playing out in my head like a French movie.

I'd secure the weekend's discount club flyers at Trax, the music shop on Greek Street. Occasionally I'd spot one of the DJs from Trade sifting through the CDs and vinyl, and be starstruck. I, too, began hunting down tunes I'd heard the previous weekend, describing them to the person behind the counter, reciting any lyrics I could remember.

I'd pick up *Boyz* and *QX*, the bibles of queer nightlife, and read them sitting in the window at Caffè Nero on the corner of Frith Street, with the Admiral Duncan in my peripheral, where the bomb had been. I was obsessed with magazines. If I had enough money, I'd buy *i-D*, *SKY*, *Sleazenation* or *Dazed & Confused* from the shop and devour them. I wanted to live in a Dior-campaign world, all glossy and tanned, but at the same time sweaty, slick and grimy, writhing around on a sports car holding a saddle bag, shot by Nick Knight. The scent of the pages was my catnip – inky print and the gentle chemical hum of a peel-off Cool Water sample.

I studied the party section of *ES Magazine* – free with the

Evening Standard on Fridays but often still floating about on a Tube carriage or found stacked in an expired pile over the weekend. In there I learned about the nocturnal activities of rich and famous people – where they went, what they ate, what they wore. I *dreamed* of pouring out of the Met Bar, Denim, the 10 Rooms, Chinawhite. I wanted a black, white and blue panelled Dolce & Gabbana jacket on my back, a cosmopolitan in my hand and massive Gucci sunglasses on my face. I *dreamed. That's who I want to be,* I thought.

Back to my reality – my skinny, blonde, Paul Frank-T-shirted reality. Old Compton Street was there to be promenaded down, as these were the days before dating apps. I'd observe, learning, ready to apply techniques later under the magical cloak of darkness in the clubs. I'd soak it all up, the hustle and jazz of Soho. To some it was a dirty place, but to me it felt maternal and nurturing. It had felt the same to folk who didn't fit into normal life for a hundred years. It was the epicentre of fun, of culture and of extravagant sleaze. It was London's thrumming heart. It was everything I loved.

———

I returned to education on Mondays energised after sleeping all of Sunday off, and revealed juicy details of rendezvous and drug dabbling to my friends. I was an open book, telling my classmates about Heaven, my clubbing friends, their sugar daddies, about how speed makes your teeth chatter, about how I saw Rupert Everett on the dance floor, about all of my boozing and carousing.

Education became the intermission to my weekends. I picked and chose the subjects I'd apply myself to, excelling in anything creative and falling behind in the more mundane and scientific. Drama class,

Art and English Literature got my full attention – they were things I could touch. I escaped through my imagination, and I'd spend lunchtimes reading novels in the library or practising piano in the music room. Maths class, however, was for gossiping and chattering – notes were passed around, the half-deaf teacher oblivious.

I'd zone out in Maths, scribbling pictures of a fantasy woman on my homework diary. She had big blonde hair, big eyelashes, big lips and was dressed head to toe in Versace. I was in awe of Pamela Anderson, and posters of her bombshell Barb Wire character were pasted all over my bedroom walls. I was obsessed with *Eurotrash*, the TV freak show on Channel 4, and in particular Lolo Ferrari, the pneumatic super-doll who'd enhanced and exaggerated her every feature. I fell in love with Grace Jones after discovering not only her music, but also her power and her seeming control over men. I was transfixed by these women. This fantasy girl I drew on my notepads using a Bic biro was a culmination of all of them. Little did I know, I was subconsciously sketching Jodie Harsh.

'Stop drawing and pay attention!' snapped Mrs Shelby, the Maths teacher. I'd answer back under my breath, some sarcastic comment inspired by the wit of the older guys I was hanging out with outside of school, in London. God, I hated Maths, and I always knew it would become redundant. 'You won't be carrying a calculator in your pocket everywhere you go,' she'd warn. How wrong she was.

By midweek, I ached for the white heat of London. When I wasn't there, I pictured myself stepping over the threshold and down into the vast humid lair of Trade and wherever else. My never-ending Saturday nights. The weekend couldn't come soon enough.

Oh, the leisure pursuits of a bright young thing who felt older than his years, who society would have tucked up in bed after a telling-off, whose mother and father thought was at a sleepover with friends down the road in Kent, not in a sweaty club in Clerkenwell.

Throughout the week I sat restlessly behind the desk at my part-time job in a sunbed shop. There'd be texts back and forth with acquaintances, some I was more familiar with and others who had been scooped up amid the mayhem of the previous weekend. My tiny red Nokia 8210 pinged into action around Wednesday evening, text messages flying to instigate phone calls, and I'd quit my game of Snake to start scheming. The landline would be taken over while my mum shouted at me to free it up so she could use the internet. A frenzy of hushed, meticulous deliberating would ensure we had our revelry locked in place.

Once Saturday finally came, we assembled in Soho – a light meal at the Stockpot perhaps, where you'd get change from a fiver for a tummy full of chicken schnitzel and chips, or perhaps someone in my group would have a new sugar daddy in tow, willing to pay for us all to have a slap-up Chinese meal at the Crispy Duck on Gerrard Street. A cocktail at Escape would be in order, if security seemed slack on ID checks. My go-to drink would be a VRC, a potent blend of vodka, Red Bull and champagne. I never paid for one myself. Failing that, pre-drinks were whatever we could club together and buy from Dodo Supermarket on Old Compton Street. I had become a connoisseur of alcopops, and in retrospect this may have contributed to the volcanic acne on my forehead that I'd coat mountains of Rimmel foundation on to hide, thus making matters even worse. We'd clink bottles and sling them back in the oasis of Soho Square, its railings a relatively easy hurdle to jump. We'd piss up the Tudor cottage in the middle, as these were the days before stinking urinals were placed around the West End. And as the daylight waned, the herd migrated south to Heaven.

As we crossed through the bright, broken lights of Soho, meandering through higgledy-piggledy streets, we trod on flyers beckoning fools to the innocuous doorway of the Astoria. As much as I hated the place and everyone in it since I'd been banned, I probably missed it. For those important hours, it had been my temporary home, a one-night stand I'd never forget. I pictured the giant bouncer who stood guard of that enticing foyer, a threshold I could not cross, my first taste of 'no'. I imagined myself attending his funeral, and how happy I'd have been at it. *I'm eighteen in two years,* I thought. *Then I'll be back. Then I'll show them.*

Half a mile down, we passed Nelson and the lions. They were poised, refined, guarding a more regal route than the salmonella sellers and the crackheads on Charing Cross Road. Our stampede crossed the Strand, with its posh hotels and theatres. *Of Mice and Men* played at the Savoy. We ascended the slope of Villiers Street, an address implanted in the memories of so many people as the gateway to Heaven, under the Arches. And there, we joined the queue that wrapped around its building under the shadow of Charing Cross Station.

There was a combustible energy in that line, a palpable anticipation of what lay ahead, a similar feeling I'd had queuing for the Vampire ride at Chessington a handful of years earlier. With time to kill, we gossiped – melodramas were maximised, the smallest reasons to dislike someone absent were uncovered. We smoked. We discussed trivial things, like the benefits of bananas for aiding comedowns and the pros and cons of belly button rings. We judged. Somebody we knew had been in hospital – they had overhydrated their brain by drinking too much water on E. We spoke about our outfits and how much they cost – I'd saved up my sunbed-shop wages for a pair of Maharishi cargo trousers, albeit the unembroidered, less expensive style. I paired these perfectly with a minute T-shirt that screamed the words *Girl Power*, that I'd shop-lifted – a feminist anti-capitalist since day one.

More toxic gossip. What terrible grudges were at play in club-land? Who was banging who? No one was off limits. Our elaborate jurying may have been laced with resentments, but Oscar Wilde reportedly said it best: 'Hear no evil, speak no evil, and you'll never be invited to a party!'

As the queue drizzled further down towards Heaven, and club-bers disappeared into it like computer game lemmings tumbling off a cliff, my heart would begin pulsing in my ears. Would I get in this week? Could this fake ID still trick those who demanded to see it? Each night was unpredictable and had the potential for anything to happen – the thought of unrestrained adventures kept me coming back for more.

We galvanised ourselves as we made it to the front of the line. The celestial name, Heaven, above the sky-blue door beckoned us in. We entered, not through pearly gates, but via a threatening grey metal detector. As I passed under its beeping gaze, I wondered if it could read my age, an alarm poised to alert the bouncers that I was, in fact, a child. But, no: a quick pat-down followed by a stamp on the wrist saying, simply, '£10', felt like a kiss on my forehead. We were through, we were in. Down a flight of stairs, we lunged into the thick darkness, briefly stopping to hand over a crisp ten-pound note, Elizabeth smizing up from it as if to wish me the best of luck on tonight's adventure.

Through a first set of double doors into a little corridor, and the bass would start vibrating though your body. Through a second set of doors, and the top-end sounds would enter your eardrums. The beats were propulsive, snares sizzled, the low end hit your chest with a thump. You were caught in a bottleneck, until you weren't – and then you arrived in the promised land of the main dance floor. It was transcendent.

Heaven was a huge, curious labyrinth. I remember trying to negotiate my way around the mapless stretch the first time I ever went. Rooms turned back on themselves – there seemed to be no logic to the blueprint. But within two weeks, I was turbocharging around like I owned the place. When I first stepped into its vast yawn of a main room, its worn wooden floor and brick walls looked mammoth but, at the same time, felt intimate. Maybe because of its position so far underground, it seemed to trap kinetic energy – love stories had been formed here, happy memories had been made, songs had been sung, hearts had been broken, and you could feel it. This room shaped my own existence, too, for a while. I was baptised there.

On any Saturday at Heaven, I was only one tiny part of the story of the night – the whole complex held almost two thousand souls. A drink at the long bar, a quick scan of the congregation on the main-room floor, and I was ready for action. Once a pill had kicked in, I dived under, breath held, my impish limbs flailing to the house beat.

Going between the other rooms was like turning the dial on an old radio – new music bled through the doors as they swung. I'd explore the Star Bar up on the first floor, and the Soundshaft if it was open. This was its own self-contained venue at the back, which occasionally opened to Heaven customers to cope with the overspill on busier nights, and, rumour has it, was haunted by a horse. Apparently, the managers and cleaners would hear it trotting about in the day, and the CCTV would pick up dark shadows. Years later, as I sat in the dressing room adjacent to the Soundshaft before opening time, I indeed heard a horse trotting. I put it down to rats and the leaking pipes in the Victorian tunnels it sat in.

After our nights at Heaven, the routine of heading to Old Compton Cafe often stuck. We walked and debriefed on kisses and drama, to a soundtrack of metal shutters and rattling bottles. We were the dawn patrol, killing time and killing brain cells. Knocking about on the barren streets of Soho, we'd chit-chat with its deviants – the call girls clocking off, the clubbers wobbling into cabs, and the familiar faces of the unhoused. There was a light police presence, but Soho was more lawless back then – and a constant, palpable feeling of mischief hung in the air.

There was shouting in every accent in Soho. If the drugs wore off it could morph into hellscape, but a bump off a key in a doorway would ward that off, keeping us going until reality beckoned. The lost fools of London, the wandering club children at daybreak.

Even on the nights when I'd *insisted* I was to avoid the place, I would leave the West End and head over to Clerkenwell, down into the hot stomach of Trade. Here it was a more aggressive hedonism – harder dancing, sex and stimulants. It was a Bermuda Triangle of decadence, and I couldn't resist the opportunity to submerge myself in the swell of its waves. Whoever said nothing good happens after 4 a.m., I beg to differ – we hadn't even started to make our way over there by then. Trade tested my stamina.

Image was everything to me. I was addicted to St. Tropez tan, and usually double-dipped with a session at the electric beach too. My white Vivienne Westwood skull-and-crossbones T-shirt collar was stained by the foundation thick on my neck. Thinking back, I wore that T-shirt every other week, my armoury of outfits small and painstakingly saved up for. A capsule collection of two full looks, on rotation. All around me, bodies were in various states of undress. I was skinny and twinkish, perfect for slipping through a crush of steroid-enhanced guys in muscle alley – a precarious place to be.

Excess wasn't just encouraged; by 10.30 a.m., it was essential. Given it was the first club in the country to be granted a twenty-four-hour licence, it required a major adjustment to one's body clock. Circadian rhythms were disrupted, but chemicals helped with the endurance.

Comedowns didn't affect me quite so much in my teens, the aftermath of my debauchery more of a faint after-smell than the hanging stenches I would later endure, but I'd still board the return train to Canterbury dishevelled and sketchy. I wonder now what other passengers thought of me, as I gurned away to a Hed Kandi compilation on my iPod. Once or twice, I missed my stop, waking up at shit o'clock in the morning as the train terminated in butt-fuck nowhere.

The truth was, I didn't want to go home.

———————

'How's school?' my dad would grunt over dinner. 'Make sure you get good grades so you can get into college, and then you can go off and do whatever you want with your A levels.' My eyes rolled. I was one of the top students in my class for all of the more creative subjects. I didn't know what I wanted to do. Something in fashion, but not designing clothes . . . something in PR like Edina Monsoon in *Absolutely Fabulous*, perhaps. Or a journalist – I could write for *The Face* and *i-D* and *Vogue*. Or something in music . . . Or I could work in nightclubs – maybe I could be the person who ticks people's names off the clipboard as they enter through that separate queue I'd seen at the front of the venues – the VIP line. Those clipboard people were always dressed in the latest clothes by Dsquared and D&G. Yes! That's what I'd do! But I didn't say it out loud – I maintained I *just didn't know*.

All the while, stacks of fashion magazines started to build, eyebrows were plucked, dance classes were attended. Signs of a life less ordinary were beginning to creep in. In fact, they were shining out of me.

'Let's have a kick about in the garden after tea,' Dad would say. His mission in life seemed to be making me appear less 'like a poof'. If I crossed my legs in front of him, he told me to uncross them; if my wrist went limp, he'd tap it into shape; if I lisped or giggled, he'd tell me to man up. He'd make me play football in the pouring rain, he took me to judo lessons to teach me self-defence, and at one stage I was even forced to join the Boy Scouts – I'd run straight home to watch my favourite musicians interviewed on *Popworld*. The word 'queer' was often volleyed about. Perhaps he was trying to protect me, but by trying to clip my butterfly wings, he was really just a bully, whether he knew it or not. *Well buckle up, Dad, you have NO idea what's to come.*

Psychoanalyse me all you like, Dr Freud: I'll be the first to admit I've gone through life looking for father figures – wise and talented friends that I could pay attention to, and receive attention from. I'd learn from them, too – a deep pool of older queens has been my secret treasure chest. Perhaps I really was always looking for someone to replace my dad, who became more and more distant as I began to get so outwardly queer. This led me into many less than healthy situations. The first of those was Mr Bailey.

Ethically speaking, a schoolteacher shouldn't worm his way into your life. Mr Bailey was the headmaster and doubled up as the

English Lit teacher. He seemed like a lonely old man, and had never married. Perhaps he always felt he couldn't come out of the closet. He developed a close friendship with me, which I look back on with a retrospective shudder – it feels inappropriate. Maybe he saw a bit of himself in me. We'd do one-on-one tutorials behind closed doors, and he'd buy me presents, which I secretly stashed away. Flashy things, like a bottle of Joop – one spray at school, but ten at Trade.

Other kids in class began to realise I was the favourite and called me teacher's pet. But it was more than that. In what could only be described as a manipulation of epic proportions, he changed his will, promising to leave everything he owned to me. What was I to say – *no thank you*? He had my family and me blindsided. Looking back through an adult lens now, I understand I was groomed.

Once, when we were alone, he pulled me in for a hug, holding me too tightly. After a moment I shook off my shock and pushed him to the floor, to escape his grip. I was a ballsy little fifteen-year-old – no one was going to take advantage of me. I was not to be bought or used. From that moment on, as he realised I was more streetwise now, his attitude towards me changed, and his glances at school began to feel vaguely threatening.

Meanwhile, a regular pattern emerged – the blazing inferno of club – club – club, walking into my house as my family ate Sunday lunch, then emerging with a sudden jolt on Monday morning to face the cold banality of school. I was working hard for my GCSEs, resolute in my determination to get good grades so I could pass my A levels, then get into university in London. That was the big plan. *London*: *that* would mean freedom.

––––––

There *was* one final night of freedom, before my train was derailed. I remember it vividly. It was a Saturday night at the end of the school summer holidays, and I was at Heaven – probably my tenth week in a row there. It was midnight – rush hour – I'd ingested a pill in the queue and another half as I embraced the dance floor. It had been a long, stifling summer; September refused to get cooler. I didn't even have so much as a hoodie to throw into the cloakroom – straight from the door on to the floor. Being only five foot eight meant at times my face was squashed into hairy chests and swampy armpits. Lovely.

I dissolved into the dance, demonised by the beat.

Malcolm Duffy was playing the music I'd waited all week to hear. Was he dancing or conducting the sounds with his arms? I couldn't tell. Bob Sinclar: 'The Beat Goes On'. Gadjo: 'So Many Times'. The bitter taste of speed was hanging around the back of my tongue. My mouth felt numb, as if I'd just been to the dentist. A pungent aroma of sexual charge and cigarette smoke filled me up, then a familiar, medicinal smell wafted my way. I reached over for the bottle of poppers. Elevating to the ceiling, I could almost touch the silver star-shaped lighting rig hanging down. My eyes were deceiving me, playing fun games. One friend had three arms. I was tripping out, but not in a scary way. It was only midnight but all five of my senses were at the absolute summit of their capabilities. The room wrapped around me and the symphonies took hold.

Further into the spiritual dimension of Heaven, I obtained a Mitsubishi, my favourite brand of ecstasy. Each pill on the menu performed its own cabaret for my brain, a slightly different synthetically produced rush. The chorus of 'I Wanna Be U' by Chocolate Puma came on – my favourite song at the time – and my friends at once knew to huddle in for a group hug. Such a special feeling.

Those days, the moments were to be lived in, partly because we weren't on our phones. I didn't grow up in the Dark Ages – we all had mobiles – but they didn't have high-quality cameras, didn't have video-making abilities, didn't have apps. We were unfiltered. There was no network coverage in Heaven, and no Wi-Fi, so we couldn't call or text to find out where someone was. It was just us, in the moment.

A cafe at the back of Heaven served bacon sandwiches and ice lollies. Business always seemed to be slow. We hung out in it, chatting earnestly – idle words falling from our jittery mouths. There we inhaled, broke up the plotline of the movie of our night, took a sort of intermission. New bonds were formed on mutual ground here in this special place, lifelong plans made in the stench of sizzling bacon. Brand-new friendships felt like a reunion after decades apart. You see, you don't just meet people on E, you sort of *melt* into them. We slurred, 'I love you, babe,' and spread conspiracy theories. We guzzled water, replacing liquids lost from dancing. We split little tablets embossed with doves. We gave each other shoulder massages.

I remember spending a lot of time in the cafe that night, flitting from friend to friend, telling everyone how my E was making me feel like I was made of chewing gum, telling them how special they were, how beautiful they looked. I didn't realise this was the last time I'd be seeing many of their faces.

At 4 a.m., we decided en masse to return to the main floor, where the bpm had ramped up. Settling into a much deeper gulch this time, we passed a key and a baggie of speed around, and I lost myself in stupid. There was something epical about that room – it became a wide shot. 'Hide U' by Kosheen flowed through my ears, the vocal chanting at me again and again, until I believed it.

That night I danced – I danced hard. I stayed in the same spot until the bitter end, wordless, savouring every last drop with the club gremlins. At 5 a.m. the lights jolted up. Not the gentle rocking wake-up call I'd have wished for after altering my senses like that. Under this stark illumination, the space was bleak, and as my retinas adjusted, I realised how much of its vastness was exaggerated by the dark. The ritualistic release was over, the remaining zombies began to leave, and the space that was left felt vacant, cold, exposing. My ears rang with temporary tinnitus. The smell of dancing hung in the air. My feet were grimy and sticky.

We emerged delirious into the shock of daylight, grounded back into existence, a gathering mass on Villiers Street. The 8 September sunrise licking our sweaty faces like a huge golden retriever. I worried people might notice my spots under the interrogation of the bright morning. My throat felt scratchy after shouting over the music. Saturday night was drawing to a close and it felt as if the last few hours were a fever dream. No Trade for me that week – I had to return back home in time for my sister's thirteenth-birthday lunch. As my dopamine and serotonin levelled out, I swapped numbers with a few new faces, kissed someone whose mouth felt familiar, and peeled away.

The white noise of the Victoria Line washed over me as I grasped the handrail, my legs heavy with the dread of facing my parents on a comedown. I ruminated on the twelve previous hours, and how summer was over, and how school was about to start up again – tomorrow, technically. The rhythmic 'Mind the gap' safety warning jangled round and round like musical hiccups. I blew my nose on the upwards escalator. A batter of speed and soot shot out.

A habitual surf at Easy Everything killed time. An attempted Egg McMuffin made me dry-heave. On the train, I doused myself in Febreze to disguise the permeated reek of smoke and party. We bumbled through Rochester, Chatham and Gillingham towards Canterbury East, a painfully slow Sunday stopping service.

On the other side of South-East England, I just about managed to disguise my plummeting comedown during the Pizza Hut buffet birthday lunch. I was a shell of a person as I tried to maintain conversation, avoiding too much human contact, my eyes still on stalks. 'Look normal . . . look normal . . . look normal,' I chanted at myself in the mirror in the toilets, returning to the clan for the Ice Cream Factory dessert, which I barely nibbled at.

A few normal days at school arrived, the start of a new term, my final year of secondary education. I bragged about my summer with friends there as we caught up, describing the clubs with an almost evangelical zeal, gushing about the boys and the pills and the music, so proud of my open-secret life. Perhaps I was too trusting, but they were intrigued. I said they should join me one night and see Heaven for themselves. They said maybe. As it transpired, I had completely misread the room.

Thursday. One step closer to Heaven. But as the school bus pulled into my stop at the end of the day, a strange thing occurred. I'd usually walk home, but that day my mum was waiting for me in the car. I didn't question it, but something felt off. She wasn't speaking much. My sister was in the back, oblivious to whatever was happening. Dinner was to be picked up on the go at McDonald's – again, another anomaly. We never ate takeaways as a family, just home-cooked meals. I picked at some McNuggets in the car as we dropped my sister off at my nan's house for a Thursday-night sleepover. Now I really felt like I was in Eerie, Indiana – nothing was routine. Rain started to splatter as I gazed out of the window at the wet road wondering what the fuck was going on.

As I arrived home with Mum, my dad was waiting for us in the living room. I set my rucksack down, removed my tie, and subconsciously knew I had to enter. I sensed a talk was about to happen, and I couldn't escape it. My stomach felt weak. I sat. I glanced at the clock above the electric fire: 5.34 p.m.

What happened next was traumatic, and I've spent the second half of my life mulling it over, being angry about it, analysing it, attempting to forgive it. I've spent hundreds of hours and thousands of pounds breaking it down, seeing it from the other side, picking at the scabs, trying to heal the wounds. I had lost the luxury of secrets – they were wrenched out of me in a hostile confrontation.

My opponents sat facing me. Mum was crying. Dad was ballistic. I've never been in a car accident, but I've heard everything slows down in the milliseconds before the crash. That seemed to be happening in that moment; I braced for impact.

'Are you gay?' I was asked abruptly; I can't remember who by. I remember the 'g' of gay sounded condescending, it was snarled. I didn't know what to say. I just looked away and answered, 'Yes.' Guilty. 'Where are you going at the weekends?' I remained mute, paralysed. 'What's all this about drugs?' Silence. They took it in turns to speak, never overlapping, their words thought out and precise. I cried, my head in my hands, my body slumped over. A puddle of tears formed on the floor. A patch of the green carpet turned dark with tears as my parade of lies was laid out before me, exposed. Through my fingers I scanned for a hiding place, but I couldn't fit behind the sofa, was unable to shrink myself any further.

The brakes slammed on my life in that very moment. I felt vulnerable. Time was standing still. The stupid brown clock on the mantelpiece seemed to be lying, relentlessly insisting on 5.34, its arms stationary and pathetic. It all felt like a simulation. I mumbled out a collection of jumbled words in my defence, making little sense through my tears.

I'd been duped. My trust had been betrayed. As it transpired, my friends at school had felt worried about me, and whether out of malice, or spite, or genuine concern, they'd gone to Mr Bailey and told him everything. Everything! Rather than coming to me to fact-check, he then took it upon himself to call my parents and tell them their son was gay, and going to clubs, and hooking up with guys, and taking drugs . . . and . . . everything. The pervert headmaster of my fucking school had blown my cover. He'd lifted the veil on my secret life and ruined everything.

After the interrogation, I ran up to my room and curled into an almost spherical shape under my bedcovers. Kylie and Destiny's Child watched over me with kind eyes, blu-tacked to the walls. I texted my London friends: *This weekend is off. I've been caught.* Some replied, and some did not. *I want to die,* I typed, which prompted a few more responses.

My duvet bunker was hot and clammy. My stomach flipped with anxiety. I darted to the bathroom to vomit the McDonald's out, the evening becoming a figurative and literal purge. For just a moment, and for the first time ever, I cycled through ways to end my life. I wrote a suicide note, because that's what I thought I should do, before snapping back into logical thinking and tearing it up.

I laid everything out practically. I was faced with a multiplicity of problems. My parents knew I was gay. My London life would be impossible to maintain. Soho was sanctioned. I was under emotional siege. So much had been lost in those short minutes. I was dumbfounded and numb.

I was out – there was no reversal. I'd had no power in the situation, no agency. That was my first release, in full, from the closet. Later down the line, another was to come, another one totally out of my control.

I never wished I wasn't gay – it's my superpower. I've always been comfortable in my own skin – even though I later armoured myself with wigs and warpaint, pomp and pageantry. I've always celebrated my differences, never hidden behind them.

But my dad didn't want me to be different. We battled on silently, arguments formed in our heads. He was embarrassed by me. He wrote a letter shortly after that Thursday night, which was slipped under my bedroom door, explaining in words how he felt. He didn't understand me. He wished I wasn't queer. He didn't know if me being gay was because of something he'd done wrong. He didn't want me to get AIDS and die. He didn't want to know anything about it or talk about it ever again. And that was that – the message was clear. We lived under the same roof for another year without muttering a single sentence to each other. Not one. He cut off his love and his parenting. He refused to eat dinner in the same room as me.

My mum, as ever, worried, but she never stopped loving me like my dad did. To this day, we remain close, the best of friends. Once she understood I was happy, she, in turn, was happy too. Eventually, the time came for my parents to part ways from each other, my mum unable to take the emotional wounds of her husband and son at war. Whether I was the only catalyst for the divorce is unclear, and it's not for me to explore. I was certainly the deciding factor in the battle of nations. Me, my mum and my sister moved away, to the other side of town, and I went to college to do my A levels – English, Drama, Music and Media Studies.

Survival mode kicked in. Rolling with the punches, I held my head high. I adapted my programme and moved the fuck on, bottling up any pain to be dealt with much later in a constant search for father figures. I dealt in triumph, not trauma, at least on the surface.

You'd think that all this stopped me from going up to London, hitting the clubs. Fuck no. I still managed to sneak a few stolen nights out – feeling like I was part of something was the best remedy for sadness. I was determined to tap into that ritualistic release a few times, no matter the risk. Clubs offered me the space to express myself in defiance of a world that would prefer to keep me closeted – and I was no longer shut inside the wardrobe. I was in Narnia.

―――――

Mr Bailey died shortly after. For the record, I didn't kill him. He'd moved to Australia after I left school, and a pattern emerged – young boys that he'd befriended, some of whom had been taken advantage of. His will had been changed, the sole beneficiary being a blonde lad he'd met out there. I'd had a lucky escape compared to the others – someone upstairs must have been looking out for me, a guardian angel or something. As for my traitorous school friends, and their Edward Snowden levels of whistleblowing? Chloe, Jenna,

Aaron, Luke . . . You bastards. No one stepped forward to admit responsibility for locking me away in purgatory, and there was no point in challenging them in the playground – the disco damage was done. Lifelong trust issues: unlocked.

In London I had two new dancing partners, and we developed real friendships in the times that I had no access to actual dance floors. Thank God for them. The fleeting rotation of club comrades had stopped replying once I dropped out of the weekly loop.

Kira fast became my emotional rock. We met up at Tower Records after bonding in a chat room, and within one afternoon of running around the West End we declared ourselves besties. She was obsessed with all things eighties – Boy George, Marilyn, Pet Shop Boys, and introduced me to the club worlds of the Blitz and Taboo in books about the New Romantics. She went to the alternative club night Stay Beautiful and dreamed of marrying Brian Molko – she even called me her very own 'nancy boy' after the Placebo song. We'd sneak in the occasional visit to the bars in Soho, where she never minded the unfavourable gender ratio.

Kira introduced me to Kingsley, who became my joint best friend. Over long, nightly phone calls, we discussed fashion, Janet Jackson, Prince and Vanity 6. Recently out as gay too, I'd be allowed to stay with him for weekends on the edge of the Metropolitan Line, as long as I checked in with twice-nightly calls home. We'd charity-shop for vintage clothes and boxing boots to wear for our stolen nights out at Heaven, and produce full-scale photo shoots in his mum's bedroom with our disposable cameras. Those occasional Saturdays became my lifeline. Kingsley was like my twin, but much better looking – he'd turn heads in town with his piercing eyes, like turquoise ponds.

What a year. Paradise found and then quickly lost. But all was about to be regained, and then some.

Before my derailment, I had left banality behind and started to feel like I was becoming a true part of the big city. I wonder, if I wasn't naughty by nature, might I still be waiting for the train to leave? Sure, the line was partly damaged in the storm. Yes, fallen trees lay in my way. But I still had my ticket. And although I hadn't quite moved to London yet, I was on track. This was no stopping service – it felt like I was about to hurtle at top speed.

If only I'd known I was at the beginning of a roller coaster. Buckle up, baby, it's about to be a hair-raising, bumpy ride.

3

FABRIC
PACHA
HEAVEN (CONTINUED)

The smell of flesh hung in the air. Translucent plastic flaps partly exposed sweating carcasses. Bodies squished together like cattle huddled in a lorry off to the slaughterhouse. As the butchers of Smithfield Market buzzed into life, people were dancing in Fabric, next door. I'd been told all about this nightspot, its epic caves of hedonism. But hearsay never prepared me for the experiences I was about to have inside.

After my nightlife coma, forcibly induced by my parents, I occasionally snuck a weekend up in London. I was rebelling against their sanctions, defiant and unwilling to slow down. They never found out – and as far as I was concerned, rules were there to be broken. The hiatus had allowed me time to study, and I passed my exams with flying colours. Oh, how I schemed. After my second year of A levels, I would be able to move to London. But one more year seemed like ages. For now, dark dance floors remained an occasional solace, a tender balm to soothe my betrayal.

There was a different mood in London in the early noughties – it seemed like the city encouraged mischief. The world was just relieved not to have been ended by the millennium bug or obliterated by terrorists, and the dark shadow of 9/11 hung over it as the war in Iraq blazed on. Social media was in its infancy at this point – we weren't living through daily digital overdoses, so the only place to really connect with your people was in the flesh. The place that gathered communities together was the nightclub. The drug that enabled this was MDMA.

Kira was the perfect alibi, and a friend of a friend of a friend of hers was going out with someone who worked for the Prodigy. It was through this tenuous hook-up that we blagged some guest-list spots for Fabric. Us, on the guest list? *Major.* We couldn't believe our luck. We'd always queued, crumpled-up discount flyer in hand, little plastic baggie of powder sandwiched in between my bumcheeks.

I'd pictured Fabric as a scary and imposing fortress, where I'd be greeted by a big fat 'no' at the door, an attempted entry foiled by a security guard like our man at the Astoria. I was used to my home comforts of Heaven, those same bouncers guarding and welcoming me in for another Saturday night. The friendly lesbian in the bomber jacket, the big-built guy with tattoos up his arms – they were there to protect us. I didn't know their names, but they saw mine as my fake ID was scanned. Maybe they knew I was blagging it in as an underage clubber. Maybe their willingness to let us pass was something like a duty of care. It kept us off the streets and under supervision. But Fabric? That was going to be new territory.

A sense of unease rumbled in my stomach as Kira and I joined a small line. We'd bypassed the main queue that meandered around a few corners of Clerkenwell, past clubbers penned in like farmyard animals awaiting their fate. It was a roadblock, but we were apparently on the guest list. I felt undeserving, and still unsure if we'd be let in at all. *What if our names aren't down, what happens then?* It wasn't really a sense of shame I was anticipating; after all, I didn't know anyone here and certainly no one knew me. I just wanted to get in and enjoy the party. We approached a wall of security, and a clipboard-wielding girl asking for our names. Relief – she found them instantly and marked a line through the print with a pen. She branded our wrists: 'COMP'. A quick pat-down, a glance at our IDs, and we went straight to the dance floor.

Fabric took the art of disco very seriously, and this particular night was extra special – 2ManyDJs were playing. I'd been rinsing their *As Heard On Radio Soulwax Pt. 2* CD to death. We hurried into the chanting of Green Velvet's 'La La Land' on that crisp sound system. The sonics were airtight, contained within the brick walls – there was nowhere for the vibrations to escape to. The wooden floor quivered under the push of the sub-bass, which tingled in my toes. 'Something 'bout those little pills . . .'

MDMA felt like a massage for my brain. It elevated me into pure, transitory joy. It pressed my pleasure button for hours, throughout which any feelings of aggression and jealousy were rendered impossible. It inspired moments of complete togetherness within my friendship circle. My anxiety melted away, and I became part of the music.

It always felt like people *cared* more when they were on MDMA. Warnings were shared among us users about proper recovery time and maintaining hydration levels. I'd grown up hearing about the pitfalls of going out, dancing, getting high – I'd seen Leah Betts on the front pages and been taught to 'Just Say No'. But drugs are never going to go away, because human beings will always want to tap into this loving feeling.

I dabbed some Mandy on to my gums, and we were off exploring. Kira didn't do drugs, but she didn't look down on my smoking and snorting. I'd have probably ended up dead in a ditch before my eighteenth birthday if she was as hardcore as me. That night at Fabric, we were excitable effusions of light in a comforting maze of darkness.

Curious in the haze, we nudged our way through the labyrinthine space. There was no time for chairs here, but we stumbled across a room full of black leather beds on which to lie. We tumbled backwards on one and stared at the curved brick ceiling, as Kira told of how she'd marry Brian Molko one day.

Back down to the front of the DJ booth in Room 1 for Soulwax. Blissful. They mixed Nirvana's 'Lithium' into a techno track just as my high took hold. The floor became liquid. A flickering strobe snapped like lightning. Each time the smoke machine billowed out its cloud of uncompromising smog, I inhaled deeply, and it smelled like batteries, or the damp earth after a particularly electric thunderstorm. And then, at 3.45 in the morning when the night was at its blackest point, having lost Kira and with no credit on my phone to find her, I slid out solo, drenched in sweat and stinking of euphoria, back into Smithfield meat market.

———

Train. School. Train. London.

The weekend after, I went to Pacha with Kingsley. We'd become inseparable by this point, and we had a shorthand. He was training to become a hairstylist and matched my obsession with pop culture and the artificial, shiny things in life. His mum said she'd blasted Donna Summer records by her tummy when she was pregnant, and his dad expressed how proud he was of his gay son all the time. I envied that.

We'd tanned, preened, pre-drank and pre-danced at his big sister Heather's house before taking a bus and three Tube changes down into town for Hed Kandi, Pacha's flagship night. I had a new part-time job sweeping up hair at a Toni & Guy salon back in Kent, which put some money in my pocket. Pacha had the potential to be an expensive – even unaffordable – night out. However, God loves a trier, and after my recent taste of guest-list fever, I suggested we blag our way in.

We arrived at 10 p.m. outside the creamy white building situated by Victoria Bus Station. It was so close to Buckingham Palace that I wondered if the Queen knew there were ravers dancing, off their faces, so close by as she slept.

We were early – doors were just opening and security people were still huddled together in the middle of their management briefing. We spotted the guest-list diva as she began her shift, and Kingsley distracted her with his charm and good looks while I read a couple of names upside down from her clipboard. 'I'm Paul Johnson and he's Sophie Webb.' And just like that . . . our cockiness paid off. We were, hilariously, unchallenged. 'FREE', said the wrist stamp, in all caps. I was getting so used to this hustle.

At Pacha we danced all night to funky, vocal house. Sweet lyrics of heartbreak, pain, release and joy filled my head. Every tune felt like it was a signpost just for me. 'At Night' by Shakedown put me in a trance. 'I think I feel much better at night . . . ' In that moment the song seemed to be sung to me, and only me. They say house music is a feeling you can almost touch, and on this night it was particularly tact-ile. I grasped on to its architecture of sounds as my emotions altered.

———

Back in Kent, with my parents divorced, my dad was the other side of the city, but not out of the picture. We built a kind of half-hearted relationship, more of a formality than anything substantial.

Strained phone calls that required a lot of energy, coffee meetings that avoided any confrontation of my queerness. 'You've changed,' clenched my dad. 'You're like a different person.' 'Maybe I've just become myself,' I snapped back. 'The real me, rather than the son you wanted me to be.' A year had passed since the trauma of being outed against my will, and I was still angry at the way he had treated me and the words that were spoken. I refused to forgive or forget, and his close-mindedness constantly nibbled away at me at a deep level. By contrast, my relationship with my mum remained stable, and although she didn't yet understand my new world, she didn't try to change me, didn't cut me out of her life.

All the while, I plugged into my studies and plotted my future. Canterbury College was pedestrian, but I knew I had to get good grades to progress to university in London. I was just getting through it. Then, on a Saturday evening in July, I marched down towards Heaven, and my life took a sharp left turn.

London was hot and sweaty, as if it were having a fever. The streets rumbled with weekend noise, awash with the smells of beer, bus exhaust, hot bins and piss. Football had been on – a Cup of some sorts – there was much cheer from the pubs. My exams were recently completed, and the very peak of summer was fast approaching. I treated myself to a Pizza Express. I dined alone, just me, my headphones and a book. On my way to Heaven, I cut through Adelaide Street towards the direction of the club, when something stopped me in my tracks outside a bar. It was a statuesque figure, so tall and commanding. A tiny black dress defied the laws of anatomy. A cloud of Dior Addict perfume hung in the air, so edible, so rich, drawing me in closer like a siren draws a sailor lost at sea.

I'd seen drag queens in the wild before, performing at the bars in

Soho. I remembered one in a red sequinned dress who'd have given my PE teacher a run for masculinity. There was a queen who lip-synced to perfection, but looked like Whitney Houston, if Whitney Houston was on an especially intense round of chemotherapy. But none I'd seen was this beautiful – didn't even come close. This was seven feet of stunning and something intensely other-worldly, with jet-black plumes of hair, long lashes, and spiky acrylic nails. Truly a goddess. Nothing could have seemed more luminescent to seventeen-year-old me. I had been developing a taste and admiration for the most over-the-top levels of beauty, becoming a purveyor of exaggeration and unapologetic strength, and she ticked this box. A fuse was lit. Nervously, cautiously, I approached her.

Brandi was working the door at Kudos, a gay bar that often served as a pit stop on the way to Heaven. 'Hi . . . Excuse me . . . You're amazing.' I smiled, unsure if she could hear me. 'What's your name?' Her neck flicked round. 'Oh, babe, you should know that,' she eye-rolled. 'I'm Brandi.' I was thankful for my fake tan, which concealed the red flush in my face. We were off to a shaky start. 'Can I get you a drink?' I asked. Gifted liquor turned out to be the way to Brandi's heart, and I crept into the bar to order something strong. Stepping back out into the evening warmth, I handed her a Baileys on the rocks. She dug her hand in, scooped out the ice, chucked it on to the pavement and chugged the milky liquid back in one go. My jaw hit the floor. *Fabulous.*

After the emblematic gesture of Irish cream liqueur – followed by several more that she forced patrons to pay for – it was clear we were really hitting it off. I laughed at her catty comments, her dry tongue cutting sharper as she lubricated. I was stunned at how voracious she was, and lost count of the number of men she greeted and groped playfully. Honestly, I was obsessed. She was like the women I drew at school – she was Grace, she was Pamela, she was Lolo. She and her friend Caiden, a muscled guy who it turned out had recently hung up his drag boots as Nicole, were hitting the same club as me. They didn't need to wait to gain access with a discounted early-entry flyer, they told me. 'Want to come with us? We'll show you a proper night out.' I was in.

Heads turned as we walked down that familiar slope under the Arches, past the drooling line of four hundred or so people waiting to pay to get in. Brandi announced her arrival with a percussive click-clacking of heels on the hot tiles. She clomped with the plain intention of being noticed, and my feet pitter-pattered beside her. On approach, a black, twisted piece of rope was detached from the front of the barrier. A knowing wink was thrown from Brandi to the butch security lady that had seen me on so many Saturdays – all excitable at 11 p.m., then high as a kite at 5 a.m. 'Made some new friends, I see?' she asked me, smirking, as if to suggest, 'You've landed on your feet here, young man.' I felt special, singled out, separate from the herd behind the railings. We rushed in, a flourish of activity, a whoosh of rippling wig, a cloud of vanilla fragrance. Seconds earlier, we were crossing the Strand, now we were already inside the depths of Heaven. It was almost too much to comprehend.

Brandi and Caiden had real social capital within the club – they seemed to know everyone, and everyone seemed to know them. As we skimmed the outskirts of the dance floor, bathing in their after-dark celebrity, I felt like I was part of some regal caravan. Air kisses were exchanged, necks swivelling with audible *mwah, mwahs*. It was like they had created their own nightclub stardom, a Warholian kind of fame, and I was feeling its gravitational pull.

These were the people I wanted to be around, the sort my father warned me about. I felt liberated, and it all felt so new. I was intoxicated.

Glamour alert. Another tall – almost giant – figure slunk through the congestion and into our line of sight. She wore a minuscule cut-off top – barely enough fabric to cover her nipples – exposing a taut six-pack, punctuated by a diamond belly button ring. Poker-straight bleach-blonde hair was topped off with a trilby hat. Pure fire. She was Petra, and she was the twin sister – and brother – of Brandi. There were two of them! 'Hi slag,' she tossed to Brandi nonchalantly.

The siblings represented a strong, powerful image of femininity, without sinking to parody. I'd always been attracted to 'tough bitch' energy, since hanging out with the girls at school that wore Elizabeth Duke jewellery and huffed B&H cigarettes. Now I was in the cool clan at my favourite club.

'Who's the new twink?' Petra asked Brandi, as if I wasn't standing there. I reached out an assuming hand to shake hers and introduce myself. She looked at it, ignored it, and pulled me into her breasts which felt hard and stuck-on, holding my head down and then ruffling my hair, like a pet. Everyone laughed, apart from the sulking clutch bag of a boyfriend that she towed two steps behind her. I laughed too. I was just happy to be there, to be honest. A duel of catty wit bounced back and forth between the sisters, before Petra slid a piece of card into my hand. 'ONE DRINK – SPIRIT + MIXER' it read on the front. The Heaven logo was on the reverse. Confused, I asked what this was. Did she want me to buy her a drink? Was this a request card for a refreshment that I must now purchase? 'That's a drinks ticket, babes, knock yourself out,' she laughed. I'd *never* seen or heard of this concept before.

With this rambunctious gang, there seemed to be no queuing for anything, no paying for drinks. They felt maternal, welcoming. A new tribe. A new home.

———

Brandi, Petra and their best mate Caiden shared a flat together on the London side of Essex, and often we'd drive back to theirs in the early hours of Sunday. We'd hurtle alongside people heading to work – anyone who clocked the gaggle of drag queens driving the Ford Fiesta at dawn must have struggled not to swerve off the road in shock.

I had found surrogate fathers, who also doubled up as mother figures. This temporary family took me under their wing, educating me about club politics and culture. If it wasn't for them, I don't think I'd be doing drag to this day. They were just three of my new firework friendships that would explode in vivid colour, hot sparks crackling through my nights, before dissipating without a trace. That's not to say they weren't important – like many of my short-term relationships, they may not have been in my orbit for long, but they would change the course of my life.

'You have to come out on a Wednesday soon – it's the best party at Heaven,' demanded Brandi on the phone. I'd heard tell of this night, seen it advertised on posters around the venue and in *QX Magazine*. Getting to London was tricky midweek because of college, but I was determined to see it for myself.

In the early aughts, Fruit Machine was Heaven's Wednesday night, and it was legendary partly for its climactic club-within-a-club, the

Powder Room. Remember that scene in *The Wizard of Oz* where Dorothy regains consciousness, and the black-and-white of Kansas transforms into vivid technicolour hues? That's how it felt as I walked in there for the first time. Brandi and Caiden led me over the rainbow.

The Powder Room was up some stairs from the main floor. Its square auditorium – one I'd traversed many times on a Saturday when it stuck to an R 'n' B music policy – had taken on a whole new dimension of warped logic. There were beautiful objects hanging from the ceilings now – and as the lights hit them I caught sight of movement. Venus Mantrap was a stunning drag creature, with eyes appearing twice the size of a normal person's because of the dramatic make-up. Their form and body were twisted through clothing to give the impression of a praying mantis as they danced in a cage, swinging from its bars. I clocked another beautiful queen – D'arcy was a supermodel who looked like Naomi Campbell, with legs up to her armpits and a pouting mouth like sin. She swished over to my gang to top up the supply of drinks tokens.

In this bacchanalian arena, queens and outsiders congregated and showed off. It was a decadent fashion parade, a baroque painting brought to life, a room of wonderment that wouldn't have made any sense by daylight. Here, gender was surrendered. The freak on the street was enticed in and thrust into the limelight. And even though the artificial was encouraged, it had soul.

This was years and years before drag queens were on the BBC in any great numbers and performing at brunch. Sure, I'd seen *Mrs Doubtfire*, and Dame Edna on Friday-night TV, but the Powder Room queens felt so much cooler, and younger – so much freakier and more fashionable. They would have been indigestible to mainstream culture. In the Powder Room, drag was a weapon of empowerment, a tribute to the divine feminine, not a joke for an audience to laugh along to, or at.

We were at the bar spending Petra's drinks tickets like Monopoly money. Brandi had ducked into the toilets to tuck her testicles back into their sockets – they had popped out in the march down from the Strand. I was introduced to Gabriel, Fruit Machine's legendary promoter and host. 'Kim Jones was here last week – do you know Kim?' he asked. I knew this name, I thought. 'Yes, I love her!' I exclaimed, as he slid away with a look of pity on his face. I turned around and was met chest-on with a huge pair of stretched male nipples. They must have been the size of saucers, the teats protruding out an inch at least. This was Roy Inc, another famous London club superstar. Princess Julia was DJing, I'd definitely heard of her. She had a mountain of jet-black hair piled on her head, and I clocked the Westwood pirate boots on her feet. They were so expensive. She was so cool. This was all, *so*, cool. Toto, I wasn't in Kansas any more.

God, I miss those halcyon days now. What a time to be alive.

As the weeks went on, I made my way up to London on Wednesdays just for the antics in the Powder Room, often staying over in Essex with Brandi, Caiden and Petra at the end of the night. My mum reluctantly permitted this, as long as I checked in with her from my mobile. She must have known that pulling the keys out of the ignition wouldn't work – if I wanted something badly enough, I'd make it happen, regardless of the consequences. It was better for her to know what I was up to.

I had to be there – I was electrified by its wild energy and its menagerie of beautiful freaks. Of course, the best intentions don't always lead to the right decisions, and my partiality to a drink would leave me entombed in a hangover all through Thursday. Come Saturday, though, I would often head back up to London, back on that train, to do it all again. I ate it up like tiramisu.

———

Later that year, another new level was unlocked for me at Heaven. It was the final frontier of the nightclub – the VIP room. I'd wondered what treasures were stashed behind the entrance to this out-of-reach, secretive space – I'd seen people slipping in and out, and I yearned to peek, just once. The queens were the ones to turn the key for me.

The Departure Lounge at Heaven was *the* place. After you negotiated the trail of tribal beats in the main room, a nondescript doorway was revealed, and the person standing guard was Meredith, clipboard in hand like an assault weapon. She was not to be messed with, and spent her night selecting and rejecting. On that list sat a jumble of names that represented every mover and shaker in the city. Oh, to be on that list. Most people I was introduced to were taller than me, but Meredith felt *much* taller. Atomic blonde and red-lipped, she smiled from the corner of her mouth, and stepped aside to let us in. 'Her boobs in that corset looked buoyant!' I observed. 'It's all a trick of the light, my love,' Caiden explained.

Brandi marched in head first, and I ran behind as if trailing my strict parents. We crossed the L-shaped, mirror-lined entrance corridor, where the queens spruced their wigs back into voluminous shape. A man in a toga with shaving foam on his head swished past, looking me up and down as if to ask what I was doing there.

I recognised him from Kira's photobooks from the eighties. 'Oh, hello dears,' he snarled to the twins. A door swung open, and then we were in. Out of the shadows, and into the Departure Lounge.

Away from the swelter of the rest of the club and into the icy snap of air conditioning – a new sensation. Surfaces in there were shinier. A bronze sculpture of a bird hung from the lofty ceiling, and the height of this room made it seem as though we were no longer buried underground. A cheerless tank of corals was built into the wall behind the bar. 'They have to replace the fish in there all the time, they keep topping themselves because they can't stand the bass from the speakers,' Caiden claimed. While the main dance areas of Heaven were dark and for hiding, the DP Lounge, as it was colloquially known, was bright and airy. This was a room for seeing and being seen.

It was theatrical. A platform to the left served as a stage for actors to perform and the audience to spectate. The principal role was played by Polly, the hostess of the room. Her head was bald and lined with a spine of silver spikes, her skin was porcelain and inscribed with tattoos of Victorian fairies, her waist was sucked in by a bony lace corset. She'd modelled for Mugler and in photo shoots for Pierre et Gilles, I was told, and I thought she looked like a beautiful alien from another planet.

Three oiled-up male models knelt before Polly on leads, as if they were dogs. A black whip was gripped in her other hand. Polly was there to stroke the egos of the chosen few, and maybe spank their bottoms. The hot breath of Polly's Angel perfume loomed as we headed over to greet her.

I froze on the spot, having clocked *the* Graham Norton sitting at a banquette next to Polly, analysing the room with a group of friends. I was such a fan of his chat show on Channel 4. 'Do you think I can ask him for a picture?' I asked Petra, fishing for the disposable camera in my bumbag. I wanted to show Kira, otherwise she'd never believe I'd met him, or that I'd been inside the Departure Lounge. 'If you do that, we're ditching you right here, babe,' Petra snapped. I put the camera back. Lesson learned: the inner sanctum was a photo-free zone.

Champagne seemed to be handed out freely in that room, but not to me. I headed to the bar to order a vodka Coke, cautiously enquiring its price first, hoping my Abbey National Visa Electron had enough cash for the transaction to go through. I punched in the pin. Success. I liked this place, this life. It felt good, and it looked right – even from my position at the bottom of the pecking order.

To my right, propping up the bar, was an incredibly tall, generously figured queen with huge blonde hair. Her voluptuous breasts appeared to be fighting a losing battle with her black sequinned gown, and I wondered at the logistics behind this optical illusion. 'All right, darlin', I'm Big Dee,' she announced in a baritone voice, offering her hand. I wasn't sure whether to shake it or kiss it – I was still picking up the etiquette. I chose a kiss, my mouth landing on a huge fake-diamond ring, as if I were meeting the pope. 'You buying me a drink too then, love?' She threw her head back and howled. I didn't think I had another £7 in my account to grant her wish.

'Don't let her pick on you,' came Brandi's voice from behind, as she handed a glass of champagne to Dee. 'She's a softie inside.' I loved the fearlessness I saw in Brandi, Petra and all of the other twilight habitués I was meeting. I wanted to emulate it for myself. I was learning their language, I just didn't quite know how to apply it yet. When we were together, I absorbed every second in their presence like a sponge.

At the queens' flat in Essex, I meandered from Brandi's room to Petra's, 'Starlight' by the Supermen Lovers and 'It Just Won't Do' by Tim Deluxe blasting out of their competing speakers. I observed their individual processes like a hawk, unaware that I was soon to become their prodigy. I'd sit cross-legged on the floor and watch their faces transform, hair pulled back in bald caps, one feature at a time carefully painted on. As the design process neared completion, and a slather of lip gloss was applied, I still struggled to make out the complete image. Finally their wigs were lowered into position, and the blurry picture came into focus.

———

Outside of my band of merry queens, I was kicking about with some people my own age that I'd met at the clubs. We were all on the cusp of turning eighteen, riding the sonic boom of youth. Conspicuously absent from the festivities was Kira, who'd found a boyfriend in the sticks who wasn't quite so keen on being dragged around Soho with us.

I'd heard a lot of noise about Sweet Suite, a new venue on Wardour Street that had recently opened with much publicity and fanfare. Like the Departure Lounge, it was for all, but not for everyone. For its most high-rolling clients, a pink Rolls-Royce would apparently drop you off and wait outside on the street. A £1,000-per-year membership was the standard golden ticket that got you in, and my friend Yanis had a boyfriend that possessed one inside his Louis Vuitton wallet. The boyfriend was much older than us – early thirties at least – and was the epitome of the 'pink pound', 'pre-crash' culture that the early-2000s marketing world loved. He was professional, had facials at the Nickel Spa in Covent Garden, shopped at Waitrose, read *Wallpaper**, shouted into his mobile phone, took a stable of twinks out for dinner at Hakkasan and paid for the lot. He was like Stuart from *Queer as Folk*. He wasn't bad-looking, and he had money. We harassed him for a night out at Sweet Suite.

We were shown to a white leather booth by a waiter who could have been a model. There were five or six of us, plus the benefactor boyfriend. It was so posh in there. Baroque artworks were blown up on to fibreglass walls, lit from behind so they glowed. Mirrors were dotted around to make the venue appear larger than it was and reflect a reminder that you, sweetie, are fabulous. Funky house played from the speakers; my feet tapped as I sucked on a cigarette, releasing a thin coil of chemical greyness from my nose, as if jaded by life already. A sushi bento box was served, a member's perk when a bottle of Absolut vodka was purchased. None of us ate a single piece, because we were doing coke.

Our night was divided into chapters, marked by the non-verbal cues of an eyebrow raise and flick of the nose – the universally com-prehensible sign language for 'Line?' At Sweet Suite there were little flat metallic surfaces jutting out of the wall in the bathrooms, their purpose never fully explained. We used them as shelves for doing cocaine off. At various times throughout the night, we'd slip into cubicles solo, racking up a few thin slivers of marching powder, leaving some next to a rolled-up note for our comrade. Other times, if we felt we could get away with it, we'd cram in together, four or five of us in that intimate *pissoir*. We were sure to wipe down the silver surfaces to cover our tracks, as if it weren't plainly obvious to the next person we were in there huffing up half of Colombia. We even flushed the toilet so the queue of people outside would think this group was simply helping each other do a wee. I took pride in my clean-ups, wiping down with gusto and leaving every surface sterile. You could eat your dinner off a bathroom surface I'd just snorted gak off. But in this world, discretion wasn't essential – drug use was normalised, and everyone was at it.

———

Back home in Kent, I anxiously awaited the results of my A levels. My admission to university, to London and my career and *everything* depended on me doing well – these grades would glue my entire life together.

Once my parents split up, I started going to dinner once a week at my grandmother's house. It was my therapy, and we'd talk about my dreams and schemes. She was the true matriarch of my family and I always felt wiser after being with her. Rules were much more relaxed in her house – I was allowed to smoke, and drink red wine.

Mary Franklin was quite a magnificent woman. She'd arrived in London in her twenties from Ireland, eager to escape the humdrum country life and plug into the electricity of the big city. Before meeting my grandad and moving to Canterbury, she'd worked as a maid and right-hand woman for Madame Prunier, a French restaurateur who owned several famous London seafood eateries. She'd share stories of all sorts of adventurous things that happened in her second act. 'We all loved the war,' she'd tell me, without irony. 'There were so many great parties during the Blitz.'

As well as nostalgic tales of dancing around town while bombs dropped, she'd describe the colourful circle of friends she kept in London. Once, she saved Quentin Crisp from a gang of youths who were taunting him, threatening to push him in the Thames. Out came her fists, and off ran the boys. She painted London to be a thrilling and rich place, but one where you had to keep your wits about you. 'That city will eat you up and spit you out,' she warned. I noted all her advice in a mental checklist, desperately wishing to apply it.

I passed my A levels with flying colours – an absolute miracle considering how much I daydreamed of dance floors while I was supposed to be revising. I had applied to London College of Fashion and Central Saint Martins to study for journalism and creative writing degrees, and as the University of the Arts London envelope landed on the doormat, I knew my fate and my whole sense of purpose depended on what was written inside. Would I follow my dreams, or stay in my provincial nightmare for ever? I peeled back the seal and ripped out the paper. *London College of Fashion. Accepted.*

Around that time, in a flurry of change and newness, I also turned eighteen. Legal. It meant my G-A-Y entry ban was lifted, and I could freely step back into the hallowed Charing Cross Road venue. But suddenly, as if a joke was being played on me, it was announced that the Astoria was to close. That man in the toilet was right – they said on the news that it was being demolished to make way for the new Crossrail. At the same time, Heaven had come under new ownership, too.

London was changing.

But you know what? I was just arriving.

4

THE SCALA
GHETTO
THE END

poured the powder on to my tongue, praying the source was reliable. Awaiting an inevitable dissolve into the dance floor, the rented nostalgia of Morrissey lyrics rattled from a redlining sound system. I hated his music. I hated all rock and indie music, it zapped my brain like a lobotomy. I needed computer-made synths and drum machines and robot-recited poetry. But here I was, looking out at a sea of misfits at the Scala, dancing like a lunatic escaped from the asylum. I saw Red Stripe cans gripped tightly, slowly warming. I saw glowing faces and sweat-soaked band T-shirts – the dewy proof of pleasure. I saw jumping and thrashing and moshing and happy smiles. I smoothed some more MDMA on to my already numb teeth and washed the chemical taste away with a swig of tepid beer.

It was night six of six, almost a week of unbroken adventuring since I moved to London, and I had truly taken advantage of my arrival. 'Come home and visit us soon!' my mum would start to say on our nightly phone calls. *I am home, though,* I thought. I had placed myself in the heart of the dance, and I started to recognise what made this city tick. London had been my North Star, and after years of pursuing its pleasures, I'd finally made the move happen. I was a rat in the rat race.

The Scala was the axis of Kings Cross. It was like Studio 54, if Studio 54 was an absolute shithole. Comparably to the legendary New York club, the decrepit venue's layout was theatre-like, having been a cinema prior to a club and live music space. Back in the early noughties, London seemed like a whole carnival of clubs, something for everyone, exciting places hidden away in basements and under arches; the only indication of the fun within being the lines of people that wrapped around the block, and the only suggestion of their thrill being the dull throb of a bass. Inside, whole complexities were at play, complete working ecosystems, like an urban anthill. It was community.

Sobering up on the dance floor, emerging from a pit of relative oblivion, I began to rebuild my psyche. I sparked up a Marlboro Light. Placebo's 'Nancy Boy' hit me like an adrenaline shot, and I thought of my friend Kira. She'd have been my party partner tonight had we stayed in touch. *She'd have loved this place.* I wondered where she was for a moment, then picked up a half-full Strongbow from the ledge. I swigged it back. It tasted strange. A cigarette butt plopped into my mouth. I spat it out.

The vibe density was weak, and there were only so many times you could get groped uninvited on a dance floor before it became an annoyance. Boundaries violated, I missed out on a secret performance by Chicks on Speed, the main reason I was there in the first place. I did a Houdini and hopped on to the bendy bus.

At the front of the N73. Headphones in, iPod Nano blasting the Knife's *Deep Cuts* album, my own little party for one. The bus inched past the derelict building with the Spice Girls 'Wannabe' staircase, and then past the British Library, and then past Euston Station. I ignored the drunks, endured the stench of kebab, narrowly avoided a mugging. A London night bus was an assault course, only for the truly brave or broke. I was both. As the red vehicle approached Oxford Circus, glowing bright in the night, a man no older than thirty stood up and pissed. Honestly, he did it so elegantly, all over the empty seat in front. Everyone else continued to stare out of the bus windows, avoiding conflict. I happily took in the view of the manhood, which was quite impressive. The Seventy-Free – so called because you'd usually get away with jumping on from the back with no ticket – really knew how to put on a show.

———

Several weeks and twenty nights out later, I was about to start university. My dream after graduating, as it stood at that moment, was to be a writer in the fashion and culture world. I'd continue to scour magazines, adding newer titles like *Pop* into my repertoire of obsession, and read weekend newspaper supplements with intent. Every Sunday I'd rush to Colin McDowell's commentary in the *Sunday Times*' Style section – once I'd scraped my hungover body out of bed and slopped down to a shop to pick up the final copy.

On a bright Tuesday morning, we new students buzzed and mingled inside the Oxford Circus campus before our introductory lecture. I was drawn to two characters. Tegan was fabulous – fur coat, vintage earrings, a nose piercing and more eye make-up than I'd seen on Brandi and Petra. She was posh and electric, and, like me, had dreams of running a PR company like *Ab Fab*'s Edina Monsoon. A new muse! Finn was an indie boy, kind of like the kids at the Scala, all skinny-jeaned and checked-shirted and messy-fringed. He'd moved to London earlier in the year to start a work placement at *i-D* before term started and was at parties with the stylists and writers there. He fast became my sidekick. I had found my little crew of friends who were on the same frequency as me.

That night, at exactly 12.01, the student loans hit our bank accounts. We knew this because we were at the Barclays ATM on Soho Square, repeatedly thrusting our cards and pin numbers in until the balance changed. I'd never seen multiples of thousands in my account before. The three of us headed to the big Balans for a slap-up Soho celebratory meal – I ordered the Thai chicken noodles, with fries. It was twice as expensive as the Stockpot. I felt rich.

I lived like a king, for a moment. But within no more than a month, funds were running low, and my inability to engage with physically demanding work to supplement my loan was really quite remarkable. Cocktails at the Friendly Society, three months of upfront rent, expensive black cabs everywhere and the purchase of a Dsquared vest that screamed 'CHIC MOTHER FUCKER' from Santos & Mowen in Covent Garden . . . Yeah, that'll do it. Down to zero.

My flat was relatively cheap considering it was a piece of fluff in the navel of Marylebone. The area was like a little village and sat on the opposite side of Oxford Street to Soho, meaning I could walk to the clubs in ten minutes. I found it in an ad on Gumtree and at £380 per month it was a steal, if you ignored the stench of onions and five unfamiliar flatmates. My bedroom had damp and would probably have been deemed a closet in legal property terms, but it was all I needed. I'd only be there to sleep. I was never, ever staying in again.

While my lodgings were affordable, London's rich social life was proving to be an expensive habit. My champagne desires didn't match my tap-water budget. I needed to make some money, and fast. Heaven came to the rescue – I took a job that paid £40 per evening to walk around handing out flyers to anyone who looked as though they might be seeking a dance. I was told to stick within the borders of Oxford Street, Charing Cross Road and Tottenham Court Road, and proudly distribute the promise of a great night. Easy, I thought. In reality, the work was too hard, too humbling. I had zero attention span for things I didn't find fun, and I couldn't bear the monotony. During my second night on the job, I ditched the entire stack of flyers into a bin around the corner from Heaven and went out drinking at Freedom with Kingsley, Tegan and Finn.

A call came the following afternoon as I was lying around hungover with Kingsley, watching *Trisha* and eating Domino's. It was Petra, who by now was working in promotional operations at Heaven during the day. My binned handouts had been discovered by a rival flyer-boy. We had to put our initials on each one so the club could count how many were returned, so there was no faking my innocence. My fraudulent flyering shortcuts had been found out, and she had no choice but to terminate my employment. I was a smart, streetwise kid, but my idiot gene had screwed me over this time. *That's one place I can't show my face again for a while,* I thought. Back to the drawing board.

My nights out were multiplying. That first month of university, Tegan, Finn and I were virtually living in the laser beams. Each week became a great omnibus of things to see and experience, and we were always in the right place at the right time. We'd go to everything: a Gauche Chic rave that felt like a warehouse party in a Larry Clark movie, cocktails for the launch of a J. T. LeRoy book at the Southbank Centre, an Islamic hip-hop night at a squat in Peckham, a Leigh Bowery theme party on the Kashpoint boat, a show-pony night called Rodeo organised by male model Wade Crescent, and the Fanzine awards hosted by Lauren Laverne at Dream Bags in Dalston. All of this before Thursday, too!

Despite hunting down the hottest dance floor to be situated on every time the clock struck twelve, our lecture attendance records remained at pretty much 100 per cent. We took our work as seriously as our pleasure. When you're young, you really can do it all.

I was in love with London. I wanted to drink it all up, savour every moment. And because I did drink it all up, I found myself overdrawn. More money was needed, now.

———

Some of my favourite nights in that first year of university were spent in a dark, musky lair called Ghetto. Despite its location nestled in the armpit of the Astoria, the two places couldn't have been more different. It was even more grungy than its neighbour, without a single drop of pretension, and it felt like something of a rebellion against the shinier bars and clubs elsewhere in Soho. To be here felt like revisiting the womb – it was moist, compact, and its ceiling was low and red. Its sound system crackled; its toilets were medieval. The floor – also red – was acned with cigarette butts and flattened plastic cups, like the aftermath of a music festival. White footwear would be a mistake at Ghetto. It truly was a charming folly, and on any week without at least one night spent here, I felt homesick. Most Wednesdays I succumbed to the siren of the dance floor, and frequented its night of mythical repute, NagNagNag.

My first time walking down the stairs into the bowels of Nag, led by Finn, with Tegan in tow, felt like I was having a sonic colonic. Electroclash was a musical genre that I'd read about in the magazines but was yet to experience with my own ears in a crowded room. It was raw and brutal, and there was something so riotous about the sounds and the scene it procured. Moroder basslines were bent, Kraftwerk-seeming mechanical sounds were twisted. Lyrics were sparse, but what was sung and spoken carried weight. The throbbing filth of Fischerspooner's 'Emerge' was omnipresent – the DJ played it three times the first time I went to Nag.

With its cheap entry and cheap drinks policy, Ghetto attracted clubbers with more sense than money. Like my first time at the Astoria, I saw people I recognised as 'like me'. The vibe was skinny and smudged, fucked up and fabulous. There was a vaguely punky flavour here, an electric stew of art school and wasters and a bit of New York Dolls-style rock-drag. It summoned those who liked a little sleaze with their beats – which apparently included one of the teachers from my course. 'Oh, hello, Mr Bonner.' We smiled and nodded awkwardly, as if to suggest 'let's not mention this in class'. No one wanted a chance encounter with their creative writing teacher on a dance floor, but unfazed, the three of us continued through into the hoi polloi.

Despite it being so long ago, I can still recall exactly who else was in the room that first night. Princess Julia held court over some posers fresh from the Central Saint Martins common room. She was real London – always in the magazines. This kid Molaroid, who was also out every night, came swishing through, disco ball attached to a thick chain around his neck. He was a stylist, and someone told me a rumour his parents owed an emerald mine. Lotta Volkova, club fixture and buzzy new stylist, spun around and around in the moshpit, the front half of her hair shaved into a V shape. Come morning, these people would be back to their real lives, signing on at the dole office, working in a hair salon, or half-listening in a lecture, but right now everyone was in the moment, in this beautiful decrepit arena built for sin.

Star status seemed to be invalid here – I noticed Alexander McQueen at the bar with Sam Taylor-Wood, left to their own devices, uninteresting to the room. Everyone was too cool to acknowledge their presence.

Twenty years since the New Romantics, and a decade since Kinky Gerlinky, people were dressing like freaks in clubs again, and NagNagNag was the central catwalk for London's bizarre and extraordinary show-offs. These were the contemporary Blitz Kids. The queens ruled the roost, but here they were punkier and more DIY than the polished girls at Heaven. The hilariously monikered Miss Kunty, with her huge inflatable balloon breasts, tribal tattoos emphasising a bodybuilder physique, and intimidating eyelashes. The rave bimbo Mikko, with her thick Finnish accent, Heidi pig-tails and sequins creating the illusion of huge lips. First prize went to Booby Tuesday, her entire body covered head to toe in a white fabric facade, make-up drawn over it, tiny holes for breathing and speaking, and a blue Anna Wintour bob. These were the divas.

Jonny Slut shouted into a whistling microphone, welcoming a new band called Scissor Sisters to the minuscule stage – if a few crates pushed together can warrant the description. The Scissors seemed to be following me around town – I'd just seen them per-forming with Pete Burns at Crash in South London a matter of nights before. Squashed in like sardines, we clambered as close to the front as we could get to hear their new song. I'd never felt a heat like it. Sweaty raindrops fell from the ceiling, sploshing on to my forehead, as if the club had its own weather system. As we pushed through the fracas, a man waved his erection at me without break-ing eye contact. At the time, I thought there was nothing more flattering than a stranger waving their boner in my direction.

I waited in line for a fluorescent-lit toilet cubicle. A harmony of sniffing and pissing came from within the row of three stalls. The stained white tiles trickled with wet. Damp blu-tacked posters advertised what was next. *Red Eye, The Cock, Don't Call Me Babe.* 'This place used to be fun before all these new children discovered it,' Miss Kunty remarked in a jaded fashion, as she squeezed past the few people in front of me, staking her position next in line. Her party balloon breasts squeaked as she seemed to ice-skate across the sludge in her plastic stripper heels, which had collected a trail of soggy tissue.

By now, club toilets were multipurpose vaults used not just for the usual functions, but for powder inhalation and sexual encounters, too. Solo drug trips were my favourite. Tiny cubicles, barely four foot deep and wide, contained a pit of excess. The smells of body, breath, waste and the chemicals to strip it were warm in the air. This heady climate often turned the stomach as one knelt face down on the toilet lid, crusty rolled-up tenner in hand, the concoction of cocaine cut with speed and crushed-up paracetamol hitting the back of the nose. It burned, and I'd gag as it diluted in my snot and passed down through my oesophagus, entering my system as the cacophony of toilet smells played on.

———

We remained in vest tops and denim shorts through the unseasonably warm autumn of 2003. The city was a golden harvest festival of light, sound and colour. But I was restless, and something was percolating. I wanted to capture some of the lightning I saw striking all around me. I wanted some kind of reinvention. I wanted to be a drag queen.

My first time – let me set the scene. It was midnight on what felt like the very last Saturday before autumn would finally throw on her big coat. One of those evenings when you're in a balmy haze and it feels like it's the middle of the afternoon, and you look at the time and it's almost 9.30 p.m. I was sitting in the dressing room at Heaven, applying a coat of high-street lip gloss on to my overdrawn lips, my dress hanging behind me on a coat hanger, and my red wig laid out on the table, ready to be clipped on. I'd visited the MAC Cosmetics store in Covent Garden where I was decorated with make-up in return for the purchase of a couple of blushers. 'I just want something very simple,' I said, as the girl painted little licks of liquid liner on the sides of my eyelids, and some soft, pastel-blue shadow below my over-landscaped brows. I got the Tube a couple of stops down to Charing Cross, sunglasses and baseball cap concealing the artificial opulence she'd just conjured, hoping no one would notice something strange about me. I feared I'd be clocked and outed as a boy in make-up by another passenger.

I ducked through the Arches and into the safety of Heaven before opening time to finish the rest of my face. It was one thousand degrees in the dressing room, nigh-on impossible to keep my make-up from dripping. A stack of flyers became a makeshift fan, my only source of moving air. A statue of the Virgin Mary stared and judged from between ripped red velvet drapes, and a pile of go-go dancer jockstraps lay at my feet. My red wig took its position on my head, that final decorative layer. I stared into the mirror, as if to introduce myself.

Hi, Jodie.

The frenzied throb of house music pulsated up through the dressing room wall and into my bones. Finn, Tegan, Lucy, Kingsley,

Brandi, Petra, Dee and Caiden were waiting to meet me out there for my drag inauguration. This was the most nervous I had ever been in my life. I felt vulnerable, consumed with self-consciousness. My brain had become a chugging factory of what-ifs and what-am-I-doings. I slipped my Topshop turquoise minidress on to my body, stuffed some crushed toilet tissue into my bra, fastened a pair of black strappy sandals on to my feet and looked once more at the reflection of a drag queen in the mirror. I took a deep breath. Showtime, baby.

I walked out through the sizzling bacon haze of the cafe, and a rapturous applause erupted from my supportive mob. Those twenty steps felt like an hour in slow motion, and I moved with burlesque precision, barely balancing on my heels, my natural movements completely stiff. As I strutted, I cursed my legs for their nervous wobble, and berated my heart for beating into my throat faster than the 128 beats per minute coming from the speakers. As I arrived at my friends, I soaked up the love and the compliments. *'You look so fab, babe,' 'Oh my God you look major,' 'FIERCE.'* Kingsley kept me in check: 'I don't think the red is really your colour, babe, no shade. Let's go and find you something blonde next week.' Sixteen beats passed by with words unspoken, before I answered: 'Fine.'

We danced, we twirled, I drank to dull the pain in my feet. I grabbed cocktails out of people's hands and threw them back into my throat, like I'd seen Brandi do. I was reintroduced to people I already knew – their heads swivelled to double take, and they apologised when they realised 'she' was 'me'. *I'm so sorry, you look so different, I didn't recognise you, WOW!'* Others did double takes and smiled. My facial features, masked by a rather amateurish make-up finish, gave the game away. I felt like a prize goldfish in a dirty pond. The stage was set for me – this was going to be my job, this was going to be how I paid my way through university.

Little did I know, this baby queen I'd unleashed was to become my lifelong shadow.

We emerged at street level as a violet dawn began skimming the pavement. I caught the eye of the lesbian bouncer. 'I know that face,' she grinned, clocking my undercover identity. 'I'd recognise those lips anywhere.' 'It's Jodie now,' I proclaimed, with a hint of fierceness. 'Well then, it's nice to meet you, gorgeous.' That exchange felt electric. To be recognised as a drag queen felt like I'd shoved a wet finger into the outlet of a nuclear power station. I was an equal to Brandi, Petra, Dee and all the other amazing people I was around. As the city awakened, a taxi was procured. 'Have you been to a fancy-dress party?' asked the driver, as I blacked out.

The following day, I woke up to a behemoth hangover, an unfortunate mess of my own making. I checked for physical damage. A bruise marked my leg and red wine spilled down my dress which meant I couldn't return it to Topshop despite its labels remaining intact. My purse appeared to have barely been opened – it seems like all my drinks, and potentially even my taxi home, were paid for by other people. I traced through a fuzzy timeline. *Was I a sensation? I think I was a sensation.*

I passed one of my flatmates in the corridor en route to shower off my make-up – half of it was still on my face, and the other half had stared back from my pillow. I'm not quite sure what he made of this sight, but I didn't care – I don't think I even knew his name.

Why did I start doing drag? I later started to ask myself this question, especially when the clamp of my wig gave me a crown of stigmata, the soles of my feet felt like I'd been walking on hot coals

and my skin screamed out for a gasp of oxygen because of the layer
of make-up I trowelled on thickly.

Why? Perhaps it's because I loved the transformative power of
dressing up – I'd loved it since school plays, since I put a face full of
make-up and a straw wig on to play the Scarecrow in *The Wizard of
Oz*. Perhaps I loved the adventure of not being me for a few hours,
inventing a new self and playing make-believe. Perhaps it felt like a
dream job, an answer to my money worries and a way to pay my rent
while I was out having fun. Perhaps it was armour – we call it warpaint for a reason. Perhaps it was a fierce protection against the society
I grew up in that didn't want me to be me. Perhaps it was a weapon
against my dad. Perhaps I wanted to break the rules and be rebellious.
Perhaps it was my punk attitude, my refusal to follow a path of linear
convention. Perhaps I wanted to shake the status quo in a pair of
stilettos. Perhaps it was theatre – I had too much creativity bottled up
inside for just one gender expression. Perhaps it was revealing a facet
of my real self, embracing and enlarging my feminine side. Perhaps
I wanted to hold a mirror up to society and say 'fuck you', laughing
at the facades and double standards that have been created to benefit
men. Perhaps I was shy and wanted to hide. Perhaps I wanted to be
loud and drag enabled me to turn up the volume and throw myself
in your face even more. Perhaps, perhaps, perhaps.

I don't know why I started to do drag and never stopped. But
without a shadow of a doubt – *an eyeshadow of a doubt* – I loved it.

The gender spectrum is wide, and that's what makes life so brilliant. Gone are the days when it's blue for a boy and pink for a girl.
My intention was not to become a girl, or even pass myself off as
one. My drag was a celebration of femininity, a tribute to those
strong women I'd known, and the heroes I used to draw on my

pad at school. I enjoyed the process of playing with gender roles for performance, but I was happy to take the wig off as soon as I stepped through the front door. I was surrounded by brilliant people who didn't conform to the binary – trans men, trans women, and every shade outside of the rigid gender lines society placed upon us. Although nightclubs and drag can often be a testing ground for gender in the early moments of self-realisation, it wasn't my story. Transvestites play with dress at home for kicks. That wasn't me either. Drag queens, like myself, do it in public for money. I personally didn't feel like a boy trapped in the wrong body, I felt like a superstar trapped in an average Joe's body.

I took my aesthetic cues from all sorts of places, trying on different hats, if you like. My visual identity was fluid and there to be toyed with – one night I'd be a Lolita in an auburn straight wig, a pink tutu and a light feminine make-up look, a brown curly hairdo and market-stall garments on another, and a mohawk and fake nose piercing the evening after. I painted my face blue, like a creature from a Michael Alig fantasy, and wore a black feathered headpiece. I stuck things to my face – little gemstones, stationery-shop star stickers, anything that felt playful. I got my ears pierced at Claire's Accessories and hung little objects from them – a mini statue of the Eiffel Tower, or a Prince CD. I scoured the bargain bins at Beyond Retro and Rockit, hunting for vintage fascinators or anything shiny. I procured outfits in So High Soho, a fancy-dress gold mine which sold incense sticks and weed paraphernalia at ground level and polyester treasures downstairs. I was like a cross-dressing magpie. Coco Chanel once famously asserted you should 'look in the mirror and take one thing off' before leaving the house. I disregarded that advice and threw several more things on.

I had a brief flirtation with eyepatches – one made of peacock feathers, for example. Covering one eye would save time on make-up, and therefore bought more time on the dance floor. I shaved my brows off, dedicated to my art and the smoother application of eye make-up, but the sacrifices were real – as a boy it made me look like an egg. Eyelashes were a treacherous affair – being so fiddly to attach, they'd usually be wonky, creating a sort of cross-eyed look. Worn so many times, they became mascara-caked, rock-solid spiders. I lost count of the amount of conjunctivitis episodes I suffered in that first year.

As the beta version of Jodie, my looks were somewhat unpolished, lacking a consistent art direction. Much like a blind participant at an orgy, I was just feeling things out. I wasn't focused on one visual brand at this stage – that was to come a bit later. I wasn't revealing truths or telling a story, I was just dressing up and having fun. But, oh, so much fun.

In the great drag tradition of a given name being a gimmicky play on someone who existed before you, mine sounded like a glamour model who was around in the papers a lot at the time, an ironic play on celebrity culture. Jodie came first – Caiden gave me that name purely because the name on my passport starts with a J. The Harsh was added months later, suggested by another friend. Harsh – totally fierce, totally memorable.

It's funny, drag wasn't really that cool back then, outside of the disco. Art and culture have progressed leaps and bounds ever since. Queens were superstars of the queer club scene, worshipped by a room of several hundred, and being *dance-floor famous* was achievement enough. Drag was subversive, and political, and provocative, a big 'fuck you' to conformity. But in the

UK, unless you were Lily Savage, the club was the very top of the ladder. *I'm going to turn this game on its head,* I thought with conviction. *I'll show them.*

———

At this stage of the early noughties – *naughties* might be a more appropriate name for this era, actually – sex was moving online. Apps were yet to exist, but websites were connecting people and helping them exchange bodily fluids. I had a profile on Gaydar that I'd log into once or twice a day to chat to boys in the local area – local area being one of the biggest cities in the world – and came across a muscled blonde Hungarian called Tomas. He had a commercial profile, meaning his sex didn't usually come for free, but we clicked, literally, and arranged to meet up for a coffee. His advert boasted of him being the most well-endowed escort in London, which sounded like a bit of a reach in a city built on the economy of sex. Pictures proved he had a horse cock. At that stage of my life, faces were more important to me than inside-leg size or brains, and unfortunately, he was a bit of a prawn (great body, a bit ugly from the neck up), but nonetheless I pushed my shallow tendencies to one side and set up a date. If anything, it would be a freebie.

Tomas gave me an address at Soho Lofts, one of the most desirable apartment blocks in Central London, all brick walls and high ceilings. I didn't even realise people *lived* in Soho. The apartment seemed to go on for ever, and was packed with exotic artefacts and stacks of Louis Vuitton luggage. Tropical butterflies hung over the walls in frames, expensive fig-scented candles were lit on every flat surface and a chorus of ancient-looking tribal masks stared down from above. This was a world traveller, an explorer, even. The bathroom was black marble, and the floor was heated from below. *Wow – who lives like this? Surely this isn't his home?* My inquisitive thoughts continued as we got to know each other.

Tomas and I hung out all afternoon – hung being the operative word – and it transpired that the apartment's actual owner was Simon, an older guy who was renting his spare room to Tomas. Simon owned a PR company which promoted London's hottest young designers and threw huge parties. He also owned a shop round the corner which sold expensive knick-knacks to famous people. Tomas explained that he was known for having a rather nuclear temperament, and that there's no way I'd actually want to meet him – he was terrifying. But suddenly, I had no choice.

Simon came bursting through the front door of the apartment in a frenzied rage, screaming at an assistant who trailed behind, spit flying, his pupils popping out their sockets. 'Where the fuck is that box of clothing samples?' he bellowed. 'Where the fuck is it – where have you put it?' Tomas was standing stark naked in the middle of the living room as chaos erupted around him, and I remained kneeling, frozen with fear, not knowing whether to introduce myself or creep backwards out of the door like a cartoon character. Cushions and clothing flew as the flat was turned upside down. Simon didn't even acknowledge Tomas, and neither did the assistant – it was as if there wasn't a ten-inch penis flopping about in the middle of the lounge in broad daylight. Much less did they acknowledge me – it was as if I were completely invisible. The missing box was found, and sweat was wiped from every forehead in the room. Suddenly Simon looked up, and his face softened. His eyes met mine, and I jumped, terrified. 'Who's this then?' he asked. I whimpered out my name. 'Are you a friend of Tomas's, or a punter?' A friend, I answered. 'Then you're a friend of mine.' And, to cut a 'long' story short, that was that – Simon was to become a close ally and something of a mentor to me for the next fifteen years.

Simon loved the wilder side of life – he'd been involved with various clubs in his youth, and received the moniker Furchild, because whenever he swanned around a party he'd be draped in some expensive animal stole or fluffy jacket. These days he preferred a consistent, unfussy uniform of white open shirt, tangle of thin chains around his neck, and ripped blue jeans. His accent was his own. He wasn't from London – very few of us were – and tweaked his once thick Manchester dialect into a posh, Chelsea tone. We were all just adapting ourselves, looking for home.

Now in his forties, Simon would often host dinner parties at his home and his kink was connecting a bento box of different people together – people who might not have mixed in normal life. A typical soirée at his might have featured a couple of escorts, a fashion designer, the daughter of a Russian oligarch, a pop star and Polly from Heaven. And then me, in drag, watching and learning how it was all put together, the inner workings. 'You need some eye candy and some intelligent conversation at the table,' he told me. 'You can't have one without the other; it's boring – London doesn't work like that. You also need good lighting.' By that he meant low lighting – so everyone looked beautiful. There were always dozens of candles everywhere – that was very much a Simon thing.

While much of my sense of humour was borrowed from Simon's fierce wit, you wouldn't want to be on the receiving end of his acidic tongue. And you probably wouldn't want to work with him. His office could be a hostile place. I'd drop by to say hi and his staff would be cowering at their desks, while he was sitting at his, seething and smoking after a scream. I'd be swiping through the fashion samples to see if there was an outfit I could nab to wear for work that night, and the room would be so silent that you'd only hear the chilling screech of hangers dragging on the rails. Anger issues aside, he truly meant well. He'd always start the day with a tray of warm croissants for the office from Patisserie Valerie down the road. A false sense of comfort to kick-start the carnage, perhaps. Anyone on the payroll would be frightened for their lives. Those were different times.

My favourite nights with Simon were spent at Soho Lofts, just the two of us, lying on the deep-grey sofas as he enlightened me with stories of the clubs he was involved with back in the day – one called Pushca and its offshoot Bambina, for example. He taught me about the birth of the superstar DJ, and his run-ins with celebrities, and all sorts of glamorous club tales. He spilled on nights at the Blitz and Kinky Gerlinky, and how he had dinner with Madonna once at the Ivy, and once threw a party for Princess Margaret. He was loyal to those he loved, but famous for his indiscretion when it came to those outside of his close orbit. We'd stay up until fashionably late, me as student, and Simon giving life lessons in cultural capital, social codes and other such important things. As homework, he made me study eighties and nineties culture like an urban forensic investigator. It was to become more useful to me than anything I was learning at university.

I became tight-knit with the professional fornicators that Simon introduced me to. The internet had brought the sex industry off the streets and into houses and apartments, and we'd often get together of an evening, drinking wine and ordering Chinese food at one of their flats, as calls and texts came in from their prospective clients. I'd answer the phone for them sometimes if they were already occupied and I'd give the punters the address. 'One hundred quid and that doesn't include any BDSM – if you want to be spanked, that's extra.' I *loved* it. We'd be lying about in pyjamas, then one of them would take a call, and suddenly they'd ping up off the sofa and start rinsing off in the shower and gargling mouthwash – such drama!

I loved these people. There was Pablo, a stallion who specialised in domination – he was so attractive, and so kind, but had a fiery temper when finances were involved. There was Katya, who had an accent that meant she couldn't be placed globally and boasted a jaw that could disengage like a rattlesnake. There was Soraya, recently divorced, so beautiful that it was like looking into the sun. But deep inside she was never happy – it was as if she was trapped in the prison of her own beauty. And then there was Ruby, a voluptuous trans girl with a trick pelvis and a ginormous pair of breasts. She smelled like Johnson's Baby Oil and had the most beautiful smile. Prejudice towards trans people was still greatly entrenched at this time, with one of the only avenues for employment being that of the sexual nature. But Ruby loved every second of it. 'The difference between sex for money and sex for free, is that sex for money usually costs less,' she'd tell me. 'Men come to see me for a few hundred then buy their wives a diamond necklace that costs a fortune – out of pure guilt. That's what love does to you, baby, it drains your bank account.' Ruby really did have men falling at her feet – she even had those huge boobs paid for in full by an Arab client who'd fallen for her.

Hanging out with these folk would have given my father an

aneurism – and for that I loved them even more. I was drawn to the erotic image of money changing hands, a pleasure transaction, love for sale. Every time one of them disappeared into a bedroom with a client to provide a fantasy, the ensemble in the lounge would have to keep voices at a hush so as not to freak him out. Sometimes, if it was taking too long to finish the job, we'd get a text from within asking us to have a screaming argument and bash things around to try to make him scarper before the business was concluded. The money would already be locked in the bedside table. Always get the cash up front, they'd say – a valuable life lesson, however you choose to apply it.

I idolised this bunch, partly because material things were very important to me at this stage of my life and they dressed better than anyone I knew. They'd be in head-to-toe Dolce & Gabbana, wore the latest Cartier bracelets, and they'd do outcalls at posh hotels with sex toys packed into black Prada holdalls. With clients, the girls would wear Agent Provocateur lingerie. The boys probably did sometimes, too! I hadn't seen major designer labels dripping off bodies like this before apart from on celebrities in magazines, and then I realised *this* must have been the fashion world's true target market.

Since I spent so many waking hours with them I considered joining in the fun, but between the drag jobs that had started to fill my nights and my student loan, I had more than enough in my bank to get by while I studied. Tomas took it upon himself to set me up with a commercial profile on Gaydar one night which I perused with intrigue, but shut down when I logged back in the following week to find a load of creepy messages from people I would not want to share a bed with for love *nor* money. *Stick to dressing up and showing off in nightclubs for money,* I thought – *virtually the same thing, anyway.* To this day, so many of my friends are sex workers or at least have links to the adult industry. There is no argument – sex work is real work. It's the oldest career in the world, and, when done safely, I've always advocated for it and those who work within it, entirely.

Drag work started as a trickle, but by now had become a flow – there was barely a free night in my calendar as it morphed into a lucrative job. I had been making connections with party promoters and club managers, and was an eager beaver with follow-up emails or MySpace messages once I'd gotten over my hangovers. It made sense to pay my way through uni with club work – I'd barely been to bed since that first night at the Astoria several years prior. I hosted the door – meaning I stood there looking pretty – at a small club called Kabaret on Golden Square several nights a week, and wiggled about on stage in front of the DJ at spots like Ministry of Sound. My jobs were adaptable but tended to be rent-a-freak scenarios. Some nights I'd double up, and at £100 per club, I was virtually rolling in it compared to everyone else in my classes.

Finn, Tegan and I were still inseparable. They would meet me at my gigs, and we'd hit some other club after I finished my shift. I'd see Brandi, Petra and the rest of that gang less and less, as Heaven felt like old news to me. The last time I hung out with them, we all got into drag at their flat and drove over to Lakeside Shopping Centre, where we caused a riot in the aisles of BHS and Woolworths. Nobody expected to see a gaggle of drag queens as they did their shopping – some people jumped out of their skin! We almost wet ourselves laughing.

Kingsley would join me at the clubs most weekends too – he was a qualified hairdresser by this point and was in charge of styling my wigs and helping me choose what to wear. We stuck to each other like Velcro, running around London clubland causing mischief.

I was having a blast.

————

Many of my nights revolved around the End in Holborn which, in my opinion, had one of the best sound systems in London. On Thursdays it was Discotec, a gay party that boasted twice as many smiles as Ghetto, which was becoming a little too cool for school. I'd blagged a job doing the door, which meant ticking people off the guest list and taking their money. I'd often slip a few extra twenties into my handbag, assuming the promoter wouldn't notice. I thought of it as a tip, a little bonus for my hard work. Being involved with that venue also meant that I could access Erol Alkan's Monday party there for free, without queuing, and that's where we danced until dawn as normal people battled through the top of their working week. That was Trash.

At midnight, Finn and I met outside the umbrella shop in Holborn that looked like it was from *Mary Poppins*, and we walked round the corner into Trash. The incessant thrumming of Peaches' 'Fuck the Pain Away' led us into the hot blackness, as we were caught up in the shuffle of social deviants going the same way as us. I was dressed as a female Captain Hook – a black-and-white striped top, pirate hat from the discount rail at Angels Fancy Dress shop, and a trusty eyepatch. Peaches gave way to Miss Kittin on the sound system – laid-back, Warholian lyrics about everyone want-ing to be famous. Electroclash was giving young people a common language, a common cohesion. I inhaled these new sounds that thrashed and twisted.

We were irretrievably drunk, having downed bright-blue WKDs prior to arrival. Within minutes we were part of a huddle of excitable eighteen- and nineteen-year-olds, rapidly spitting new discoveries and theories, huddled in a corner, bumping. A tune by Justice bled through from the next tunnel along – I think James Murphy was DJing. I'd arrived with some ketamine – an impulse buy, really, as I didn't usually do much of the stuff at that point, but when in Rome . . .

Up until then I'd just do other people's drugs as a rule, rarely having much of my student loan left over for sherbet fare, but I had started earning some serious money in clubs. I was a high roller, with emphasis on the 'high'. We clustered and passed around a grotty front-door key to snort little bumps, while someone stood guard on the edge of the circle to look out for security or other such threats. I smelt the metal and the chemical compound of the powder as I huffed. It's a wonder I didn't get hep C off those keys.

Without Wi-Fi in clubs or WhatsApp on our mobiles, and with text messages requiring phone service to send, communication was sparse once we were subsurface. Finn and I would often get separated but gain new friends in the toilet queue or at the bar. I met pals for life by the iconic landmark water fountain at the End, and on the dance floor I recognised Hedi Slimane and Tim Burgess and people that wrote in the magazines I read. Tegan never touched drugs, and barely drank, yet she'd be out with us almost every night. Once, I found her curled up fast asleep next to a bass bin at Trash, the vibrations having rocked her to sleep, some much-needed kip before our IT lecture several hours later.

It was discombobulating to tumble out of Trash into the barren nothingness of Holborn, into the crisp deliciousness of a London morning. The stares we'd get, early on Tuesday, cramming on to the bus, dishevelled and pie-eyed . . . We didn't care – we knew we were the future, about to change the world.

———

Life was on fast-forward. Painting my face nightly felt cathartic as I anticipated the adventures to come. Sitting on my bedroom floor looking into the broken mirror, I concealed my tiredness, dusted some sparkle, and drew on a smile. I wondered if I was covering over the scars from my past – my dad's disapproval, maybe – and then I would crack into a laugh. Nothing riles up the haters like someone having a bloody good time.

Drag was allowing me to be both visible and invisible. It was an anchor and a release. It was a coping mechanism against the banality of real life. It was introducing me to all the right people, and it was also introducing me to all the wrong people, too – and I *much* preferred being around the latter. I was getting my education in the day, and simultaneously doing my master's degree beneath the gutters of London at night.

I must have spent thousands of hours on dance floors that first year, always in pursuit of the next place, an unceasing chase of the night, injecting myself into the pulse of London like a needle into a vein.

So, here I was. Jodie Harsh. Welcome to the party.

5

MINISTRY OF SOUND
THE CROSS
CANVAS

By the end of 2004, I was going out eight nights a week. I kamikazed into every room of excess where music could be danced to, from the witching hour until *at least* silly o'clock in the morning.

Welcome aboard the cross-dress express! Deep into my second year of university I was working at clubs in some capacity almost every night of the week, earning my keep in the world's most overpriced city.

Jodie was at the forefront of everything I did. I was constantly assessing new wigs, new ways to do my make-up, listing clubs I wanted to work at, promoters I needed to get friendly with in order to generate business. I would go out to have fun, but also to be seen. University was my priority, but drag even crept into that forum – I showed up at lectures dressed up a few times, having not slept from the night before. I'm sure my professors found it amusing and knew exactly what I was up to – half of them were going to the same clubs as me.

Inspired by Ibiza, straight clubs in London had started to desire some window dressing to break up the masculinity of the spaces, and that came in the form of drag. We were mascots for the club, confectionary for the eyes, a shock of bling in the grime. We brought order to the chaos, helping to keep everyone's behaviour in check – especially the more rowdy hetero boys. Us queens and our go-go-dancer colleagues were hired as show ponies all over town, hyping up the room in all our regalia. In the party pecking order we were nowhere near as important as the DJ, but still an important ingredient; an antidote to the realities of life outside. I wasn't the best dancer – more of a marionette up there on the stage – but I put in the effort, and I liked to think my image was an effective apparition in the streaking lights.

———

One Saturday near Christmas, London wore a thick, fluffy cloak of snow. My senses were frozen before I even got to Ministry of Sound. I rarely went this far south – crossing the river to Elephant and Castle felt like crossing the Russian border.

I'd left the house hours before, grabbing a dinner-and-bitch session with Kingsley at Mr Wu on Old Compton Street. It was cheap and cheerful – an all-you-can-eat, grand-tour-of-Asia-style buffet that could line the stomach for five pounds. Gambling on food poisoning here was half the fun.

The powdery ground surrounding Ministry looked not unlike the inside of my nostrils on a typical night out. Thawing out inside the venue, I stood stage-left with my colleagues. Me, Jonny and Vanity were awaiting our cue to jump up and give the crowd some theatre to mark the very centre of the weekend. I worked the club circuit with these two a lot, and our friend Johanna. We'd last been together at Fiction the previous Friday, which felt like a lifetime ago. Eight days really seemed like for ever back then. We'd been in DJ Fat Tony's 'Decade of Dance' room until dawn, working it on little wooden podiums that raised us above the throng. He'd dropped 'Finally' by Kings of Tomorrow, the four of us caught each other's eyes, and I was lifted to another dimension. When the long intro gave way to the vocals I felt their sentiment fully.

Vanity was a twisted vision of punk and androgyny. An oversized safety pin punctured her cheeks, and red PVC boots with ginormous platforms made her tower at over eight foot tall – she was a whole stage unto herself. Witnessing the contortions she'd have to execute to fit into taxis was hilarious. Her drag was aggressive, but she was a softie. Jonny was a sharply tailored queen with a quiff who worked as a creative director for a major high-street chain in the day, so had access to the best accessories. Jonny had been diagnosed with testicular cancer, which was metastatic, but she was *never* downtrodden at the rave. Chemotherapy made her body hair fall out entirely, but the thickness remained on her head. 'At least I don't have to shave my chest for drag any more!' she'd laugh. 'And tucking is *so* much easier!' Drag was her escape, nightclubs her release.

These queens were older than me and teeming with wisdom. 'It takes fourteen muscles to smile and seventy to frown, so get up there and give the punters something happy to look at,' said our team leader Jonny when she noticed I was flagging. She was right – this was *work*, and even though I was shattered from the thousand gigs I'd had over the weekend, I needed to give my full focus to this final job on the schedule. No one wanted to see a knackered drag queen when they'd just paid £20 to get into a party.

Right . . . where am I? I thought, shaking myself back into the room. I'd been at so many clubs so far that weekend it was difficult to remember where I was in that exact moment. 'OK, Ministry – let's do this.' I did a quick bump of nose candy off the corner of my overdrawn debit card – a little amuse-bouche to soften the butterflies in my tummy. I chased it up with a shot of sambuca, and followed that with a further, more mountainous bump.

Showboating on stage required lots of energy and bravado, and I found that cocaine was a great enabler for both. I was serviced with free booze everywhere I went, and the act of spending money on consumer goods such as drugs was becoming a distant memory. Plus, I was being *paid* for this wild carry-on. What a life!

I wore a red suit, black boots and a fake white beard attached to my face. I was dressed as Santa, or Mrs Claus, I wasn't sure which. Who cared anyway? Gender was merely a construct here. I'd coated my wig with enough hairspray to fell an asthmatic elephant and contribute massively to the hole in the ozone layer. My make-up was accidentally asymmetrical since I'd painted it on in the cab on the way over. My lips were skew-whiff, as was the rest of my face. I looked like a stroke survivor. The beard would come in handy.

Ruby arrived, late and panicked, making our group an even four – two for each side of the stage. We bumped cheekbones and made loud, greeting foreplay sounds. 'Fuck, I'm so sorry, baby, oh my God, I couldn't get a fucking taxi in this fucking snow!' She'd been taking more club dancing gigs to make up for her lack of regular escort work, a result of her recent gender reassignment surgery. She was thrilled to have the vagina she had yearned for since she was little, but many of the men she did business with preferred her previous anatomy. 'Fuck those bastards. I am who I want to be now.' Couldn't argue with that. 'Who wants to see my pussy?' she asked, as she began lifting her dress. We gave it a rapturous round of applause.

'That Sound' by Steve Lawler connected the room in its piano riff. Strangers cheering in unison, channelled to the same frequency. I couldn't wait to get up on stage. We took a final shot and strutted out. I noticed that not many people turned to look. *Never mind, we're just here to create ambience,* I thought, *not turn Ministry into a sit-down dinner show.* As we moved, we drew a few curious glances and nods of recognition. A man crushing a beer can began to heckle with gusto before being hushed by the girls in his group. I was used to this – us club folk were an irresistible vision to some, and a freak show to others.

The crowd was stroked by sweeping disco lights, illuminating their faces in soft caresses. Still, barely anyone was really watching the stage – it was a room full of people ignoring our efforts. *But that's not the point,* I told myself. My exhibitionism may have been unimpressive, but from up here I could see the collective mass looked happy on the floor.

No one wants to admit it, but dancing is all about sex on some cosmic level; it's carnal, and a night out is often one big open audition for a partner. Even if you didn't end up pulling, or weren't looking, the atmosphere in clubs certainly facilitated a feeling of sexiness. I observed these mating rituals from above the cavernous room of Ministry as I danced jubilantly for money.

The beats amped up. I was whirling at breakneck speed, reaching up to the rafters as if engaging with my ancestors. The opening bars of 'Destination Calabria' wriggled through, and a collective chill spread across the stage. For me, dancing was an outlet for my pent-up anxiety and anger. It was a sanctuary. As Crystal Waters began to sing, my head became vacant, and my body moved in time. I bungee-jumped into the beats that enveloped me, free-falling into the drums and percussion, and the bass and the saxophone melody.

But suddenly, my jerky, subconscious movements ground to a halt. Something was bubbling up from my tummy as I froze like a statue. My eyes couldn't compute with my brain and my ears lost track of the music. The room began to spin, and all those human faces became a warped blur. I could feel an acidic surge roiling in my throat. Sweat started to pour off my forehead from underneath my festive hat. I knew what was coming. *You* know what's coming. I covered my mouth with one hand, lip gloss transferring on to my palm. Noticing I was in a bad place, Jonny waved to get my attention and see if I was OK, and in that very moment I projectile-vomited on to the dance floor. I redecorated the room, showering hundreds of people with the contents of my stomach. I had never seen so much liquid forcefully leave a human body before, much less my own. It was operatic. Mr Wu had left the building.

Mortified, I leaped off the stage and tumbled back into the dressing room, leaving the aftermath of my dinner to the front-of-house crew to clean up. I stood at the wall mirror and began to pick pieces of sick out of my formerly shiny white beard. Jonny and Vanity burst through, and they didn't look pleased. Vanity tipped back a shot to calm her nerves – which made me retch again – then refolded her arms. I defrocked, keeping my drag on from the neck up but changing into the hoodie I had arrived in.

Ima Diva, a Peruvian drag queen, walked in. She wore thigh-high boots that would sway when she did ketamine, which was always. She was hardly a monument to classical beauty – I'd describe her as boisterous. She had bright-green eyes, which pierced through the dark. An ever-present halo of white powder was to be found around her left nostril. Ours was a friendship of obligation, as she danced and hosted at some of the same parties as me. She wasn't nice to me.

'You really fucked it tonight, bitch,' Ima slurred as I got up to leave the dressing room. She was fishing out some more K from the bottom of a tiny vial, so I thought she'd better get the rest of her words out now before she lost the ability to speak completely. 'You're just a kid.' I stopped in my tracks and attempted to retaliate, but she interrupted me with further venom. 'You're at the bottom of the ladder, and I'm at the top. Remember that.' Everyone in the room was stunned into silence, and her cutting delivery left little opportunity for a comeback. I bottled it up.

The venue manager stormed through the door, blood boiling, shouting at me for ruining Christmas. He'd been passing through the dance floor at the time and had got splattered in the cross-fire. I'd embarrassed myself at Ministry of Sound, a great bastion of British club culture, and I lost my job on the spot. The manager was right to let me go – a few weeks back I'd dared to stage-dive off the bar, the crowd had parted, and I'd landed flat on my face, breaking the top of my nose. I was so inebriated I hadn't realised there was no one there to catch me, which is usually an essential for this manoeuvre. An ambulance was called, and I had caused quite the disturbance that night. I was becoming a liability.

'You're welcome to stay for the rest of the party,' the manager said, 'unless you're planning on giving us another Jackson Pollock piece.' I think he didn't want me disappearing into the snow in such a vulnerable state. I rattled some Tic Tacs around my palate and headed back down into the guts of the club.

My desires flowed freely. I kissed the closest pair of lips, despite having thrown up a little while before. He seemed up for more. Within minutes we'd zipped our coats on, jostled with an umbrella, and flung ourselves into one of the hawking minicabs. We briefly glimpsed the incandescent light of a crisp winter morning, a snowy December dawn. Day had started to rumour and there were strangers on the streets negotiating a fresh layer of snow. I spent half of my hard-earned fee on the cab home with him and passed out on the sofa in my Mrs Claus beard before we even made it to my bedroom.

I awoke the following lunchtime to a familiar sense of crushing shame, a particularly weighty hangover and a bad case of disco dementia. The guy had gone and hadn't left a note. *Oh, sambuca,* I groaned as I chipped diamantés and dry spirit gum from my cheeks. *You really are my enemy.* By the time that evening came around, I had been resurrected from my sorry state, and prepared to do it all over again. *It'll be fine this time,* I told myself. Delusion had always been my strong point.

———

Even if I was blindfolded to it at the time, I can see now how unhappy I was. I was worn down, physically and emotionally. I'd stopped reading books – clubs had become my only escape into fiction, my exile from reality. I'd stopped making plans to see friends in daylight. I missed calls from my mum and forgot to return them. While I wasn't quite morally bankrupt, I was certainly short of change.

Sometimes London felt like my playground, but on weekends like this it felt big enough to swallow me whole.

———

London is criss-crossed with Victorian railway lines like veins mapping a body, and empty, gaping arches are two a penny. Back in the early noughties, the area behind Kings Cross was a desolate wasteland that sprang to life once darkness fell. A handful of nightclubs formed a fleshy bond within its brick and concrete intestines. Their entrances were no more than one hundred feet from each other. Their insides supplied illicit capers until dawn.

One of these places was the Cross. Its arches had been used as a goods deposit since the mid-1800s, and in the early aughts club-bers filled its carcass all weekend with hedonistic abandon. Out of its carefully curated line-up of events, a monthly spectacular called Drama was *the* main moment. I'd felt tremors about the night but was yet to experience it for myself. It was alleged to be the best party in London – unleashed and wild, a place to see and be seen at. Everybody wanted to be there. A week after the Ministry incident, I went to see it for myself.

As a rule, midnight was the prime time to arrive at parties and I'd been pre-drinking champagne at Soho Lofts with Tomas, Ruby and our erudite friend Simon since nine. We pulled into Kings Cross Goods Yard right on time, just at the clock struck twelve, a reverse Cinderella. Set far back from the terminus, this was a shadowy, neglected corner of the city. Overbearing gas holders framed the distant horizon. Our feet slapped the cobbles as we moved through the industrial complex towards the Cross.

A swell of bodies gushed towards the mouth of the club, which was flanked by two flaming torches. A guest-list-wielding figure shouted for everyone to get back, but the battle was being lost. A whole cross-section of London club society swarmed – straights, gays, club kids, queens, freaky fashion victims. There seemed to be a widespread entitlement to bypass the actual queue – which wasn't moving at all – and the door picker was flocked by desperate faces as he tried to maintain control under the pressure. Knowing how doors worked, I didn't envy him. A Scottish accent yelled out

– 'Simon, Jodie!' It was Terry Hart, the night's promoter, dressed in head-to-toe Westwood squiggles, pushing through the six-deep wall of desperation. He grabbed Ruby's hand and pulled us through the squish. We entered in a conga line.

Inevitably, some nights are a disappointing experience, with the heady anticipation of a fun time becoming impossible to live up to if the place isn't that busy or the vibe is off. All that planning and chattering and getting ready can feel unjustified. But not tonight, not at Drama. I'd been obsessed with going out so much over the past few years, but walking into this party changed everything for me.

The Cross was a series of interlocking arches, almost like a Roman ruin. Filled with people, the place boasted the colour grade of a Fellini movie. Velvet draped over exposed brick – a layer of opulence masking the building's industrial decay. Huge bunches of flowers were positioned on the bar. I'd never seen flowers in a club before – at least, not ones that weren't fake. Golden gilded mirrors hung everywhere – to trick the eye and increase the scale. I glanced at myself in one – my legs looked good. The DJ was playing 'Make a Move on Me'. Delicious.

Curiosity carried us into another arch. Everything was bigger at Drama – budgets, heels, shoulder pads, lips, tits, egos. This was not a dress rehearsal; this was opening night. I saw radical flamboyance and colours like the plumage of a jewel-coloured bird. Through again into another arch, darker there, and menacing shadows were revealed to be a chorus of masked faces as the disco lights slithered. I saw elaborate costumes with double meanings. I squeezed past the texture of lace and caught the shine of imperial crowns. Greco-Roman soldiers spun on the dance floor. Dodging historical accuracy, Tudor queens spun beside them.

We submerged into a world reminiscent of a Salvador Dalí painting on steroids. Chance encounters filled the next hours. I met Gina Love and Daniella, otherworldly divas. I met a family of drag queens – quite literally a family, made up of a husband, wife and adult daughter – who all wore matching Pucci-print outfits. I met It girls in garments that reminded me of fancy desserts. Something flashed past me – at first glance it looked like a giant silver scrotum. I saw the supermodel Alek Wek. I met Julien Macdonald. I met Skin from Skunk Anansie. I met Patrick Cox. I finally met Alexander McQueen – he was so nice. I met a straight couple from Stoke who said they had nothing like this up there. I met a supply teacher who'd bought tickets for this the day they were released. I met Heidi Licious, a pink-haired drag queen from Australia, like a John Waters take on *Whatever Happened to Baby Jane?*, who spritzed the atmosphere with her own blend of candyfloss perfume. I met somebodies and wannabes. 'It's all so chi-chi la-la,' professed Simon. 'It sort of reminds me of old London!'

For once, I felt underdressed. Those around me were adorned in the most fantastical attire I'd ever seen. Without a fashion loan from Simon's PR office, I was left to my own devices, and that entailed a trashy denim miniskirt, a canary-yellow vest, huge toilet-paper-stuffed boobs and a slutty strappy shoe. A baseball cap was tightly placed over my poker-straight auburn wig, on to which I'd glue-gunned porno playing cards. I wore plastic jewellery from Tatty Devine. It was not enough. On this night, I realised I needed to step up my game; image was everything, and I had to take it seriously. The ripples I was making in clubland needed to be a tsunami. In my head, I forged a quick sketch of a plan. My flat was to become my dressing room and my rehearsal space, and London was to become my stage.

An older man cornered me at the bar, a service twink in tow, asking me how my night was going. He looked like Fagin but smelled like money. I politely feigned interest in his conversation, maintaining eye contact, sensing the offer of a drink was soon to come. But then, from the edge of my retina, a movement caught my attention, and I stopped listening to the man. I saw a black slip dress and a nest of luscious black hair from behind and smelt the undeniable Dior fragrance that Brandi wore. I hadn't seen or spoken to her for a year. I wondered what she'd think about me working in all the clubs, my fledgling career as a queen taking off now. Surely she'd have seen me in the free clubbing magazines – she had helped conceptualise me, really. I chased her through the packed floor, pushing through dancing bodies, sweat transferring. When I caught up I reached out to touch her shoulder. The figure spun around, and Brandi vanished. It wasn't her. It was a tall lady, with a similar build and hair, but a different face. I wondered in that moment if I'd ever see Brandi again.

Hours into the night, we moved like a cavalcade to the outdoor terrace. The garden felt Balearic, or a bit like I imagined Thailand to be, all palm fronds and Buddhas nestled among bamboo. We grouped together for a picture, the only memory I captured that night on my disposable camera. Clubbing was an entirely different state of mind for us back then. We weren't recording the vibe for thousands of friends to see, or tweaking our make-up with apps and filters, or even facing the DJ when we danced. As clichéd as it is to say, we were living in the moment, and the moment was now.

Red and green lighting drenched the faces of my friends in a warm glow, and, perched on an outdoor sofa, we watched a sunrise bleed through cinematically. 'Too much of a good thing feels wonderful, doesn't it?' asked Terry. He'd finished producing the night and could now relax for thirty minutes before it was time to shut the music down and kick everyone out. The world that Terry had constructed for us was a pumping heartbeat within the jagged edges of London.

Through people like him, I started to learn the science of club-land. A perfect alchemy could create *the moment*: the metaphorical and literal performances that are enacted, the importance of a family behind the scenes, and the planning and efficiency required to enable the 'organic' fun that happens on a dance floor. It was an invaluable peek at the enterprise behind the velvet curtain.

As the night drew to a close, the picturesque turned stark under the shock of the house lights. It smelled familiar in here – the lingering odour of cigarettes, stale champagne and armpit. I smiled. I'd been to some great parties, but this one was biblical, like diving through a magical vortex into another universe. At Drama I felt I had found the soul in the superficial. Honestly, it ruined clubbing for me, because after that night nothing I went to really felt quite good enough.

A mass of bodies collected by the taxi rank. Gormless faces from other Kings Cross venues merged with ours, a sociological cross-pollination. They weren't like us, with their loud energies. It was all getting a bit Costa del Crackhead.

A hand reached out to offer me a brown package exclaiming 'DON'T PANIC' across the front. What secret mission was this? Back in those days, London club nights were promoted via a curation of flyers in these envelopes. They'd be crammed full of little pieces of card advertising what's on next weekend at Fabric, Cable Street Studios, Plastic People, Canvas, the Egg. They were distributed outside venues, and sometimes even contained a lolli-pop, a sugary treat for the ride home. We had a flick through the selection and agreed seeing Tiga play at Bugged Out could be fun next weekend.

But, sleep? No, no, why would we do that? It was only 5 a.m. The tangle of an after-party felt appealing. We'd whittled down to a core group of three – Tomas, Ruby and me. Simon, who was near-ing fifty but wasn't usually one to call it an early night, had made a French exit a couple of hours ago. Without his vast Soho Lofts apartment, the options for a fabulous soirée were limited. Everyone we'd met and kissed and danced and drunk with had departed – perhaps it wasn't de rigueur to stay out until closing among these circles. Perhaps being under the floodlights as the music stopped and the cleaners swept in was too exposing.

Back to Ruby's for an afters. We'd stopped at a petrol garage ATM to withdraw cash for the coke guy – throwing my full £100 limit into the ring. After a typical dealer delay, I crafted lines across a Basement Jaxx CD with my Oyster card, walloping up the equiva-lent of an entire night's pay cheque. I rolled back into my own bed at noon, the glamorous memories of Drama already distant in my anaesthetised mind.

———

One month later, we were back in the grubby grasp of Kings Cross, heading to Canvas. It was an ashtray of a place, but thousands before me had called it home, and the ghostly energy of myriad nights seeped through its walls. That Saturday I was on hosting duties for a special edition of Drama. 'Just come down, look glam, talk to every fucker in that room and bring the party,' Terry instructed. I followed the call of the disco ball, and the smell of a £100 cheque.

A muggy storm was breaking open as I stepped back on to those familiar cobbles with the same troupe as the month before. The path was slippery; sheets of rain spattered my made-up face. Canvas was a coal warehouse once, then a film studio, then it lay dormant and derelict for years. In the eighties it was reimagined as a club called Bagley's, and helped shape how a generation dressed, danced and celebrated. As industries left London or became redundant during the recession of that era, so many incredible buildings like this were repurposed into churches of the dance. We really didn't appreciate them enough, until they were gone.

Ruby, Vanity and Jonny were also booked – we were not dancers this time, but hosts. The premise of the job was to bring a few fabulous friends down, who would get comped at the door, drink for free, and cause a stir on the dance floor. They'd stand out amid the usual ticket-buying crowd and help it feel like the place to be. It was a financial arrangement we were happy to accept, and the unspoken rule was to give the impression that you'd chosen to be at this party, rather than raving for a fee. And, of course, we'd dress to the nines and add a topcoat of gloss to the proceedings.

A queen called Hollywood was also on the committee. She wore a towel on her head as if she'd just stepped out the bath, and dazzled in layers of imposter-diamond jewels. My friend Amber was there, so I knew it'd be a scream. She was a Northern riot, and taught pattern cutting at Saint Martins in the day. I called her Amberlicious and she called me Jodicia. Kunty was there in all her highlighter-pen colour-coded glory, along with her comrades Stix, so called because she was tall and lanky, and Chicken, who wore a rubber jockstrap and cheek piercings, and little else. A beautiful girl called Sahara brought feminine energy to the group, her entire body illustrated with creeping vine tattoos, and another queen who shall remain nameless in this tale. Let's call her Vixen. To know her was to hate her. She wasn't very popular and wasn't big on presentation either, so I wasn't sure why she'd been booked. We were not friends.

We endured a draconian security search, more thorough than I'd experienced elsewhere. They combed inside the linings of my and Ruby's handbags, and fingered inside Tomas and Simon's socks. The vibe inside was already feeling wonky – and that was just how we liked it. It seemed to be one of those *anything-can-happen* nights. The energy was up. Discarded cups were bouncing to the vibration of the bass on the speakers as we propelled into the main room, adjusting to the unfamiliarity of the space, searching for Terry and his magic bag of drinks tickets.

We found him in the dressing room. I checked my hair up close in the mirror – it all seemed in place. A hint of the Jodie Harsh style I would become known for had taken shape that night – blonde, backcombed, over to one side, but no fringe yet. The glitter I'd splashed like melodramatic tears down one cheek was peeling off in the mugginess, but I liked the effect. Drag had become like a second skin. I liked the way it confronted and scandalised, even if I wasn't quite sure what it was confronting or who it was scandalising. I was head to toe in Basso & Brooke – dressed to impress the punters, and depress my haters, like Vixen.

And then I heard that unmistakable voice. 'Jodie Fucking Harsh, what a delight to see you again.' Sarcastic in tone and miserable in face, I saw Vixen behind me in the mirror. Yikes. 'Oh hi, babe, you look nice,' I mustered. She didn't, though – it looked as though she was wearing an NHS wig, and she seemed to have brought bad vibes to the club. All positive energy was immediately sucked out of the room. She was holding a can of hairspray and had an unlit cigarette hanging out of her mouth as we exchanged our fake pleasantries. She went to light up, then held the can next to the flame and pushed down on the nozzle. I'm sure it was a joke, or a little playful threat, but a roar of fire shot out, right up to the hair on the right-hand side of my face. Being synthetic, the side of my wig melted in a hot flash. Human hair would have just singed. I had no time to jump out of the way or even comprehend what was happening. I was shocked. The room gasped. Even Vixen gasped, realising she'd just taken things a bit too far, a hostile act of sabotage thirty seconds after greeting me.

In drag, you have to be either a runner or a fighter. In that moment, I was a fighter – I smacked her in the face, a full fist punch, the only time I've ever used violence in the workplace. The rings on my fingers drew blood on her chin. Somebody called out for the HR depart-ment – which was Terry. He rushed back in and mediated our resulting argument. I was vexed. Vixen was sent packing, and as she slowly left the dressing room, seething, we all cheered. I was just relieved the flame didn't reach the other side of my face where there was no pro-tective shield of hair. We were never booked on the same gig again.

After that cuntquake, I needed something to take the edge off and settle into the night. My fleeting love affair with ecstasy was pretty much over by now, and I preferred the wobble of a vodka or champagne along with the stabiliser of some cocaine. That combin-ation was the secret sauce that kept the wheels turning when I was working late at night. It gave me a rush of control, an Olympian endurance. But this particular Saturday felt like a good night to be naughty – I was craving some old-fashioned bad behaviour.

Simon often carried an apothecary of pharmaceuticals within the lining of his coat. 'No pills and potions tonight, babe, I just have a bit of MDMA.' Sounded like a good plan. 'It's strong, though,' he warned, handing me a little bag of bitter beige powder. I headed into the scuzzy dressing-room toilet and, in the name of research, rubbed some of it over my gums. Then, I dipped in again and did the same. And then once more for luck.

There were so many rooms ripe for exploration at Canvas. We found a little side space to slot into, a wide sofa in the hinterlands of the venue, where the crowd was less dense. Simon said something and I leaned in closer. I couldn't hear what he was saying over the music. He repeated himself. 'Are you OK, J?' His voice had dropped down a semitone, and the words appeared to fall from his mouth back to front. He used my real name, breaking the rule of calling me Jodie when I was in drag. This was serious.

The MDMA started to flow through me, I could feel it. A sudden whoosh. Avenue D were due on stage in the other room to perform their song 'Do I Look Like a Slut?', but my legs were too shaky to move. I asked the group to stay with me for a moment, anticipating a bit more of a rush. Everyone agreed – they could see I was peaking too early. And then it came.

I tried to hang on to my reality a little longer, but I felt it slipping away. I counted bars of beats in the music in an attempt to stay afloat. One, two, three, four – one, two – three, four. Doof doof doof doof – doof doof doof doof. I lost awareness of my limbs, one at a time. I stood up, trying to face the thudding machine-music, and collapsed back down.

MDMA was buzzing in my brain, and I couldn't find the exit. Any feelings of warmth from moments ago had been lost with a sudden turn. Simon, Tomas and Ruby multiplied into a sea of gurning jaws; their faces warped as if in a hall of mirrors at the fair. Their lustreless eyes rolled back and became pure white. Any euphoria had departed – I was jostling with a sense of panic in this demonic parliament.

My perceptions of time between 1 and 3 a.m. were nonsensical. Did it feel like a month? Or did it feel like one second, as I was sucked through the wormhole? Shapes hunched. The room pulsed. I stared at my hands – insects were crawling out from beneath my fingernails. My friends remained close but felt far away. Their words of concern were spoken in tongues.

The basic laws of physics dictate that what goes up must come down, and I eventually landed back after a couple of hours in deep space. I couldn't recall a single record that the DJ had played, as if I'd been in a vacuum.

'I'm so sorry for ruining everyone's night,' I said, back in the dressing room, as dancers changed back into their daywear. 'Don't be silly,' responded Simon. 'But that was scary – you need to be careful. We might not always be there to look after you.' My friends were now getting worried about me.

My days being an oral compulsive were up. It was decided, I was never again going to touch anything that made me lose control. *Nasal only, from here on out.* I called it a night, stopping first to hand over my invoice and pick up my cheque from the office.

———

The courtiers and queens of Soho had become more of a family than some of my biological relations. I rarely returned to Kent at this stage – I couldn't bear to be away from London for a single night. When I did visit, as much as I enjoyed my mum's cooked meals and sleeping in my old bed, I couldn't wait to stir back into the lather of the city.

My dad still looked at me with contempt, barely mustering up the words to ask me how I was. He knew nothing about Jodie. My mum thought it would be the last straw of our already dismantled relationship, so I hid my alter ego away in a secret compartment. Mum was growing to love what I did for a job, especially as she saw that 'doing Jodie' was paying the rent – and then some. My sister was extremely supportive of it, too – she'd just turned eighteen and had started to enjoy the free guest-list spots I could organise.

I dated a massage therapist called Fabien – not his real name; that was George. He advertised professional treatments, but clients often went to him because of the extra services he provided – a secret spa menu for sexual satisfaction. I was obsessed with him – codependently so. But that relationship was short-lived, because he was sober, and I was . . . not.

Now I was deep in my final year of university, and spent the first half of 2006 chipping away at my dissertation (subject: drag!). But I still ran riot in clubs most nights. While I barely cracked the spine of a reference book until the eleventh hour, I managed to find time to carry out some work placements. Still resolute that I'd be retiring my wig and becoming a writer within a year or so, I thought that building connections within the publishing world would be a practical way of getting a job. I helped out at the lifestyle magazine *Attitude*, which soon gave me the title of clubs editor and allowed me to flex my word skills for real eyeballs. I assisted on the fashion desk at *Heat* for one week – Fashion Week, of course – purely to secure tickets for some shows, which I went to in drag. And then I worked at *The Face* for a short time, playing third assistant to the creative director, Grace Cobb, and writing little news items on the features desk for Eva Wiseman.

'We need flowers for John – send some gorgeous flowers to John!' Grace bellowed to the office one Wednesday morning. I quickly worked out she meant John Galliano. Rather than send them to his home address, I thought of something way more fabulous. With my ear to the ground, I knew he was going to NagNagNag every week at that point, so I picked up a huge bunch of peonies and delivered them to him – in drag – at Ghetto that night.

I graduated from London College of Fashion in the summer of 2006 – with a 2:1 degree, which felt like a blag considering my distractions. It was time to work out my next moves. I wanted to be a literary star, a magazine editor, a creative consultant, a manipulator of word and image. But a real-life job – albeit a glamorous one at a busy magazine – didn't feel like it was going to feed me what I needed as much as a life in the shadows and the music. There I was earning decent dough, hanging out with people twenty years older and twenty thousand times more successful than me. It was a rat race still, but a more appealing one. I decided to forget about finding a real job. I realised I had an aversion to early mornings and conventional work anyway, and I lacked any desire to be normal – if there even was such a thing. And so it was decided, I'd remain on the fringes of society, and in clubland for ever.

———

My post-graduation nights were even more packed than before. So many things to do, so many places to go, so many people to meet . . .

9 p.m.: something miniscule to eat at Cocoon on Piccadilly, a white room with swivelling Austin Powers chairs and padded walls, presumably in case diners had psychotic breakdowns when they tasted the food.

11 p.m.: a drink at Sketch, a London institution and sensory overload. £17 for a cocktail? That really burned – I regretted buying a round. Those giant egg toilets were disorientating – *so* hard to do coke in. I drank at an unusually glacial pace, at approximately £3 per sip.

Midnight: a dance at the Grill Room for Stunners International, a baroque-and-roll club night thrown by two male models, in a space that felt like a scaled-down Versailles. Tara Reid was there, and the Kills. Too many neckerchiefs and too many cunts. Hated it, and left.

Finally, the umbilical cord of Heaven pulled me back in.

I'd only been there once in the past year, when I entered a Halloween costume pageant. Dressed as a blood-soaked vampire bride in a structured basque, I walked off the stage at the end of a round thinking I'd lost, and bolted to the Departure Lounge to sulk. Tegan and Finn came running in to tell me Polly had been shouting for me into the mic, but as I was nowhere to be found they had no choice but to give the £1,000 cash prize to a topless man in red PVC horns.

Back to the scene of the crime, one year on. I really felt like I was *somebody* on the club scene now – I took up cultural space. But the shaven-haired lady bouncer on the door was nowhere to be seen. Despite thinking my face carried some cachet, Kingsley and I were asked to step aside and await the return of the guest-list person from their toilet break. In the arrogance of youth, I fumed at the insult. I waited, huffing and puffing, mortified at being asked to *wait* to get into *Heaven*. I even teetered on bringing out the 'don't you know who I am?' card.

Things had changed since I stopped going to that club; the family I'd formed so tightly there had slowly slipped away. I learned from a barman that Brandi had stopped doing drag; she was focusing on her day job. The Powder Room was no longer a thing on Wednesdays. Dee was still there, at the edge of the bar in the Departure Lounge. I went to say hi, and she turned her head away. We sauntered about, trying to distinguish who all these new faces were. We tried to catch the rhythm, but the music just didn't sound the same.

As we were nearing the end of our night, Kingsley had started chatting to a guy. Kingsley was *always* chatting to a guy – he was, after all, so good-looking and charismatic, and I was, intentionally, the freak best friend in a full face of make-up. When we walked into a room, mouths would drop – he was *that* striking – and I'd be beside him wincing with jealousy. This guy worked in fashion, and they'd go on to be boyfriends.

Over the course of their one-year relationship, I spent a lot of time at Kingsley's boyfriend's house in Notting Hill. He had the most epic archive of fashion – Westwood, Helmut Lang and BodyMap – and a very impressive collection of art hung on his walls, even some Keith Haring pieces. He taught me about *Paris Is Burning* and Leigh Bowery. He dressed me in priceless, delicate clothing to roll around club floors in.

That night they met, we ended up at Fran Cutler's house for some late drinks. Fran was friends with Kingsley's boyfriend and the gatekeeper of the London showbiz scene. She was the ultimate host, and orchestrated group pleasures by way of organising celebrity birthdays, launches, baby showers and weddings. She was the party engine that kept the shakers moving, always revving, flashing her ample cleavage. Despite her being the absolute queen of the scene, there was nothing regal about her language and her dirty laugh, and for that we loved her. According to Soho folklore, her parents were publicans at the Spice of Life, so she'd grown up around the buzz of the West End – there was no doubting she was the real deal. Fran Cutler's mission seemed to be to have more fun than anyone else in London, and it was pretty much always accomplished.

After scooping up some party people from Heaven, we arrived at Fran's house in a convoy of black cabs. She was notorious for overseeing an impenetrable scene, so I was nervous to meet her. In the living room, Lily Allen was on the sofa, smoking and chatting to Courtney Love. As we passed by the kitchen, actress Samantha Morton was searching for fresh glasses with a rock star I recognised – one of the legends. It was all quite overwhelming, even with my armour of drag on. In a fluster, I went to use the loo, just as a Royal somewhere in line for the throne strolled out before me, asking if there were any hand towels around. Blimey. And then I met Fran – I was face to face with the voluptuous brunette the press had dubbed the Party Rottweiler because of her fearsome notoriety and the way she protected her friends. 'All right, treacle, you look bloody gorgeous,' she exclaimed, making me feel immediately welcome. She pulled me into a cloud of expensive-smelling Oud perfume for a hug. 'Come and sit down and have a drink – have you met Lily?'

Within an hour, I was in the legendary Cutler closet being dressed up like a doll. 'Work it, bitch!' I wore a gold sequinned McQueen jumpsuit, the most expensive thing I'd ever been zipped into. 'God, that looks stunning on you,' exclaimed Fran. 'It's only a sample size, look how tiny you are!' I left her house that night with a couture Dior dress on my back and a load of very fun new friends.

The wheels were in perpetual motion. I was rolling with the A list. Now I had a seat at the table. I was right in the trenches of the twilight world, ripping up the rule book and deconstructing what a drag queen could be. If there was anything new or interesting happening, I had made a blood oath to be there, right in the centre of it all.

At twenty-one years old, I was still just a baby. I truly think that these were the best days of my life. Every night was a different scene, a different party. It was as if I had the keys to the city, and I was constantly doing bumps off them.

6

TOO2MUCH

'd been thinking about Jack. Way back at primary school, I was forced into a friendship with him by my parents. He was less than popular, and initially I resisted the alliance. Our mums were friendly, and they'd sit together to watch us in school plays. In *The Wizard of Oz*, I played Scarecrow and Jack was a Munchkin. He was harmless but slightly odd, which my mum put down to him being an only child. He suffered from a speech impediment, which made it quite difficult to understand what he was saying, and expressing himself seemed to be challenging at the best of times. His mood often seemed to change suddenly, which I found testing to be around, but as we spent time together, I found him to be an ultra-sensitive, kind soul. Once I saw him being roughed up a bit in the school corridor by some of the lads. The teachers didn't do anything about it, and I knew it was my responsibility to be his friend, an ally to lean on.

One summer's day he had a birthday party. He was turning ten – a momentous occasion. The entire class had been invited, even the boys that bullied him. His mum had crafted beautiful handwritten invites to each child, and they drove around together hand-delivering them through letter boxes. We were promised fun and games in his back garden, and lots of delicious cake. They had a little swimming pool with a fence around it, so we were told to bring our trunks and a towel if the weather was nice.

The sun was indeed out that day and Jack was dressed in a

colourful checked short-sleeved shirt with a red bow tie, and red shorts. He answered the door beaming and gave me a big bear hug that lifted me off the ground. He was delighted I had come to help celebrate his birthday. He proudly walked me through his home, past a buffet table with a cake spelling out his name, through the French doors and out into the garden where strings of balloons were tied to empty chairs. In that moment I realised I was the only person who had turned up to his party. We spent the afternoon playing games together in the sunshine with no mention at all of the absent guests. He just seemed so happy to have a friend that understood him.

Several months later, in an assembly at the start of the new school term, our headteacher Mrs Carpenter fought back tears as she told us Jack had died. His mum had found him the day before, floating face down in the swimming pool. His funeral was in the newspaper, with a picture of the little coffin and white flowers spelling out his name. I couldn't get my head around the fact that he was actually in that wooden box when he was so happy at his birthday.

I've carried Jack with me ever since.

———

Twenty-one, and I had never thrown a party for myself. Well, there were certainly birthdays with pass the parcel and jelly and ice cream when I was a nipper, but I'd usually throw a tantrum and be sent to my bedroom at those birthdays, overwhelmed and full of rage, a victim of my own anxiety. I think the last time I had a party like that was when I was just six or seven – my parents couldn't take the stress any longer. And now, at the grand old age of twenty-one, it was time to mark a milestone. Operation Big Birthday was on.

Firstly, I needed to find a venue in which to throw the party. A place of indulgence but nowhere too sleazy, a place that was grand but not *too* posh, and a place to be flash but not too expensive. Soho was still the centre of this misshapen city to me, and in its black heart, down a little alleyway, there was a notorious bordello. You could still pass through the narrow walkway and see shops selling recorded fantasies behind concealed entrances. The buzz of a tattooist's gun filled the air. A pissy parfum insulted the nostrils. Seductive neon promised 'GIRLS GIRLS GIRLS' and hand-written signs on doors described thrills that could be bought in the parlours above. Look closely, and an unmarked set of opulent carved gates were the veneer guarding a glittering jewel in the centre of Soho's rusty crown. It felt like a miniature Moulin Rouge. *This* was the place for me.

It was a decadent palace that had fallen slightly in stature since its heyday as the Raymond Revue Bar. Way back then, the Kray twins had frequented this joint, and Sinatra would visit when he was in town. Decades later, I'd stopped by with Finn and Tegan during its final breath as a strip joint: we found it at its lowest ebb – a collection of sad, hollow-eyed girls, a room of great emptiness. Glamorous one-on-one sex theatre was nowhere to be found, despite the legendary tapestry of its past. We stayed for five minutes, without even buying a drink. Subsequently, the girls were shipped out, and the party was shipped in. It was revamped and renamed – Too2Much, the new Soho clubbing hotspot and the perfect place to gather my friends to celebrate my birthday.

I had become quite the girl about town. Barely an evening would go by without an invitation accepted, a door managed or a dance floor destroyed. I was working on the club scene and working every room, and Jodie Harsh was becoming *the* name on people's lips. I was in make-up so much that drag was barely a performance, hardly an act, it was merely an alternate side of my personality. *She* was *me*. There was day me, and night me, and the twilight escapades were all I could think about in the afternoons. I was going everywhere and meeting everyone, my Nokia crammed with new names and numbers at every twisted turn. With a date set, I extended my birthday invitations to everyone via email.

Creating a party is almost like scoring a symphony. The trick is in bringing together different players and sounds and allowing a melody to take shape. You can't just have one type of instrumentalist – the music wouldn't sound rich or dynamic enough. I invited practically everyone I'd met over the past few years, every professional exhibitionist and reveller and artist. I put the theory I'd learned from people like Terry and Simon into practice and leaned into this event almost like a chess move. I was soft-launching Jodie 2.0.

At 11 p.m., I arrived for drinks at Simon's flat in Soho Lofts. While the party at Too2Much had started an hour or so earlier, it was essential that I turned up fashionably late. Truthfully, although well lubricated by now, I felt extreme pre-match anxiety. Would all the right people show up? A lot was riding on this, and a bad night would be an epic public relations disaster. I studied my reflection in a floor-to-ceiling mirror in the black marble bathroom. *Twenty-one, eh? Getting old,* I thought. I wore a huge wig that weighed a ton and defied the laws of gravity, and a pink and mauve sequin creation on my body. My make-up was heavy. You couldn't miss me.

'You look great,' Simon reassured me, grabbing my hand like

a proud father. As we left the flat to walk the few streets over to the club, I blazed on a cigarette profusely, wrecked with nerves. Another followed immediately as we approached the alley.

At precisely midnight we commenced through the front vestibule of Too2Much. Ascending its twisting staircase and crossing the little bridge over Walker's Court, anticipation burned in my face. The main auditorium was exactly what you'd expect from such a historic palace of indulgence – blood-red banquettes, tiered levels of seating, small lacquer tables illuminated by bronze lamps, a grand central chandelier nestled in a golden dome, a stripper pole to your left, a stripper pole to your right, and a stage framed by twinkling lights. The double doors swung open, and I gazed across the busy room. A cheer exploded and I waved as if I was the Queen arriving on her balcony at a jubilee. Externally, I looked full of joy; and internally I felt relief.

What a delightful massage for the ego a birthday party is. A room full of friends and acquaintances telling you how fabulous you are. As my eyes swept, I clocked Alexander McQueen at a table, Peaches Geldof behind the DJ booth and Amy Winehouse at the bar. Drag queens – check. Uni friends – check. Fashion people – check. Celebrities – check. My mum and sister – check. *Everyone was there.* It was a triumph. I think Jack was with me that night, too, in spirit.

————

In the second half of the noughties, London's party scene was at its zenith. It was an extraordinary time to be invited to shiny, showbiz events, because there was so much money spent on everything. Guest lists were tight, production was big, carpets were crimson and cameraphones were non-existent. Maybe it's because I was in my early twenties, not yet jaded, but everything felt exciting. At the very least, there'd be crateloads of orchids on every surface, and pyramids of champagne glasses on arrival, like in the Ferrero Rocher commercial. These truly seemed to be the last glory moments before everything crashed down into a recession, and I was fortunate enough to experience a quick flash of this absolutely insane excess.

At the start of October, Terry Hart, the promoter of Drama, was involved in creating a humongous event for Faceparty, the online platform. Social media was still novel. It was to be held at the Truman Brewery on Brick Lane, and rumours circulated about it costing multiples of millions. Getting to know the entertainment business, I personally suspected it could be some kind of tax write-off masking as a public relations exercise, and honestly, those can be some of the most fun parties to go to. I went with Simon, Tomas and Ruby. It was a Tuesday – the start of our weekend.

We had dinner around the corner at Les Trois Garçons before trotting over. The restaurant's exterior tricked you into thinking it was a mere pub, but inside it was a bonanza of stuffed animals, including a giraffe whose head formed an arch over our dining table. Handbags hung from the ceiling like in a souk, threatening to decapitate you before the arrival of your bread basket. I ordered the offal, to show off. I wondered if it came from the giraffe. It tasted revolting, but gastronomy wasn't really the point of our reservation – it was the hot place to be seen. Sienna Miller sat a few tables away. I couldn't work out what was on her plate either.

The Faceparty event was evidently going to be everything it promised to be from the outset. Lasers cut dramatic green shapes in the London sky above like in *Batman*, and two separate entrances were presented to the guests – 'Virgins', and 'Sluts'. Purely out of irony my group headed straight for Virgins, where we were checked in and handed a package of drinks tokens tucked inside the type of small plastic baggie we were well accustomed to at the clubs. Tomas had spent the majority of dinner negotiating a business deal with a rich client on his mobile, something to do with water sports, which explained the amount of Evian he'd been tanking up with at dinner. He had to leave, but no matter. Our group would often splinter off – someone might get called away for work, someone might pull, someone might over-consume and head home, someone might get bored. We didn't complain, and rarely needed to explain.

The giant halls of the former brewery had been transformed into immersive showpieces – it was like walking around a movie set. The first room was a rainforest, dense with palm trees and steam, with a crashing waterfall in its centre. People were dressed as tigers, and some as 'savages' with spears, which I guess seemed fine to everyone at the time. A dark dungeon room contained all sorts of erotic she-nanigans – the 'Sluts' entrance brought you right up to this floor. A gimp slid past me like a slippery fish, the wet-look rubber suit only allowing their eyes to be exposed. They jumped on a platform to vogue, badly, limbs lolling and thrashing. Then they stopped, statue still, sustaining eye contact with me. The situation felt erotic-ally charged, until I noticed the catlike gaze. It was Ima Diva – I'd recognise that green glare anywhere. I fake-yawned so wide it gave me lockjaw. 'I thought she'd been deported,' Ruby wondered aloud, as we swerved towards the bar.

Fran Cutler's parties were unmissable – there'd be at least one every week. To be in the 'Fran club' was to have a fast-track pass into the hottest things in town – she was a conduit between the art, music and fashion scenes. A few days after I'd first met her, I saw her name light up my mobile. Fear hit me – she had quite the tough reputation in this city, and I thought she might be calling to ask for that dress back. But, no, she was calling to invite me to a 'faaaaab party, dahlinnn". I replied yes before she even told me what it was for. It turned out to be a night celebrating the launch of the John Galliano menswear line. I gagged with excitement – at twenty-one, it felt like I was being offered a seat at the grown-ups' table.

The party was at Harvey Nichols, the department store known to Knightsbridge residents as 'the corner shop'. Its Fifth Floor restaurant had been flooded with so many flowers it felt like a mafia funeral, and the heady essence of Galliano Diptyque candles made it smell like a church. The lights were low and flattering, and the room had taken on a baroque aesthetic – no sign of the mini-supermarket and sushi bar that lurked in its shadows. You see – the power of good lighting can transform a place.

I'd brought Kingsley as my plus-one, and we arrived composed and confident. It was deep midwinter and, as we stepped out of the cab, I instantly felt the icy air seep into my marrow. I was wearing very little – a black waistcoat barely covered my skinny torso. White panstick chalked my face and I'd drawn charcoal and red details around my eyes. I wore no wig, instead strapping on a stuffed fox – face and all. Animal rights campaigners would have thrown paint over me given the chance. I felt like I was walking in a Paris couture show, but looking back, it was quite a grotesque look. I had a licence to provoke, and I'd just laugh every time someone glanced at me with shock or disgust. I owned it – I had the power to create that reaction. We marched straight to the front of the line.

'You're not on the list,' declared the evil person with the clipboard. Her words hung frozen in the air. 'Oh, we definitely are,' I argued. 'We're on Fran's list.' She looked us up and down. A power struggle was clearly at play . . . and it was me that was struggling. I shivered like a little orphan in a Dickens novel; my fox was animated. 'Sorry . . . no.' And that was that. I was mortified. We'd been denied because of some miscommunication along the way – I didn't know I had to send an email RSVP. But you can sense what's coming, I'm sure. I wasn't wasting that outfit, and Kingsley had come all the way in from Middlesex for this. Plan B.

Ever enterprising, Kings thought it would be smart to find the loading bay and try our luck there. We dipped into the yawning entrance that displayed the word 'deliveries' out the back of Harvey Nics and told the guard in the tradesmen's cabin that we were there to work at the party. 'We're here to hand out the vol-au-vents,' stated Kingsley. I corrected him – 'Canapés.' Kingsley mumbled something about prawns. The guard stared at my fox and winced at the gnarly face staring back. 'All right, go ahead,' he muttered, looking perplexed. Our plan had worked. We were in the goods elevator within moments travelling up to the fifth floor.

In the hot room full of London's hot people, we began to thaw out. A tray of pink champagne cruised by – we took two glasses each. The famous Galliano newspaper print was on most surfaces, and most bodies. We paraded around, air-kissing cheeks we didn't know and accepting compliments about my 'major look', which Kingsley took full styling credit for. We drank until we were drunk enough to dance on tables as if it were a rave, and smoked until we ran out of people to ask for cigarettes from.

Oh, the social advantages of rolling with the rich, famous and beautiful (no one was ever all three at once, by the way). PR agents darted about shouting into walkie-talkies, and we laughed at their panic. We didn't see Fran – she was probably in a secret VVVIP room with some VVV famous people. We blew out as many Diptyque candles as we could, ran a few laps around the room, and half an hour later when the wax was vaguely dry we scooped them up like we were a couple of Artful Dodgers. With the still-warm glasses rattling in our pockets and bags, we left, this time via the main entrance.

During the attempted assassination of our night on entry, we really thought it was going to end in tears, but instead it ended with a party until dawn at a suite in a five-star hotel. We jumped on sofas with Galliano himself and saw so many faces I knew from the magazines. I'd find myself in all sorts of fabulous, flower-filled rooms over the next months, but I knew I needed to forge a career path of my own, and, coming from a working-class background, I knew it was going to take pure hard grind and hustle. Nothing was handed to you in this town. Time to get to work.

———

A few months later, at the crack of dawn – it could have been as early as 10 a.m. – I was startled awake by the annoyance of ringing coming from my handbag. I prised my eyes open, still caked in last night's mascara. Shards of light stung like bleach fumes. I'd been out until late with Camilla Fayed, whose dad owned Harrods. She'd been drumming up a bit of attention, hitting the scene most evenings in her personal London black cab, which came with its own driver in a flat cap. We'd been at a party for the Elton John AIDS Foundation in collaboration with Grey Goose, which would explain the half-full bottle of vodka I was spooning resolutely in bed. Flashbacks of dancing in Covent Garden Piazza with David Furnish and Liz Hurley popped into my head, as did raising my arm in an auction for a Jake and Dinos Chapman ice-cream van. I came to my senses around the £45,000 mark – my bank account was almost empty.

I winced. 'Uhhh, my hair hurts,' I uttered out loud, before realising my hair was in fact lying discarded on the floor, staring back at me. She looked exhausted. I answered the call.

'Hello?' I croaked, trying to centre myself in the spinning room. My eyes began to focus, and I wondered whose room it actually was. It wasn't a rare occurrence to regain consciousness in a bed that wasn't my own. I did some quick calculations – a huge chandelier above my head, and a fluffy Maine Coon cat staring at me, perched atop the bedside table, next to a framed picture of Dodi and Diana. I guessed I was still at Camilla's, then, in one of her guest rooms.

I'd forgotten I was on the phone. 'Jodie, darling, are you there?' I coughed up half a lung. 'Oh, hi, sweetie, it's Fred from Too2Much.' I bolted upright and fumbled around in my bag for a cigarette. 'We loved your birthday party, darling, and we wondered if you'd like to come and take over our Fridays at the club.' This was the invitation I'd really been waiting for, a move in the right direction. I'd give it a go, and, hey, if no one turned up, there was always going to be a plethora of guest-list jobs and podium-dancing gigs out there for me. 'I'm just in a business meeting,' I lied, 'but I'll ring you back. I'm interested!'

I hung up, and rolled out of bed, cringing at how embarrassing it was going to be, leaving a posh apartment building when I was in such a poor state of repair. I sucked it up and showed myself out, scuttling down Park Lane with my wig under my arm and my heels still on. The daylight was incessant.

————

Since I'd exploded into London like a heat-seeking missile half a decade earlier, I'd earned my keep after dark, when most people were asleep. I loved my sideways existence, and its antithesis to normal life. Not for me the routine of waking up at 7 a.m. and commuting to a job I hated. I was built for glittering in the shadows, built for the graveyard shift. I needed the brilliant and couldn't bear the banal. Like a werewolf, I'd committed to a moon-lit life, and realised that everything so far had been a dress rehearsal for this very moment. After my successful soft launch, I was ready to become a club promoter.

I set about organising the first night, channelling the teachings of people like Fran, Terry, Simon. The party was to be called 'Circus', a name that was informed by what my life was becoming – they do say you should allow your personal life to inspire your creative work, after all.

Andre J. was to handle the guest list – a fierce New York diva with a tough facade – and protect the doorway to the party. Once lured in, the punters would dance to my favourite DJs from the scene – Luke from Horse Meat Disco, the Lovely Jonjo, Tasty Tim, and a kid from up north I'd been chatting to on MySpace called Nick Grimshaw – Grimmy – who'd do the warm-up set.

There wasn't a strict music policy set in place – it was a play-what-you-want, mixed-bag vibe. I preferred the DJs at Circus to bring their own personality to the dance floor and curate their set like a movie soundtrack.

I'd met a magician called Dynamo and booked him to go from table to table doing tricks. Paloma Faith, a cockney red-headed cabaret singer with dreams of pop stardom, was engaged by the venue to croon in the upstairs bar. I hired a pair of pole dancers – a girl called Francesca who'd worked at the venue in its previous incarnation, and a boy called Hugo who worked in the City as a banker by day, and stripped down to a thong at night, like a kinky Clark Kent. This was my little team – my version of the Warhol superstars, my Hollywood studio system. We were set – an intergal-actic party generator was about to land in Soho.

I'd made it my mission to create the most potent punchbowl of people in that room. At just gone midnight on launch week, I looked out across the red-felt room. Opulence and trash were duelling, and it felt like some twisted hallucination. I was a glutton for the most over-the-top, attention-seeking characters – the more dazzling the exhibitionist, the better. I saw the bio-queen Holestar, who described herself as a 'tit in a wig' and was a dominatrix by trade. I saw the identical twins who were omnipresent around London at that time, whose names I never learned before they dis-appeared from the scene weeks later. I saw Shelly Would, Kabir, and a person painted from head to toe like a zebra with a bleach-blonde mohawk. There was an angelic boy on roller skates. There were flowerpots on heads. There were a lot of big shoulder pads. The face and form were technicoloured and distorted. Everything appeared so wrong, and at the same time, so right.

Big Dee came down, our unspoken beef seemingly behind us, as did a group of older drag queens who used to sneer at me, and who we'd secretly call the Dog Squad because of their unfavourable looks. There were famous faces, too, and the designers Matthew Williamson and Kim Jones. Because all these people were there, I was sure the rest would follow week in, week out. Success was surely coming my way.

Meanwhile, that night the hedonism had been turned up to high. I peeked out from the stage curtains and observed dancers gyrating body to body, just as I'd seen on other dance floors across the city. Friendships and love interests looked to be germinating. I watched, stirring the punch. With a full house, and powered on cocaine and champagne, the dopamine hit I got that night was off the scale.

But then we had to do it all again. After the volcanic eruption of week one, the second Friday presented itself as an anticlimactic dribble of lava. At 1 a.m. I stood behind the DJ, with a girl called Twigs who was a bit of a fixture in the booth in those days. I wallowed in embarrassment as Jonjo's music echoed around the empty dance floor. It was a humbling experience and suddenly it became clear: I'd have to work harder and smarter to build this empire. I piled a ski-jump of cocaine on to the back of my hand, a tonic to see me through. Daniel Lismore barged past wearing ginormous puffball sleeves and knocked the powder to the ground, an expensive snowstorm wasted.

One mundane party can often sound the clubland death knell, but for me, failure was not an option. I got to work. A photo shoot was organised for some adverts that I'd placed in *Time Out* and *QX* magazines — mad scenes of debauchery inspired by my favourite photographer, David LaChapelle, with me front and centre, sur-rounded my club-freak friends.

By day I traipsed around the West End's hair salons and fashion boutiques like the Pineal Eye and Kokon To Zai distributing piles of flyers. I'd hang out with the staff, try on clothes, and play music. Kokon To Zai had the best selection of electronic music on vinyl, and it felt like a daytime club in there.

I curated a team of hosts, like the glamour-puss Mika Doll, to bring a band of merry men, women and everything in between to sit at a table and drink Absolut vodka; some venues were known to decant Tesco own-brand vodka into high-end bottles, but not here. It worked – within weeks the club was rammed, and we stopped paying for promotion, applying a 'never advertised, always spoken about' school of thought.

MySpace was fast becoming a useful medium for connecting and promoting, and we posted bulletins on there, announcing who our guest DJ was each Friday. I brought in special guest performances from the likes of Amanda Lepore, the New York trans icon, who stepped out of the taxi wearing literally nothing but high-heeled shoes. Empress Stah would spin around on a hoop above the dance floor, body entirely aglow with glitter, which would sprinkle down on to everyone's heads, catching the light. While hindsight tells us the glitter was not very environmentally friendly, her twirl-ing dazzled – the finale would see a diamond necklace pulled out from an orifice. The performance artist Rhyannon Styles played a sad clown on stage, disappearing into a human-sized balloon and blowing it up with air from within until it burst. The room lapped all of this up.

Word of Circus became contagious. I had truly begun to deliver a great party and a great big ker-ching for the Too2Much cash registers. You could feel the manic panic coming from outside in the alley as people pressed against the door, literally fighting for Andre's attention, announcing they were on the guest list. Andre was great at pulling up the drawbridge if they didn't fit the vibe of the club and loved sending people to the back of the paying line if they couldn't see them written down. 'But I'm on Jodie's list,' was the plea most commonly heard rattling around Walker's Court. Several months ago that had been me, begging for entry outside Harvey Nics.

By the end of the first month, it felt like you didn't need to go out anywhere else, because everyone you knew was there in that room. Inside, Circus was like Weimar Germany meets New York's Area club. Outside, it was bedlam. Photographers snapped the then underage Pixie Geldof, Kelly Osbourne, Pete Burns, Jeffree Star. Every Friday, I walked through those heavy double doors in Walker's Court, having been scooped up by my security guard from the cab that dropped me on Brewer Street, took a deep breath, and braced for impact.

Oh yes, that security guard. I'd cajoled the club into hiring him to walk around the dance floor with me as I greeted guests in the maelstrom. I'd intended for it to enhance the drama, but I'm sure it came across as obnoxious. My likeability was becoming questionable in work scenarios, but the club was full, so what others thought of me rarely raised my concern. I was acting as though I was still at my birthday party, but with the indescribable buzz of turning a tidy profit. I was not immune to delusions by this point – in fact, they were rampant in me. In my head, producing a party gave me permission to act like both the studio and the movie star. In my little corner of clubland, I'd been elevated into some pantheon of micro-fame.

As part of my deal with the venue, I took the door fee – for £10 you could have the time of your life chez Harsh – and four hundred times ten was a lot of dosh. Banking piles of cash got me truly feverish. Add to that the loyalty card with my dealer, and an open bar tab . . . Those were high times.

I hired a godsend of an assistant called Dan who held everything together as I fell deeper into the dark hole of party notoriety and egotism. I barely remembered non-celebrity faces – names were met with amnesia. Dan would whisper into my ear to remind me who people were. In the daytime we worked hard on keeping the club exciting and fresh – new DJs, new dancers. Dan would meet my hangovers with bravado, trying to keep everything shipshape, including me.

On Friday afternoons I called around whoever I'd bumped into that week on the party circuit, ensuring the right cocktail of people had been invited these were the days when everyone spoke on the phone. Once twilight set in, we'd head to the party and get in among the night-blooming flowers of Soho.

Behind the scuffed velvet walls, down a grotty corridor, past a kitchen, and through a smelly stock cupboard was the Too2Much dressing room. It was a funny little curiosity of a space, untouched since the strip-club days, and was used to store props from the stage shows at the venue's other nights. I'd sit on one of the little stalls in there, taking off my stilettos to unpick cigarette butts from their grooves, and satisfy my insatiable lust for club gossip with the dancers and performers. While the main room was like pagan Rome, back here it was an intimate situation room, where inside stories were swapped under stark lighting, and secrets never left.

'I heard Madame Jojo's got raided by the police last night,' reported Empress Stah, as she lubed up her diamond necklace ready to insert it for her show. 'There's a footballer that's about to be busted for doing coke off my mate's tits in her strip club, the *News of the World* have got pictures,' Francesca alleged, fresh from the podium. Hugo, her pole partner, was sitting on the busted armchair wearing just a thong, knitting, minding his own business.

When fully loaded with booze and drugs and satisfied with gossip, I'd head back into the main room, the security guard pushing everyone out of our way as I showered in the confetti of a glorious, packed night.

Circus was my statement of intent – it was brash, colourful and played great music. It revealed the fun and games that became my brand of party. As cocky as I had become, I always understood the concept of the club as a home. I wanted to house the daydreamers and the weird kids of the playground, just like the Astoria, Trade and Heaven had housed me.

In the very best clubs, every walk of life is manifest. Regardless of your upbringing and your resources, your race, your generation or your identity, I wanted you to feel welcomed into the magic. I wanted to provide a safe place for you to dance away humdrum daily life. I wanted to endorse the unique and support the outsider. I wanted to hold the door open for other people like Jack who didn't fit in, and give them the best party ever. Life's too short not to.

7

BOOMBOX AQUARIUM

London was fucking me somewhat, and it had ripped the condom off while I wasn't looking.

On Monday morning I came to in a puddle of dribble, with coke bogies crusted into a ring around my nose. A list of missed calls flashed on my Sidekick, and a couple of angry-looking text notifications. What fresh hell was this? It seemed I'd fucked some people off and allowed havoc yet again to have the upper hand in my life. I punched out an apology reply to one and parked the rest for later. 11 a.m. was far too early for real-life dilemmas. This day had no business beginning just yet, thank you very much. My frontal lobe throbbed – self-inflicted. This hangover was colossal.

I dragged my aching corpse to the bathroom and pissed – a thick, acidic yellow, dehydrated kind of piss. It stung. I was supposed to be off the booze – a course of antibiotics to clear up a visit from Ms Chlamydia was working its way around my system. You can't trust a nun in London. I shook, turned, gripped the sink – it felt like the poison I'd consumed was about to return. I dry-heaved, spat strands of saliva into the porcelain, then regained composure. No puke. Result. See? A professional.

I glimpsed my reflection in the bathroom mirror. A strange creature stared back at me. A zombie. A vampire. Half a face of mushed make-up, bloodshot eyes, rough textured skin poked by brittle beard hairs. *If only Dad could see me now*, I chuckled. The chuckle hurt.

I've slept six hours since Circus on Friday, I thought, impressed by my quick maths. I winced at the sexually transmitted chafing in my upper legs as they hurled me back towards the nurturing cocoon of my duvet. I glugged from an open can of warm, flat Diet Coke – a failed attempt at tethering myself to the present. I hated it here. The sun had become a nuisance. I'd wake up mid-afternoon and spend the final gasps of daylight ordering food from Deliverance and DVDs from LoveFilm to my door. I was much more at ease in the early hours, saluting the moon, adventuring through the streets as the city slept.

A nebulous timeline of my night began to reveal itself. There seemed to be no distinguishable order to the places I'd been. Fragmented memories flashed into my peripheral vision. They felt thin, like a sticky residue on the bottom of a clubbed-out shoe.

A high-pitched ringing in my ears fought against half-memories of Tiga, Miss Kittin, Felix da Housecat . . . I could feel the palpitation of a bassline in my bones – it pummelled my head further, so I tried to focus on the ringing. I opened my laptop, which glared judgingly, typed DirtyDirtyDancing.com into the browser, and scoured for pictures of myself at the club hours before. I refreshed twice, in case the website was glitching, but no, it was me that was glitching, and it was too early for last night's upload. I moaned, feeling unripe for human consumption. Accepting that this was the type of hangover Nurofen Plus could not fix, I turned and became foetal, melting back to sleep, hoping for a new body by the time I awoke.

————

Let's put a pin in that for a moment and wind back the clock to twelve hours earlier.

Every Sunday, we went to Boombox. No exceptions, that was the rule. For a year, to miss a night was to miss an important strand of that club canon. It was the centre of gravity for the entire fashion and pop cultural worlds. We'd converge on Hoxton Square, where a mass grave of plague bodies was buried deep under our feet, clambering on top of each other like a dance floor of death, paving the way to our bohemia.

A decade before, this area had been a derelict wasteland, a cesspit of crime and poverty. By now, Victorian warehouses were luxury flats of exposed brick. High art was hung at the White Cube gallery, £10 bunches of tulips were bought on Columbia Road, cronuts were eaten on the street. For a minute there, the West End felt kind of embarrassing, and the gentrification of the East End was the main conversation piece at posh dinner parties and in *Grazia*. From Old Street roundabout to the shiny new Shoreditch House, twats were everywhere. It made London swing again.

The spectacle of a frothing queue always builds the exterior of a club into quite the theatrical production, and nowhere was this quite so apparent as Boombox. Its corner of Shoreditch was brought to a frenetic standstill every Sunday evening, as word of the show inside was passed around from mouth to mouth and magazine to magazine.

As the door picker of Boombox, Jeanette had the most important job in East London. Club kids and international fashion students pushed forward, clenching their teeth with rabid determination, desperate looks upon their make-believe faces. Jeanette, in head-to-toe Giles Deacon or Gareth Pugh, always remained composed. Desperation was sniffed out like a truffle, try-hards were rejected without remorse. This was a casting, of sorts – an audition. 'Yes.' 'No.' 'Not tonight.' 'Come on in, sweetie.' 'No, sorry.' While appearing elitist, Boombox cost nothing to enter, and the fun was democratic inside. Some level of disco dictatorship had to take place – after all, the club was a nucleus of only six hundred or so people in a city of ten million. But, oh, that queue – sometimes we'd leave the premises just to battle back through the baying mob and head in again. The dramatics on the street felt even more thrilling than the party inside. The most fabulous fact of all: clamped on to Jeanette's silver clipboard was a lone piece of blank white A4 paper – there was no guest list.

My nights out had become turbocharged with camera flashes and cocaine, and a phalanx of new characters was in my gang. On this particular Sunday, my party partners were Kelly Osbourne and her best friend Omar. Kelly was one of the most famous girls in the country – wild child daughter of Ozzy and Sharon, attitude-heavy star of reality TV, tabloid sensation. The three of us marched straight to Jeanette on the door, who was inflatable and shiny in something architectural and unmistakably Gareth Pugh. We air-kissed and greeted in an elaborate pantomime, before being ushered through – straight in, no lube.

Boombox's venue, Hoxton Bar and Grill, was a sort of *nothing-special* space that was transformed by a menagerie of vibrant creatures every Sunday evening. The smell of the day's burgers always hit you first – it was open as a cafe from noon. The Sunday-brunch grease diluted in the earthiness of the haze machine come twilight. The pong of beer hit you next. I never really got the appeal of fizzy hop water but respect its popular trajectory. Cigarette smoke added to the alchemy, plumes upon plumes of Marlboro Lights. It all muddled together, and it smelled like trouble.

Heads tilted – spun! The drag queen at the centre of every party, and the It girl from rock-star lineage. We *filled* the room. There were three distinct spaces within the venue – but there was so much overspill between the divides that walls lost their meaning. You arrived through a front bar, where widescreen glass opened on to a cinematic view of car headlights as they snaked round Hoxton Square's back alley. To the right was the food bit, a spot where we could hang out and chat away from the blaring decibels. The main dance room had a DJ booth and a big stage where people moved and peacocked, creating a sort of gauche tableau. In truth, it was nothing but a black box. The surroundings were unremarkable, the people were what made it really special. It was packed with all of London's pace-setters, its shakers and makers; adventures *thrashed* within it.

That night the place was filled to the brim. Rex the Dog was DJing, and later Jerry Bouthier was taking over. Bodies were stuck together like frogspawn in a garden pond. There was a beautiful tension in the room – there always was at clubs back then. Sexual, insecure, giddy tension. Kelly grabbed my hand, which was moist and squidgy with sweat, and winked at me. She led the way through the assemblage.

Gwendoline Christie called out to us from atop the dizzying bar. A six-foot-three powerhouse of a lady, she was a permanent fixture at Boombox, and always felt to me like an anachronism, a glamorous Studio 54 character who landed in the wrong decade. Gwendoline's stardom shone so brightly you needed sunglasses to look at her. I reached out to help her down, and we chit-chatted about the acting auditions she was going for that week. We left her to the bar, her stage.

Boombox was the connecting tissue of the mid-noughties

London fashion world, and we kissed faces from the pages of *Vogue* – Roksanda Ilinčić, Giles Deacon, Christopher Bailey from Burberry, the eternally cool Pam Hogg, the hot new supermodel Agyness Deyn. Further through, Kim Jones was sitting at a booth with the stylist and editor Katie Grand. She cast me on the spot for a shoot with Mert and Marcus the following day – a respectable 1 p.m. call time. The writer Tim Blanks joined the table with an armful of drinks sploshing. I helped him lighten the load, picking out a vodka tonic, before Kelly, Omar and I carried on our merry way.

The stylist Judy Blame rushed past, shimmering with an outfit covered in pins and needles. Gareth Pugh was leaning against a wall outside the toilets, deep in conversation with writer Hanna Hanra, who made a nodding gesture to acknowledge my presence and suggest a later conversation, which didn't materialise. That was the thing with these heaving nights – if you didn't catch someone the moment you bumped into each other, chances are you'd never see them again once you were swept up in the current.

Booby Tuesday was there, overheating in her bodysuit. The steamy climate was not a great pairing with her fabric. Dampness seeped over her face, which I felt and smelt as we hugged. The moment we let go, my eyes continued to scan the room and my mind continued to strategise. Over there was Randy Rockstar, always a good time, her occupation an unanswered question. 'I am obsessed with this shirt, diva,' she yelped, pointing at the 'NOBODY KNOWS I'M A LESBIAN' slogan across my chest. At home, I had one that shouted 'ASK ME ABOUT MY PENIS', which I planned to wear the following week. God, I was hilarious.

Speaking of penises, a man brushed past wearing nothing but a smile and trainers – not even a pair of socks. Kelly squealed as if she'd never seen a cock before. I'd seen two that day. Naked Man was omnipresent in London clubland in this era, I saw him everywhere. He seemed free and happy to be nude in public and accepted for it. He, and his willy, were just part of the furniture.

Richard Mortimer, the event's promoter, gave us each a drinks ticket at the bar. He'd been running parties in this neck of the woods for a few years, including the nights Golf Sale and Family, where I'm pretty sure Björk once came up to me, stomped on my food with force, laughed, and ran off, leaving me completely agog. Mortimer's revels were always similar in tone and were not built to last – I reckoned we'd have about three more months before he shut up shop and moved us on. Boombox was a temporary, noisy reaction to the grey, barren dullness that was creeping into the country in 2007 . . . The economic climate was overcast – worlds we created at night were the antithesis to everything on the news, an escape from the sorry state of reality. These were the last days of decadence as we plunged into national debt. We just didn't fully appreciate it for what it was yet, because we still had it – even if it was starting to slip from our clutches.

That night, such bleak thoughts were still being held at bay. Walking further through Boombox I happened upon the kaleido-scopic Lavinia Co-op, a grande dame of the drag world, her face painted like a circus clown. 'Miss Harsh, you skinny little cunt,' she heckled, as she raised a pair of golden opera goggles to her eyes. 'Have you got any gossip?' Sadly, and unusually, I didn't. The music was loud and bassy so I watched her lips, doing my best to decipher the words. I caught some titbits. Seemed juicy.

We journeyed through. Was that Princess Julia? It was. I shouted

'Juliaaaaaaa!' at her, but she was engrossed in conversation with Wolfgang Tillmans, and I didn't think she heard me, so onwards. Theo Adams, the performance artist with permanent orthodontic braces, was hanging off a vibrating stack of speakers, wriggling about to Uffie's 'Ready to Uff'. A titanic new kick drum cut through the margins – the Chemical Brothers, 'Do It Again'. Great tune. Gary Card and Matthew Stone seemed to be in hot debate by the fire exit. There was Carri Mundane, the designer of Casetteplaya, and Kabir, in a Grace Jones hood and two-inch-thick painted eyebrows. Looks upon looks!

An exchanged glance – a guy I'd had a little encounter with last week. We'd cruised in a WHSmith and ended up back at his. Did he know it was me? Did he recognise the boy through the make-up, the wig and the extra few inches the heels gave me? Although I was concealed behind a wall of artifice, you could still see the sketch of J underneath. He came over. I screamed internally. He said, 'Hi, nice to meet you.' He had no idea.

By this point, there were very few 'boy nights out' – it was either full-on Jodie Harsh, or a rare night in. The two versions of me were contained in their own temperature-controlled boxes. Wanting to be part of the in-crowd is very exhausting – I could only do it with one of my personalities. Out of drag I felt a little awkward, even a little shy, but in my warpaint I felt invincible, as if I were wearing armour. It became clear that my sweet spot was a very public work life, and a very private real life. Hannah Montana had nothing on me.

I waved at Mr Bonner, my old teacher from uni. He seemed to be out dancing more than me. I saw Millie Brown, whose party trick was vomiting up coloured paint in the name of performance art. I bumped – literally – into Russella, a drag queen whose schtick was cooking a pancake in the middle of the dance floor. Anyone who cast their eyes on this vision was spellbound by her cosmic mini-oven and batter-flipping technique. My wig got caught in her red sequinned apron as we collided in a cloud of pancake frazzle, and Kelly prised us apart.

My eyes wandered, cataloguing. I spied Cozette – always good for anecdotes and tattle. Another old pal was back on the scene, too – Ruby was perched on the bar, head to toe in a white Grecian robe, an angelic outer shell concealing the discreet devil within. We caught up: she'd been focusing on moving her work from the bedroom into the boardroom. After running away from her Catholic parents a decade before, she'd found solace in club and sex work. Now, it was time for another reinvention. She was planning to leave the club scene altogether as well, she said. I felt bemused at that admission – why would anyone want to leave all this? Nightlife was the centre of everything. I quoted the timeless Meryl Streep in *The Devil Wears Prada* – 'Everyone wants to be us.' I said that a lot.

Moving into the core of the club, we sliced through to the DJ booth, which was roomy, and allowed everyone to see us. A swarm of fashion students buzzed over like moths to a bright light. 'Hustler' by Simian Mobile Disco was playing. I knelt down next to the DJ's feet and hoovered a line of the devil's dandruff up my nose from a Kitsuné Maison CD case as Kel stood guard. I wobbled up, tasting the bitter stream down my throat. I scanned the room, drinking in the vignette. It was a poser's paradise in there. *Just the right mix of new school and the old guard tonight,* I thought.

The photographer Alistair Allan from the Dirty Dirty Dancing website spotted us. His voyeuristic archives of hedonism were uploaded every Monday for hungry eyeballs and ravenous egos. He snapped the famous faces and the talented people on the fringes of the mainstream. Hundreds of images would document every party, his trademark filter portraying a hyper-airbrushed version of events. I faced his line of fire, doing an impression of sobriety, throwing my arms around Kelly. I covered my dilated eyeballs with my fingers in the peace sign, and she mirrored me. Pose, pose; click, click; flash, flash. And then he was gone, off hunting, on a Shoreditch safari. At Boombox, people didn't want to disappear on a dance floor, they wanted to be watched, wanted to be seen, wanted to be immortal-ised by the lens, and they dressed competitively for that. This room was a catwalk for London's least boring people, embellished in looks from eras past and ideas for the future. Alistair's camera became an incentive to push aesthetics even further. If you were over the top, you weren't trying hard enough, and if you were there, you wanted everyone to notice it.

I shuffled over towards some commotion – a petite figure seemed to be drawing focus. I thought I was tripping – Kylie Minogue? *That really looks like Kylie Minogue.* It was, of course, *fucking Kylie Minogue,* dancing on the bar with her stylist William Baker, as her song '2 Hearts' blasted. The room swirled into a frenzy. Kylie twirled in the distance in a skintight leather dress, and on the dance floor Kelly spun and I stomped. We shared little snatches of dia-logue over the righteous kick drum.

Two more hours remained, and my bouncing powder wasn't working. It was kind of just levelling me out, a plateau of numb-ness. *Fuck it,* I thought, *I'm gonna find some Ketamine.* I knew who'd have it, and I knew where to find them. That club was so predict-able. Girls' toilets, second cubicle in.

Minutes later, back on to the hot dance floor's wet embrace. The K was burning my nose and the music sounded lighter. At once my legs felt like they were made of cotton wool. I sank slowly into the ground as if it were quicksand, the horse tranquiliser coursing through my blood, cushioning me. And just like that, without warning, I found myself lying on the floor, a dense forest of shuffling legs like trees around me. Kelly yanked me up. 'You just fucking stacked it,' she shouted at me. 'Fucking idiot.'

The last track of the night played out – Gossip's 'Standing in the Way of Control'. I'd heard it everywhere that weekend. I took a hit of poppers. Apparently, someone had dropped an entire bottle of amyl over themselves at Boombox the previous week and was then set alight by a stray cigarette butt, but I wasn't there to witness the inferno. I huffed from the bottle again. My head rushed. Kelly disappeared, and I mirrored an invisible dance partner. She came back into focus, and we looked at each other and laughed.

The lights went up at 1 a.m. and we scurried out from their harshness like bugs from an upturned rock. Back into the abrasive, music-less reality of Hoxton Square that reeked of hot bin juice, looking for the after-party. I'd recently moved to Hoxton, to live in a flat above the Breakfast Club. I'd taken over the lease from the musician Tim Burgess, and the selling factor was its convenient location, a twenty-second strut in a heel to Boombox. My afters suggestion was accepted, our destination secured, a building full of neighbours pissed off, likely an email from my landlord incoming. *Fuck it,* I thought. I *always* pressed the fuck-it button. 'The more, the merrier – all back to mine!'

The rest of the night became pixelated, but I had photographic flashes of drag icon Jacqui Potato laying an egg on my living-room floor like a chicken. This was her party trick, and it's not hard to imagine which orifice the egg plopped out from. It was still there at 11 a.m., uncracked, a perfect ingredient for a cooked breakfast once it'd been rinsed off.

A rhythmic pattern of pre- and after-parties bookended most of my nights. Sometimes they turned into a solo finisher, where I'd ping about my flat in a face full of make-up with no wig on, polishing off the leftover powders and liquid. I'd chase that up the following morning with a shot of shame, a teaspoon of regret, a line of pain. I flirted between raging highs and aggressive lows. Moments of 'feeling normal' were rare and dulled down. Ever in the party spirit, I strived to keep the glass half full, but by now the glass was spilling over with vodka.

'Are you maybe an alcoholic or, like, an addict?' asked Finn. The words impaled me. I'm ashamed to say, I removed him from my friendship circle soon after. Yet despite my dismissive response to his and other friends' concerns, I had a gnawing sense that I wouldn't be able to ignore them much longer.

———

Fast-forward to where this chapter started – in bed, demolished by a hangover of Greek tragedy proportions. My liver was pissed, and I had a photo session to get to in an hour. An omelette, two Marlboro Lights and a fistful of ibuprofen brought me back to life – the breakfast of champions.

I made it to the Mert and Marcus shoot for *Pop* magazine. It was themed around London's beautiful and damned, and starred Kate Moss, Lily Allen, Peaches Geldof, Jonny Woo and a cast of night flowers from the club. I was half-naked, my lithe frame balancing on a pair of Westwood stilt-like platforms, nipples painted pink. Katie Grand and a team of fashion assistants styled me, pulling and tugging at corsets and pantaloons while I struggled to stay afloat in my hangover. And as I stepped on to set, Mert asked me if I'd take my wig off. The photographers shot the pictures while taking turns wearing it on their heads. The images looked beautiful in print.

———

The flat by Hoxton Square was my danger zone. It placed me in the axis of the N1 and E2 action, a base to start and end my night crawling with all sorts of unsavoury people. A long grey balcony looked out on to Old Street, and I'd sit with my legs swinging above a huge fake human spine attached to the front of the osteopath clinic below, chain-smoking. I never emptied the ashtrays, and when it rained they became a black sludge of toxic waste. A cancer soup, of sorts.

There was a surge of club nights popping up all over the space of a few square miles, and most of them were run by friends. There was Nuke Them All, and Trailer Trash, and All You Can Eat, and Slimelight. There was 333 if we wanted a cheeky one but didn't want to leave my actual street, Bistrotheque if we were hungry for revolutionary cabaret, and Beach Blanket Babylon if we felt posh. There were so many enticing and exotic things to do – what a shame it would have been to have stayed in. We had to go to everything, urgently, as if time was running out – and it's true, some parties seemed to close before they even opened.

Too2Much had changed hands and transformed into Soho

Revue Bar, and I had ants in my pants. I moved Circus over to what I'd now consider a lousy venue on Shoreditch High Street, which ended up being a big mistake, and taught me not to mess with a party's location. It didn't hold the same appeal for my clubbers, who quite enjoyed the jaunt into town for their Fridays in a luxe Soho venue. In Soho I'd walk into Circus and know everyone in the room, but across town I recognised very few faces. The hysterical melee outside had become more of a murmur. What was bedlam in Soho became a deflated balloon in Shoreditch.

For our opening night, I booked in a performance from a girl who'd been messaging me on MySpace called Charli XCX. She was dropped off at the back door by her parents because she was only fifteen at the time. It was one of her first gigs as a baby pop star, and she performed to an early-doors crowd of perhaps twenty people. She owned the stage and sang like she was headlining an arena, and I knew she was going places.

I walked around with a live six-foot snake around my neck, accompanied by its handler from a company called Animal Actors. It spent the whole night shitting all over me – bright-yellow, runny, smelly, serpent shit. It was not the Britney moment I'd envisioned. Apparently snakes only defecate once every few weeks, and my wriggly friend chose that night, potentially because of the stress of being a python in the middle of an actual fucking dance floor.

Circus needed some buzz. I threw a one-off party at the top of Centre Point and lost a fortune on the bar – huge fail. I took it to Café de Paris, the iconic venue that had housed events like Pushca and Kinky Gerlinky in the past – and the biggest storm of the decade hit that night, so everyone stayed home. Huge, huge fail.

And then another: Circus took over an area at Lovebox Festival in

Victoria Park, and I booked Felix da Housecat to close with a DJ set. Nile Rodgers from Chic arrived at the side of the stage and asked if he could have a live jam during his set, but he was turned away by one of the kids I'd booked to manage the arena, who didn't recognise my musical hero. I was doing gak in a Portaloo somewhere. Fail, fail, fail.

An email came through from a DJ in Liverpool called Yousef who owned the trademark for club nights in the UK called Circus. I was so clueless and wrapped up in my own self-importance that I barely looked outside of this microcosm I inhabited. Google told me his night was huge, and Yousef was – still is – a legend in the game. That was the final nail in the coffin – it was time to wind this night down and think of my next move. It had paid the rent for a few years and given me a stencil for my flavour of club nights in the future, but it seemed cursed. That was it – no more room for failure.

At the Shoreditch High Street venue, I held a funeral-themed night for our last party, which was sparsely attended. A fake Jodie Harsh sculpture lay in a coffin on the stage. I set it alight half an hour before closing time, which created much bigger flames than expected. I stood and watched a burning effigy of myself, face melting and contorting, thick black smoke polluting the room, people running away from pretend-me coughing, shocked at my reckless stunt. The fire brigade was called because the entire building's alarms were set off. One final fail, and Circus was cremated.

———

Throughout 2007, musical tastes were shifting. Nu rave nudged in from the outskirts of culture, bringing with it wacky aesthetics and some absolute characters who glanced at life sideways. Unlike other youth movements, it seemed to have no set soundtrack, which made it difficult to anchor – it was a megamix of electroclash, grime and indie sleaze. Bands like the Klaxons and Gossip were its superstars. Frankmusik, Kissy Sell Out and Bip Ling were its underground hotshots. The visual focus was irreverent, the nerd and the outsider were celebrated. Metallic lashes, bruises and fake blood were applied, reminiscent of the New York club kids of the nineties. Dayglo skiwear was worn; gold spray-painted phones were on heads as accessories. Every weekend, a new direction was passed around like a whisper. For all of forty-eight hours, the nu ravers were even fashioning frog and sheep masks into their looks and calling it 'zoo rave'.

Decades earlier, pop art forced people to look at the 'normal' and consider it as serious culture. But nu rave flipped that on its head. It forced the viewer to look at the abnormal on the surface – the extraordinary, the freak – and consider it as *normal*. It was certainly about upending the establishment, but it wasn't angry like punk was, for example. A generation had passed since the days of illegal gatherings in fields up and down the motorways, and these were the spoilt children of the original ravers. With self-promotion egged on by the fashion press and the Sunday supplements, it was commercially savvy and ready to be commodified. But fun was always at the very top of the agenda.

For the first time, social media, identity, promotion and performance started to mingle. We met on MySpace, the worldwide shop window where your status update said more about you than anything else in your entire life. It was less about consumption, and more about connection and expression. MySpace was the attention economy's soft launch, where we traded not in likes and follows, but in requests for friendship.

We also kept abreast of what everyone else was up to via the pages of *SuperSuper* – a hallucinogenic trip of a zine that became our bible. It was like *Vogue* for club kids, the *NME* for the 'me generation', and it disappeared without a trace after issue 10. But most importantly, we met on the dance floor. Nothing could replace the nightclub for physical connection.

Every Saturday, the club to be at was AntiSocial. Enter Scottee, a new character in the movie of my life. He was one of the night's organisers – part performance artist, part court jester, part promoter. His costumes would fluctuate in scale and structure week by week, and he'd often pay homage to Leigh Bowery. We first connected on MySpace, of course, and he soon found his way on to my Top Eight. 'Girl, come down and DJ for us at AntiSocial,' read the message.

I'd never really considered being a DJ before, much like how I'd never really pondered the concept of writing a book until the idea was placed in front of me. But it made perfect sense – I loved music – I had a vast collection of it and an encyclopaedic knowledge of the dance world. I'd spent virtually my entire childhood in the Our Price record store in Canterbury, and as an adult, I was ravenous for new music. I loved to give people a good time, loved technology, loved to be out and about. *Loved* the attention. Maybe I could indeed become a DJ – just once, at least. Perhaps my inner jockey had been waiting in the wings, unconsciously trained up over the last seven years by dance floors around the city.

I arrived at the glass-fronted venue – Bar Music Hall, on Curtain Road – with a case of CDs and no headphones. I'd been practising with my DJ friend Kris all week, who'd told me a set is a declaration of taste. I was taking this as seriously as I could. I planned to open the performance with Princess Superstar's 'Perfect (Exceeder)', which was an incessant tune at the time. I wore a gold sequinned flapper dress for the occasion with a pair of Topshop pumps – great for the aesthetic, terrible for the ingrown toenails – and a red wig punctured with roses. I looked fantastic, I was sure. But I was irreversibly drunk. I'd been at a Klaxons gig, and on this occasion, I had to be carried *into* the club, rather than just out. Leopard print never changes its spots.

Scottee and his best friend Buster ran the night and DJ'd together as Yr Mum Ya Dad. In private I called them 'You're Scum You're Sad' until Scottee reached out that time and invited me into their world via the DJ set, therefore sealing us as allies. They met me outside the club and seemed visibly amused as I fell out of the cab, on to their feet. We went on in. It was rammed inside. I spotted lots of Henry Holland slogan T-shirts, lots of fascinators, lots of stickers on faces, lots of oversized pussy bows, and golden American Apparel leggings so tight that sperm counts must have been compromised. There was glitter, which I had learned to avoid as it showed up in hard-to-reach places. There was neon fluff, as if a Mad Hatter's tea-party was being thrown on Sesame Street. No Bra were on stage – they performed exactly as labelled on the tin. Nu rave London was out in full force for my debut.

The basic skill set required to DJ is relatively low – if you can control a Nintendo, you can *probably* wing a set. But to be great at it is a whole other story. A DJ must be part musician, part shaman, part tech nerd, part crowd psychologist. It requires skill, but it's also about feeling. That first night, I played like an amputee. As soon as I walked into the booth, everything I'd spent the week learning evaporated. My eyes glazed over as I stared at the mixer

– I could have been looking at the cockpit of a plane for the first time. I couldn't remember what a single button, dial or lever did. Scottee ended up taking over the whole second half of the set as I pointed at tracks and said, 'That one next!' while dancing about in the booth.

The following day I awoke from what could almost be described as a medical coma. I fumbled over a glue gun and a pile of cut-up vintage clothes, remnants of a Kingsley visit that had turned my flat into a fashion atelier and hair salon, and missioned to the living-room table, which functioned as my office. I plugged my digital camera into the USB socket of my computer and dumped the photos of the DJ set on my Flickr account. I stared at them, smiling as they uploaded. I was a DJ. It looked right. It felt right. Something had been unlocked in me that night.

———

After a night out, or a night of work, we'd often carry on at illegal venues dotted around the local areas. A rave barge on the canal, a fully kitted-out dominatrix's dungeon, that sort of place. There was an illegal party parlour in the back of a kebab shop which stank of salmonella and rat poison. You had to knock three times to get in there – if you gave a fourth knock, they wouldn't open the door. Inside, half the floor was missing, and we drank cups of straight vodka surrounded by crooks at 5 a.m.

We'd go to Gary's Place, a speakeasy at the top of a tower block that overlooked Bethnal Green. You'd pull open the heavy door of the mildew-coated elevator and find what looked like the interior of a medieval castle in front of you, tapestries and all, and a bedroom converted into an English pub. Playwrights, artists and reprobates could be found there. There'd be the people that made London tick – a Fran Cutler, a Chapman brother, a Lily Allen. Actual Gary himself resided there. He'd be telling stories and hosting the congregation as Hackney twinkled twenty storeys beneath us. It was unlicensed and felt illicit. The party would close down when Gary wanted to go to bed, which was rarely ever. Same, Gary, same. Live east, die young, they say! Well, I was certainly trying.

Some of our regular watering holes were actually *above board*. I barely left the Macbeth. There was the George and Dragon pub, great for an early shot and a nosey at the White Cubicle, potentially the world's smallest art gallery, in a former loo. There was the Royal Oak pub, on a council estate off Columbia Road, which opened at the crack of dawn for the flower sellers on Sunday, and therefore became our place to carry on the Saturday sesh. We loved the pokey little Russian Bar on Kingsland Road, which seemed to be populated exclusively by a mix of club kids and actual villains. There was the Joiners Arms – heading there would guarantee a much darker circumstance. That hole kidnapped people – you'd arrive at 9 p.m. for a nightcap, and miss the whole following day of work, utterly ruined by its seedy temptations. Its canary-yellow walls and ceilings of barely two metres created a sweatbox of sin, a coven of dancing silhouettes, ruinously high in the sleazy darkness.

And then Aquarium, in Old Street. Oh, Aquarium. Disgusting venue; mythical reputation. It was a sensory overload, that place. It had a little swimming pool in it – or was it a jacuzzi? Regardless, the water was grey and murky, and the stench of its staleness hit you hard. The whole place smelled like feet. If that didn't knock you for six, the thump of the sub-bass did. The music galloped faster in there – minimal house and techno, far from my flavour.

I'd been out and about in a dark and run-down corner of London, boozing at Miquita Oliver's birthday party, then hopping around the East End chasing something or other. I was telling everyone I was 'clean' that night – proud not to have touched a single grain of powder. Unfortunately, I more than made up for it with alcohol.

In Aquarium, I poured more vodka into the cup I was holding to disguise the taste of Sprite. I virtually fell into the decks, slurring at the DJ to switch up the music. 'Play "Perfect (Exceeder)",' I pleaded. I crawled over to the pool. Club kids seemed to be sitting around it in K holes – it looked like a surreal pop art installation. Jacqui Potato was there. Jacqui Potato was everywhere. Her face was smudged from the humidity and stubbled after a weekend of raving and laying eggs. Allegedly she had a sister called Trish Fingers, who I never met.

As if on a Mediterranean holiday, I slipped off my heels and dipped my feet into the swampy water, breaking the grey film seal that floated on top. Athlete's foot was of no concern to me. 'I should have brought my bikini!' I screeched, raising no laughs. I was drunk – deep-in-the-black-abyss drunk, and the room appeared soft-focus. My final memory was of submerging fully into the putrid water. In drag. In public.

I awoke the following morning and looked around, no idea where I was: I seemed to be in a tiny cabin-like coffin. I was sopping wet and I stank. My wig was next to me, I'd been hugging it like a teddy. My face was numb, having slept on a cold tile. It was then that I realised I'd fallen asleep inside a toilet cubicle. The management or security must have skipped the toilets in their final checks before they locked up. I scrambled for my Sidekick – 10.47 a.m., Monday. I was locked inside the club. *For fuck's sake, J.*

A cleaner had the fright of his life when I stumbled out like a zombie from *28 Days Later*. He let me out into the harshness of Old Street roundabout, and I meandered home, looking – and smelling – like a fucking freak.

The slivers of daylight that touched my skin here and there felt lethal. My hangover was apocalyptic. I pinned the blame on Mercury, for we were in retrograde.

But it was me. It was my fault.

I was out of control.

8

MAHIKI
BOUJIS
MOVIDA

Britain was broke. It's all we were talking about. The strippers felt it first. 2008 was going to be tough.

While the country was financially down and out, many of its club scenes were popping off – especially in the bulletproof Wild Wild West End of London. Within the hyper-wealthy village of Mayfair, the streets were paved with Tories. Under these roads, a subterranean circuit board of dens could be found that watered more richies and wannabes than you could shake an Amex Black Card at. And unlike its neighbour, Soho, which wore its sleaze on its sleeve, Mayfair concealed its sins under a thin layer of gold plating – you just had to know where to look for it. At its very centre, around the corner from the Ritz hotel, in the bowels of a grand townhouse with a white facade, was Mahiki. The name was Polynesian for 'tunnel to the underworld', and I found it much more fun there than the other hedge-fund hellscapes in Mayfair that seemed to attract the worst type of finance bro. For a while, I was what you'd call a regular; I went every Monday, kick-starting a week of rampage.

Late May. London was heating up for a summer of economic loss and social anger. The perfect time for a recession procession down to Mahiki, where a cocktail could cost almost a whole day's wages for the average citizen. I barely paid for a sip any more – the venues showered me with liquor, on the house. Kingsley and I were heading out to this parliament of privilege to gawp at American heiress

Paris Hilton. We were obsessed with *The Simple Life*, the reality TV show she starred in where her role was to go to work like a normal person. She was hosting the party that night, which entailed very little other than arriving and leaving. Rumours circulated of a £70,000 pay cheque – the *Daily Mail* worked out what her appearance was costing the club per minute. It was a lot. Most people in the country were struggling to make their rent.

I roared up to the door with Kingsley in a rickshaw. I'm sure you can picture it: pink fluffy upholstery, Abba's 'Dancing Queen' blaring, mini disco ball spinning. For some, an arrival like this would have been the absolute kiss of death, but I could get away with levels of gauche and camp that very few in this town could. I was Jodie Fucking Harsh – queen of the scene.

We had rattled down Piccadilly from Soho Square, pulling right up to the entrance after speeding past a long parade of panic. The great and the guest-listed were queuing from the tip of Dover Street, but I never queued any more. I thrusted a twenty-pound note into the rickshaw driver's hand, and the red velvet rope was lifted. The security guys chuckled – they were used to a bit of chaos when I was down. The previous week I'd rocked up with Sarah Harding from Girls Aloud, who was there to support her DJ boyfriend. As we tunnelled into the dance floor, some drunken buffoon grabbed my wig, ripping it clean off my head. I was maimed and mortified. A room full of people stared, aghast. Sarah came to my rescue, punching the guy straight on the chin, before recovering my wig from the club floor. I was found crouched in the corner like Gollum, shocked and quivering, clutching my scalp.

One's entrance to a discotheque can be like a high-stakes board game – sometimes a well-thought-out move has to be executed to create the perfect impact. My rickshaw pit stop was no match for the absolute earthquake Henry Conway pulled off that same night. It was his twenty-fifth birthday being celebrated at the club, and a horse-drawn cart with elaborate gilding trotted him up to the door, totally outdoing my pathetic cycle. The crowd waiting in line cheered as he stepped out of its cabin like a prince, all regal in his frilly shirt and Regency cosplay. He'd been making a bit of a splash in the papers as his dad was an MP who'd found himself in a spot of trouble, and the sudden rush of media attention proved to be a worthwhile launch pad for Henry's career promoting parties. He knew everyone young, beautiful and loaded, and like me was friends with pop stars and heiresses. He had a mane of golden locks and single-handedly led the white-trouser movement. He boasted a reputation for effortlessly tossing out compliments and kindness with favour. 'Hello, chicken, thank you for coming out tonight,' he gushed with ceremony as our feet met at the entranceway. He was as well mannered as ever. 'My apologies for upstaging you there – nice rickshaw, though,' he laughed, extinguishing his skinny pale-blue Vogue cigarette on the ground as we whooshed through the carved wooden doors. I laughed too – 'You bitch!'

Henry was ever so dignified, but this was not the court of Versailles we were stepping into, nor Buckingham Palace. It was something far less classy than that. Mahiki was a kitsch, overly themed tiki bar in a part of town that otherwise took itself seriously. Inside, smiling waiters in Hawaiian shirts greeted us, missing the geographical mark somewhat – cultural accuracy had little to do with anything in the noughties. The familiar falsetto of the Bee Gees blurred into Wham!'s 'Club Tropicana' – Toto, we weren't in Fabric any more. The club was larger than expected from street level. The atmosphere was that of a nocturnal carnival and the interior was like something you'd find in Disneyland – plastic bamboo-effect walls, with fake palm fronds hanging down from the ceiling. But if you went to Mahiki, you were kind of in on the joke.

We were surprised to find the club half full. Vacant chairs sat at empty tables, and there was a soulless, anticipatory atmosphere. There may have been more waiters than customers, playing musical statues. Why, then, was there such a huge queue outside? There was plenty of space for all.

We were shown to our area. Rattan chairs were pulled out for us, and a wood-framed menu arrived with a little LED strip light attached to it. My finger skimmed the list and I gazed gluttonously at the syrupy options. I already knew exactly what I wanted – the 'it' drink. Soon a wooden box was hurled on to the table, usually priced at a recession-denying £400 but, to us, on the house. The Mahiki Treasure Chest was the stuff of legend in these parts – a concoction of coconut rum, Dom Pérignon and juice, loaded with ice, garnished with sliced fruit and tropical flowers. It was stabbed with twenty long straws so everyone around your table could jump on in and start sucking. The backwash alone surely added another half a litre.

'Go easy tonight, eh, Harshy?' laughed a waiter, as I leaned down to start lapping up the sugary contents. I had no idea what he was referring to – the past few times I'd been here, I was sozzled, and what happened then was no business of mine.

It was just Kingsley and me that night, meaning there was a lot of Treasure Chest to go around. The two of us sat there, slurping the family-size, high-proof liquid, waiting for Paris to arrive. Maybe we'd catch Prince Harry – he'd been down a few weeks before.

Maybe he'd sat right where we were sitting, perched on the worst table in the house, the first one you came across by the draughty door – virtually Outer Mongolia.

Where was Paris? We glanced around. A higher-than-average turnout of socialites and debutantes had flocked in, perhaps hoping some of the glam Hilton magic would rub off on them. We saw sulking girls at tables, on the meter, surrounded by rich men. Lots of international student types, too – it was as if LSE and Imperial had a special deal with the club. There were husband-hunters, slightly past their prime, on the prowl for a lucrative catch – a tech millionaire, or hotshot city banker, or a toff from noble stock – old money was the hardest fortress to scale. A couple of terminally tacky Hilton wannabes were table-less, free-range and shuffling about, impatient for their idol's arrival. One had clearly fought a losing battle with her hairdresser.

A slurring, insufferable man plonked himself down on a chair next to us, uninvited and unwelcome. I recognised him – but couldn't quite place where from, some tenuous connection of a fair-weather friend, I expected. He told us he was vaguely related to a European royal family. He explained how he was too rich to do cocaine and tried to sell us on the merits of doing heroin. He'd just returned from Monaco, so he said. 'We lost the yacht but at least the hookers there are tax-free.' Kingsley and I didn't even need to look at each other – we had the power to communicate without using words. This haemorrhoid of a man had to go. I called security over to deal with the situation.

While he was being carted off, I ran to the toilet, on high alert for any groping hands that might lurch towards my wig. En route, I was cornered by a second-rate It girl I couldn't stand. In terms of social climbers, she stood at the summit of Mount Cunt. She was blue-blooded and bleached blonde. At almost every party I went to, she was there, reeking of nepotism. That was the thing in those days – there was no hiding behind a screen, there was no blocking, no muting. If you didn't like someone, you'd still be face to face in a room with them three times a week. As she talked centimetres from my face, I smelled stale champagne, and I strained to stop my eyes glazing over. She chewed my ear about Henry's horse-drawn carriage, knowing full well we were friends. 'I can't believe how scandalous that was,' she hissed. 'The papers are going to have a field day over it.' I did my best to appear interested and animated as she talked at me, exhaling her death breath into my nostrils. 'Money talks, wealth whispers,' she exclaimed with her California twang, a souvenir from years of fucking mid-rate American actors. 'Right, yeah,' I mustered back, my internal dialogue wondering how she got her moisture-less skin to turn such a shade of mahogany. I excused myself before a vast monologue continued – 'I'm so sorry, I'm about to piss myself,' I pleaded, as she scrunched her face up like a bulldog.

I emptied my bladder and boshed some coke up my nose in the cubicle. Pretty much everyone did cocaine in the circles I moved in then, and it was my sole drug of choice – any powder that made me relinquish control was pushed aside by now. It's funny how people's favoured chemicals seem to reflect their existing personalities. I liked how cocaine rushed through me, made me feel superhuman – at least for fifteen minutes, after which I craved more. I liked the ritual of it, chopping out the lines on a shiny surface. I loved the social aspect. I even loved the sniffing and the running and the way it made me rub my nose in a weird reflex – it felt rock 'n' roll. Some of the people around me didn't feel the same passion for my use of it. It made me bolshy, and rude, and impatient. It made me argumentative and obnoxious. It made people not want to hang out with me.

Often, due to consistency of use, the medicine cabinet failed to work: this was one such night. The vibe was off, my social meter was running low and the room had become too busy to relax in. The clock struck one, and Henry's coach had already turned into a pumpkin outside – it was time to call it a night. As we ascended the stairs back up to street level, we were caught in gridlock. Kingsley had escaped through the door at the top. Without a chance to work out what was happening, I was thrust aside by the same security guard I'd shared a laugh with on the way in. Suddenly I was pinned to the wall by a mob of black suits moving in the opposite direction to me, surrounding a sparkling dress and an angelic halo of golden hair. Paris, protected in the middle of them, stopped suddenly, raised her glasses, locked eyes with me, and simply declared, 'That's hot,' before carrying on down. And that was all I needed.

———

My social status in the London clubland hierarchy had progressed from ingénue to hot property. I was surrounded by interesting people, and music, and nightclubs, and glamour. And tonight, like most nights really, I wanted to live like a star. Picking up on the recent groundswell of interest, supermodel Naomi Campbell had booked me to walk in her Fashion for Relief charity catwalk show at the Natural History Museum, a place I had been astounded by on school trips.

That day, my friend Rowan picked me up from the Hoxton flat. We cruised along the Embankment to avoid the West End at rush hour; the grand dome of St Paul's Cathedral appeared tiny in comparison to the glass blocks that were being erected all over the city, forming a bigger, bolder corporate backdrop. Houses of God and commerce lined the banks, just as they always had done. The river cut through a city divided by extreme wealth and extreme poverty, and with national debt piling up, we were constantly reminded about being in a sorry state in every headline.

We arrived at the 6 p.m. call time. I had my picture taken with Vivienne Westwood, Princess Beatrice and the other celebrity models. I smoked in the toilets and swigged champagne on an empty stomach. By 9 p.m., when I strutted out as one of the final models, I was obliterated. It all went by in a blur, but I remember the room cheering for me as I walked the runway, and I remember how good that felt. Doing special things like this allowed me to believe I was making a mark in the world I was obsessed with when I was a teenager. But deeper than that, moments like this made me feel accepted in the city I called home.

My drinking was cranking up and cracks were appearing under the bonnet. I was numb, perhaps feeling undeserving of the joy I was receiving. Perhaps it was my way of coping with high-octane situations, or perhaps it tricked my brain into feeling like I belonged in a scene packed with nepo babies, rich folk and superstars. But sometimes you've just got to fake it to make it.

After the fashion show, I jumped back into Rowan's Range Rover. He lived next door to me, and while we were from very different upbringings, he thought I was entertaining to be around. For a while we'd hit the clubs together as a double act. Being in drag, I'd be a bit of a magnet for girls asking how I did my make-up, and where I got my dress from. That would lead to an introduction to Rowan, who very much enjoyed the opportunity to talk to pretty ladies. We cruised through Kensington and swung into the Roof Gardens, which was empty – just a couple of old grey flamingos pacing on the terraced garden. An urban myth circulated for years that one of the flock had been thrown off the side of the building.

We continued across our route of the Monopoly board. Nobu wasn't far – the original one – so we dropped in to find something microscopic to line the stomach with. As a general rule I didn't eat in drag – lip gloss! – but sushi rolls were easy to drop into the gullet without touching the sides. The usual shouts of '*Irasshaimase*' followed us as we were shown through the packed restaurant to our table. Although we were deep in financial depression, the Mayfair bubble appeared determined to ignore it. I was hard to miss, and it felt like the whole room dropped their chopsticks and stared at me. And wouldn't you? A man in drag, in 2008, at a posh restaurant, was not one of the usual sights you'd expect from your sushi dinner on Park Lane.

Blackened cod digested, we made a pit stop at Whisky Mist under the Hilton hotel next door. I called it Whisky Pissed because they'd drop a bottle of vodka in front of me within a minute of walking in – I used that place like an off-licence. Then, we careened to Kensington proper. The destination was Boujis, a pocket-sized festival of wealth in a town that could barely keep the lights on.

I'd started to take DJing more seriously and made a real go at it as my main source of income. London responds to heat, and gigs were flowing in, and I was hustling – exhaustively – for more. But I was living in my overdraft, only just scraping by with my rent payments. This was an expensive town, just leaving the house cost you £50. Thankfully, drinks were usually free, wraps of coke traded for spots on guest lists, and I'd often get given clothes to wear by the fashion designers I hung out with in clubs – so the most important things were covered gratis.

Boujis was fantastical, if you were a person that had never stepped foot in a nightclub before. It was no comparison to the places I'd been and the things I'd seen. These 'bottle shops' were like one giant VIP room, all roped-off tables and gigantic mark-ups and cunts everywhere. I disliked the us-and-them divide that a VIP area created, so hated an entire venue of it even more. A formula was followed, elitism ran rampant, and the true culture of clubbing seemed to have been chucked out of the fire exit. I yearned for the feelings that other venues gave me in those weightless former years. I missed being sixteen, seventeen, eighteen. I lamented the Astoria, Heaven, Ghetto. However, I won't lie – I loved the vulgarity of acting like a trash can here in the Royal Borough of Kensington and Chelsea. But the places I was going to now just lacked some soul. Maybe I was becoming jaded. I'd pretty much stopped dancing altogether.

———

When big money moves in, authentic culture usually gets shunted to the side. One thing that really bothered me about clubs like this was that the sound played second fiddle. The venues I enjoyed more were built on the foundations of a love for music, whereas these rooms prioritised privilege and the process of prising money out of people ahead of beats. They bastardised everything I believed in. And for a certain breed of punter, obtaining things – access, expensive drinks, sex – was of top priority. The clubs seemed to be built solely on commerce and ego. Further evidence of this could be found in the dance floor at Boujis – it was the size of a box of cigs, almost like an afterthought. In clubs like this, tables took up the space where ravers should be, and there was little dancing happening at all.

We parked up round the corner from Boujis and went straight to the front of the line. A lowly paparazzo lurked to the side, in case a minor Royal rocked up. He took my picture – just one sad little click-flash. Inside, the red and purple room bore the atmosphere of a morgue. Perhaps we'd arrived too early, but it was way past midnight.

We did a lap. It took thirty seconds. It girls sat guarding their It bags. Sloane Rangers roved. Girls in tiny dresses rubbed shoulders (and the rest) with banker types. I clocked Lord Freddie Windsor and some of the other turbo-toffs. No sign of William and Kate, or Harry and Chelsy. Caprice was there, though, and Lindsay Lohan, caught in a social whirl. No sign of her girlfriend Samantha Ronson. Sexual tension hung in the air, agitated and impatient, mixing with the heady pheromones of privilege.

A lady of a dubious age bracket and tombstone teeth slouched over a man who looked not unlike a gargoyle. Challenging the dress code, he wore flip-flops on his feet and his belly hung out of a T-shirt that pronounced GUCCI in large letters. The next table presented an array of augmented lips and terracotta tans, and that was just the men. A journalist cornered me, fishing for a titbit. I vaguely recognised her from the masthead of a red-top showbiz page, and she was circling for a story. She'd be out of luck – I wouldn't kiss and tell on my mates, and I was a difficult one to crack.

On each table, luminescent Cristal champagne bottles sat in

sweating ice buckets. Now that summer was approaching, clubs would soon begin to clear out as the jet set relocated to Saint-Tropez, Ibiza and Mykonos. Eid would guarantee a busy influx of top spenders from the UAE, and table spenders would try to outdo each other with bottle shows paraded through the clubs. The bulging wallets of the oil-rich pissed money all over London – and our economy was grateful for it. I once got caught umbrella-less in a particularly heavy champagne shower at Boujis, and left sticky as hell. I thought it was such a waste of money, all this pomp and circumstance. But I still partook.

I glanced around at the flashy landscape and the bourgeois show-offs. On *my* dance floors, no one cared about where you came from or what you earned – but here, it was all that mattered. I much preferred hanging out with the disreputable folk – the queers and the clubbers and the sex workers, these were my people. Aspirational, upwards mobility was something I was used to, and indeed possessed myself, but it all seemed a bit desperate in a room where the drinks had a 900 per cent mark-up and the music was crap.

There was nobody here I could chat with about house music – not even the DJ. I enjoyed wearing that expensive costume for a while, the gold-plated mask. I just couldn't get my head around how blowing £10,000 on a night out could make things any more fun for some. It felt like a mirage.

A 'Crack Baby' shot was squirted into my mouth from a syringe by a stranger with his own security personnel – the unmistakable sign of recently acquired wealth. The liquor burned my throat, and I was sedated a little longer.

———

As the country hurtled towards the crash, and reeled from its impact, new venues continued to open up in the West End. They added to the consumption extravaganza that continued for certain scenes. Many were owned by the same events groups, and they'd cannibalise each other, the weakest sibling closing without fanfare, a little sparkler sizzling out. The 'hot new thing' included Crystal, which was never a guaranteed good time. There was Paper, where I sat on an adjacent table to P. Diddy's, suffocating under the cigar smoke and bad vibes of my neighbour, and there was Hedges and Butler, an old wine cellar tucked behind Regent Street. This spot was kind of murky and the decor reminded me of my grandmother's living room. But after-hours, there'd often be a lock-in for all the people who worked in clubs across town. You'd get away with lighting up here, a godsend as the smoking ban came into law in 2007, so it was a place we went often.

Movida – another pleasuredrome of showy hedonism, next to the London Palladium – had been causing a bit of a stink in the papers. At the peak of the financial crash they launched a £35,000 cocktail. Yes, £35,000 – more than the average annual salary . . . for one drink. It was called the 'Flawless', and the huge cup consisted of Louis XIII cognac, half a bottle of Cristal Rose champagne, some brown sugar, a few flakes of 24-carat edible gold leaf. An 11-carat white diamond ring sat at the bottom of the glass. It arrived flanked by two gnarly-looking security guards. Anyone could see this was a bizarre menu addition, two fingers up to a nation buried under an avalanche of bad credit. I thought anyone who bought this might as well be setting fire to a pile of cash. This was the grotesque side of clubland.

You can't buy a good time, but you could buy my birthday party. Movida offered me their hospitality for my twenty-third birthday, organising a drink sponsorship deal with Grey Goose, a cake and five hundred mini Kobe beef burgers. It was a fair trade-off – half my friends were famous, and they got into the papers via the paparazzi waiting outside, securing both them and the club some priceless press. Everyone was a winner.

It really did feel like I knew everyone at this stage – artists, actors, indie boys, models and pop stars filled my phone book and filled my party, and it was a who's who of London. Mark Ronson, Skin, Róisín Murphy . . . I hate to name-drop, but this kid from Canterbury was gagged that some of my musical heroes were at my birthday party.

My mum and sister were my guests of honour. We were closer than ever, a tight-knit family of three, and I'd involved them in as many special events like this as possible until the witching hour came. I'd make sure they were on the train back to Kent as the cocaine came out. If my mum were to find out I was taking drugs she'd have been worried sick, inaccurately blaming herself for some wrongdoing in my childhood, which couldn't have been further from the truth.

The paps pounced on the three of us as we rocked up to Movida, cameras jostling in our faces. I wiggled my moustache-tattooed finger under my nose for them, and threw the other hand into the air. Inside, I had one of those nights that make you feel like you're in exactly the right place at the right time.

I'd laid some chemical foundations throughout the party and was keen to build on them. Among friends and acquaintances, it was quickly decided we'd double down on the night, committing to relocate to an afters, which ended up being split between my flat and Rowan's next door. He was not happy, but I was gently manipulative back then, always preferring things to go my way. Back at our apartment building, sound systems were cranked, corridors were trashed, neighbours were awoken. Word spread, and friends of friends of friends turned up to join the double sesh. At one point I looked around my living room and didn't recognise a single person there. I think someone might have been smoking a crack pipe in my kitchen. We ended up disconnecting the buzzer to my flat that night. Everyone in London seemed to know my address, and chez Harsh was at full capacity.

And then, and then . . . At 2 p.m. I woke up face down on my smashed glass coffee table, in a pool of blood. My head hurt, a lot. I couldn't quite piece together what had happened, but concluded I'd woken up and stumbled to the kitchen to fetch some water, before tripping over on to the glass, knocking myself unconscious. I sat in A&E for hours, my face tinged red, waiting for stitches, reading about my birthday party in the *Evening Standard* newspaper. This was madness. And what did I do later that night? I went back out again.

Not to put too fine a point on it, I didn't know when to call it quits any more; I never wanted the night to wind down. More often than not, a club or a party or a DJ set would simply be the precursor to an improvised tour of our metropolis. Geographical bounds and curfews didn't exist. It always seemed like a good idea, before the sun rose. And when it did, you'd either power on through, festering in some mansion or some sin-ridden place of rot with the curtains drawn, or creep back home in a cab at 8 a.m. In that case you'd hope and pray that the taxi driver didn't end up being a chirpy fellow who wanted to chatter away as you were pinned to the back seat in a comedown-induced state of fear. As neighbourhoods fell away, you'd see normal people go to work, and experience complete terror if a police car pulled up beside you at a red light.

Some afters would be intimate affairs, just close friends assembling around a coffee table as if it were a campfire, words slurred of love and life. It was as if we were poets at a salon or philosophers, theories tumbling over each other in duel. Competitive lying appeared like a sport. Sometimes there'd be wigs and lip-syncs. Beyoncé would be pulled up on YouTube for the sake of choreography. Funny videos would be thrust into your face, demanding to be watched until the end. Cocaine would be shared, soggy rolled-up tenners passed around. Games of 'who would you rather rim' would be played. Self-indulgent stories would be overshared and exaggerated. Curtains would be closed. Paranoid hushes would be demanded by the host. Dealers would arrive, cash would be gathered, the stock replenished. Nights would melt into mornings and occasionally into afternoons on bank holidays. Bonds would be tightened or broken. Sleep would feel like a retaliation against stimulants.

Other afters would be much bigger affairs. I've been to after-parties of up to a hundred people – and indeed, you need friends with very big houses for those. I lost entire mornings screeching along to top-ten hits on karaoke machines while the artists were present, laughing at the charade.

Lily Allen could often be relied on to host a great house party – I went back to hers after she was carried out of the Glamour Awards, and bumped into everyone I knew in one moment. Lily had a gig overseas, so she had to fly out the following night. When she returned from the concert, we were all still there, still partying. That's how mad it got sometimes.

I danced and DJ'd and wore daft hats at so-and-so's house, gathering around vast lacquered dining tables with some of the most recognisable faces in the world. Sometimes, genuine Warhols were hung around us, in Mayfair. Financial status wasn't a deal-breaker though, so long as drink and drugs were available. But honestly, I made some quite meaningful connections at these places. I saw a few butts, too. I burst in on a famous actor – straight, by the way – having a shot of coke blown up his fun-hole. In my circle we called this move 'cocainus'. I'd rarely leave an afters empty-handed – a rock star gave me one of his Grammy Awards once. He had plenty more left on the shelf.

The threat of the party ending was too much to take for some. I remember once a group of us were attempting to harness the dark and suppress the morning at a flat in Clerkenwell. It was perhaps 6 a.m., and daylight was a mere whisper away. A man whose name I didn't know, but who had been with us in the living room moments before, had a full psychotic episode on the roof, threatening to jump. Police arrived and cordoned off the building while we remained inside, barricaded, continuing to rail lines off an upturned mirror. He ended up not plummeting to his death, and once it was all over and the flashing blue lights outside the curtains went away, it still didn't feel like time to call it a night. That is the sort of insanity that felt normal back then.

Some people could handle an afters with gusto – usually the ones who weren't consuming chemicals. Scottee was always hilarious, and we'd ride haphazardly into the night together, as a second wind would make way for a third, off to pillage the bar at some house in Hampstead or a hotel suite made of glass on the river. 'This is so camp, girl!' he'd remark matter-of-factly, as we bundled into the Primrose Hill home of someone very famous, up very late, up to no good. We took a dip in the basement swimming pool of a major celebrity after their divorce party. Those twilight scavenger hunts were some of my most hilarious capers.

As a professional facilitator of fun, I've developed a sixth sense for the exact time to arrive – and leave – a party. But back then, fuelled up on drink and drugs, things were not so linear. I had a little trip home planned, back to Canterbury to see my mum and sister. I'd been out partying – surprise, surprise – and had ended up in a flat by Borough Market. I'd passed the point of reason, and getting a train to Kent was beginning to feel utterly unrealistic.

Something roused in me to do just one more line – 'literally just one more, then I really have to leave,' I announced to the room of unfamiliars. Three plates lay before me, as if in a TV game show. Three piles of powder: one was coke, one was ket, one was meth. Multiple choice. Just because it's on a plate, doesn't mean it's breakfast, but I wasn't one to pass up on a little nightcap, for the road. I didn't think to taste, didn't think to ask. I picked up a rolled-up note and inhaled a long, thick line. The very moment the powder hit the back of my throat, I knew paralysis was imminent. I tasted ketamine. Enough ketamine, in fact, to fell a horse. The TV game-show buzzer let out an abrasive sound to let the viewers at home know I'd lost the challenge. The lights dipped and the studio audience booed. My nasal canal stung as the K permeated my mucus membranes. It pinched in my eye sockets, and my tongue went limp and speechless. I dissolved into my chair, K-holing, inanimate like a statue. Mad hallucinations appeared before me, and a thirty-minute deep dive into the most traumatic parts of my brain began. I saw my dad, I saw Mr Bailey, I saw friends from school who'd betrayed me. And then I saw nothing.

9

THE HAWLEY ARMS
KOKO

4 a.m. My taxi crept round a cobbled lane behind Camden Road Station lined with ivy-covered brick buildings. We passed through a long Victorian brickwork tunnel. By day, trains rattled overhead. There was a mechanic's garage, a couple of houses, and little else. It would have been an unremarkable backstreet if it weren't for the poised paparazzi. We stopped outside 25 Prowse Place, where the scrummage of cameras gathered in the gloom. A new bin liner to rifle through, a twitch of a curtain, a late-night visitor – all would be documented here. This twenty-four-hour front-door surveillance meant that lenses were always just a few feet away from Amy Winehouse, the global superstar whose torch songs and chaotic antics had the whole world captivated.

My cab door opened, and the cameras fired out strobing pops of flash, flash, click, click, click, click. I was momentarily blinded, but I was used to it by now. I had a trusted technique of throwing back my shoulders and walking proud, eyes set on the destination, ignoring the shouts of insult and entreaty. When I got to the door it opened barely more than a crack and I was pulled through by a thin, tattooed arm. A cockney voice greeted me with a little, ''Ello, darlin'.' Amy was the same as ever, chirpy and warm like Barbara Windsor, in a Fred Perry polo shirt and the famous beehive hair pinned on to her head.

I'd been DJing at the opening party for a restaurant called Mint Leaf in Mayfair, kicked off the decks early for some kind of unruly

195

behaviour – how predictable. Each night was always going to be 'an early one', and would subsequently become a jaunt around London in a series of black cabs and Addison Lees, hopping around nightclubs, people's houses, and pubs for lock-ins. It was repetitive, like Groundhog Day.

———

By now, Camden was the after-afters area of choice for the terminally restless – in a series of texts and calls, a party pad would be secured, and a location locked down. Sometimes it would be round the skanky flat of some new indie band lead singer, or at Sarah Harding and her DJ boyfriend's penthouse by Kentish Town Station – the concierge guy in that building was always a difficult negotiation at 5 a.m.

To some, Camden was a stain on London's cartography, but I adored it. I remember driving through when I was young, on a day trip to London Zoo, which was just over the hill. Passing through the High Street, avoiding the meander of mohawked punks and black-lipped goths, the acid trip sculptures that hung outside kaleidoscopic shops and restaurants enchanted me. The dragon outside the Chinese restaurant, the huge boot outside the Dr. Martens store and the flames outside the tattoo parlour implanted a vision of Camden into my brain that evoked a fun-filled theme park. Posters advertised nights at the Electric Ballroom, plastered on to graffiti-smothered walls. Street art was everywhere – decaying neon shapes crawled across decrepit, crumbling architecture. Words, letters, Banksys, faces of the area's dead musical heroes. I wound the window down and took a lungful of the sooty air. Camden could be whatever you wanted it to be, and you could be whoever you needed to be inside of it. It was raw, and it was unfiltered. And now, I was living there, first in a flat behind Mornington Crescent, before moving to Camden Road, a few minutes up from Amy's, right in the middle of the action zone. Mischief was in my DNA, and it could be found in abundance in this sticky honeycomb of pubs and clubs.

Camden was mucky, and I loved its scuzziness. Everyone's houses stank, because we all smoked back then. Just imagine the pollution of twenty people crammed into one space sucking cigarettes down to their orange-flecked butts and immediately lighting another. The aroma of Marlboro was baked into my clothes. Cocaine – my usual stimulant of choice – really heightened my paranoia. I could often be found peering out from behind closed curtains, a tiny crack of daylight threatening to kill the party buzz. I recall being so fucked-up once that I must have spent a full hour peering out through the peephole of someone's front door, fossilised with fear, on high alert for MI5.

The papers had started to dub us the 'Camden Caners', successors to the party thrones sat on by the 'Primrose Hillbillies' a decade earlier, most of whom had kids and had been to rehab by now. There was a new crew in town who looked up to this set – it was Nick Grimshaw, who had been my resident DJ at Circus and was starting to make waves as a TV presenter. It was Peaches Geldof and Kimberly Stewart, who had famous rock-star dads. It was Kelly Osbourne, a veteran of the celebrity scene after her family practically invented the concept of reality television, and had just moved back to London after living in LA. We all missed out on the era of the Met Bar and Chinawhite, but we entered a brand-new London with gusto. And then there were the fame-adjacent, but not famous. The hangers-on, the groupies who wanted to be as close as possible to bright shining stars.

Many nights, Amy's house was taken over by the decadent and the deranged. It turned into a modern-day gin palace, a booze-soaked after-hours club, keeping the neighbours awake until the sun came out. She'd lived for years in a flat around the corner on Jeffrey's Place, but the new digs on Prowse Place had become the true central hub of the North London action. Every day, this postcard of a street in the backwaters of Camden was beamed into the consciousness of the globe as Amy's fame, and antics, grew stratospheric.

Before Amy became a superstar, as famous for her behaviour as for the spiritual wonder of her voice, she was another bright talent in a pool of creative friends. Don't get me wrong, she was already a big deal when her album *Frank* came out, but she hadn't won the five Grammy Awards for the sad songs of *Back to Black*, she wasn't yet dubbed 'Wino' by the papers.

As well as a core gang of best friends Tyler, Catriona, Naomi and Chantelle, the Prowse Place late-night door-knockers included scene types and musicians that Amy trusted and kept close – Sadie Frost, Noel Fielding, Mark Ronson, the photographer Blake Wood, and Pete Doherty and Carl Barât from the Libertines. These formed a loyal inner circle. But often the crowd at Amy's also included randoms. They seemed to pop up everywhere – the unidentified plus-ones, the sort of leeches who'd orbit around famous people without much explanation of what they did for a job or story of how they got to be in the living room of Britain's biggest music star.

We weren't only moving in the moonlit hours – Camden was the heart of so much of our social lives. On some afternoons we'd meet up at the Hawley Arms – none of us had real jobs to be at, after all. It was just another London pub, all brushed wood and darkly lit side rooms, with a beer-tinged carpet and greasy spirit bottles lining the walls upside down. Like any boozer, anywhere, it sounded like clinking pints and chatter and the Maccabees. It was right around the corner from MTV Studios, so you'd get a stream of music people popping in for a pint after work.

We'd usually drop our anchor at the table by the jukebox, downing pints with Kelly and whoever else was up for it. Amy would get up and start singing the Shangri-Las, stopping everyone in their tracks. As her fame climbed to its highest peak, it began to feel like every pair of eyes in the room was fixated on the table by the jukebox. There was a small private room upstairs with black walls where we'd go when it started to become suffocating in the main pub. We'd drink until the last bell, then stay on for a lock-in.

Eventually the Hawley became a tourist trap, and people would travel from far and wide hoping to see the 'Rehab' singer behind the bar, pouring herself a pint. As her fame became a behemoth, the closer the net pulled around her and the more she retreated home. Every time I went there, it felt like the four walls of the sitting room drew closer. She had become a superstar, and her music formed the soundtrack to someone who was, willingly or not, slowly killing herself in public view.

When I picture Amy, it's always marching through the night with ravenous delirium, the Pied Piper to a merry band of North London revellers. But she's free, running from pub to party, ending up in her house to settle into the sofa for many more hours.

KOKO was somewhere else I'd go often, a vast cathedral of music and the North Star of Camden's landscape. In its earlier guise as Camden Palace, it had presented Madonna's first ever London show, and Steve Strange notoriously guarded the door for its club nights in the eighties. Chewing gum scarred the carpets. There was a balcony with ragged sofas on which we'd watch bands strumming and sweat-soaked forms colliding.

I'd first met Amy at a Boy George gig at KOKO. We were introduced by our mutual friend Kelly on that balcony, and we'd struck up an immediate kinship. 'You're that Amy Winehouse, aren't you?' I asked. 'You're that fucking Jodie Harsh, aren't you? Fuck me, pull up a chair, darlin', we've gotta be mates. Got a fag?'

Amy was a fan of Culture Club; all those soulful lyrics about heartbreak and pain were probably quite influential to her. We watched as George belted out 'Karma Chameleon' and 'Do You Really Want to Hurt Me', in between dipping in and out of the toilet to chop out lines. The first time she beckoned me into a cubicle, she pulled the little baggie of cocaine from within her beehive – and yes, I know how remarkably camp that sounds. She was *the* woman of the moment in British music, splashed across the tabloids for her crazy antics every day, and here we were crouched on the floor of a toilet in Camden, connecting like instant besties, a new union forged by our love of music, big hair and drugs. From our first meeting we were firm friends, and I'd often find myself at Amy's with Tyler at all hours of the night and way into the morning; the promise of another cheeky line making an early night impossible.

You didn't have to be an alcoholic to be out in Camden, but it helped. The truth was, booze and drugs were at the centre of everything for me then. Sometimes I couldn't work out if they were the consequence of my late nights, or the cause of them – but there was barely an evening that I didn't slip in and out of toilets railing whizz while my mates hung off balconies smoking spliffs. I tipped back vodka with vigour, as if to test the absolute limits of my slight body. From my first E at fifteen, I'd really taken to the idea of getting high, and, frankly, never encountered anyone in those years who felt differently. The thing is, it didn't feel like a problem back then – it was just friends, staying up late, having fun. For the most part, it just felt like a glorious fucking adventure, if sometimes a little turbulent. But the drugs Amy was doing were even harder, and soon the whole world started to see it.

The evening I went to Amy's after getting kicked off the decks is the one that's imprinted on to my brain. The one that I immediately flash to when I think about her now. There's a photograph of us together from later that night, our beehive hair towering over mugs of tea, two in each hand, on Amy's doorstep. For the public it seemed to sum up who they thought she really was – the chaos and the kindness. As ever the truth is better and worse than what the photos showed; there's a vulnerability to this story, but it's full of Amy's wicked wit too. In many ways it was just another night in Camden.

Roll forward from that ''Ello, darlin',' and being enfolded in her arms. By the middle of the night, I was sitting on Amy's bed on the mezzanine, looking out over the group in the living room below, wearing a black Fendi dress she'd been gifted from Karl Lagerfeld. She'd received a box of stuff from the label that day and wanted me to have most of it. That was typical Amy – generous through and through. We'd discarded my old outfit and dressed me up in expensive couture. She was wearing a little heart-shaped pin in her hair that spelled out 'Blake', and her winged eyeliner was smudged; likely first printed on her lids days ago. I took a Rimmel pen and some hairgrips out of my bag and reapplied her make-up and tightened the block of hair on her head as we smoked cigs.

Amy and I bonded from the get-go over our love of big barnets, mine inspired by Dolly Parton and hers by Ronnie Spector. Both larger than life in design, an exaggeration of femininity and a nod to our pool of references. Wigs are great for both repelling and intimidating people, while being camp and fun. A hard, aggressive look helps you get the job done and makes you memorable, two important things in our professions. 'Find one style and stick to it,' Amy once articulated. 'People should be able to draw a picture of you in ten seconds; make sure you have something about you that is iconic.' And with that, my refusal to ever change my hairstyle was born. Like Andy Warhol, Anna Wintour and Amy Winehouse, I'd finally found my freeze-dried style – blonde, swept to one side, with a fringe. The formula was in place.

It was 2008 and 'Back to Black', a single from the 2006 album of the same name, was still all over the radio. In the video, Amy attends her own funeral – a bleak foreshadowing – and the song increased her global fame. She'd become the voice of a generation and an instantly recognisable, iconic British superstar, but right then, she was my mate Amy, sitting cross-legged on her bed in her little house in North London, crying over her boyfriend as I reapplied her eyeliner and pretended not to notice the red marks up her arms where she'd been cutting herself. I saw beyond the Amy Winehouse caricature. She was the sweetest but most tortured person I'd ever met. Life seemed too painful for her, which you can hear in the songs she wrote. She wore her heart on her sleeve, the ink of ex-boyfriends' names on her chest, scars on her limbs; disarray recorded by cameras every time she left the house wearing Marigold gloves and with a silk headscarf over the beehive.

At Amy's, unwrapped gold discs leaned against walls, never to be hung. Guitars were strewn on the floor. There was a seldom-ignited sunbed. Her room was filled with piles and piles of clothes – Fred Perry tops, printed dresses and ballet pumps. In seemingly manic bursts, she'd get the urge to clean the entire house from top to toe.

After I'd finished her eyeliner and smoothed her hair down, she sprang to her feet, putting on that wicked Amy grin, ready to return to the world. Downstairs at her coffee table a pack of people were talking over each other – a few of her best childhood friends and some scattered, unsavoury Camden Caners. One had the letters DBT tattooed on his throat. 'What's that about, then?' I asked. 'Your nan's initials?' I teased. He answered, simply, 'Dead By Thirty.'

Amy took centre stage, playing host and topping up her guests' vodka Cokes. She'd flit over to her computer to look at pap shots of herself on gossip blogs, which would scrawl penises and write 'mess' across people's drunken photos. Amy would look at everything on these blogs and news websites like MailOnline, checking what the press was saying about her, obsessing over pictures taken earlier that day of herself popping into various pubs and newsagents' around Camden in her little vests and skinny jeans. Years before the internet warped the way we critique our online image, it was strange to see one of the most photographed women in the world sitting at her desk, googling pictures of herself.

Mental health issues weren't at the forefront of people's minds back then. They were generally ignored by – and perhaps even vilified by – the press. In retrospect I think I saw the music industry and the media take advantage of a vulnerable person, grinding her further down when she was at her lowest. Certainly, it seemed the public in general enjoyed her downfall, as if it was for their entertainment. Hunting Amy was like a blood sport to the papers, and she was 'fair game'. They just didn't care. As much support as possible was given inside her friendship circle, team and family, but Amy was a strong-willed character. She said it best herself – they tried to make her go to rehab, and she said 'no, no, no'.

I suspected the damage I was witnessing first-hand was just the tip of the iceberg compared with what was going on inside her head. That night she seemed at once more electric and sadder than I'd seen her in a while, and I knew it was all tied in with the fractious nature of her relationship, and the intensity of the scrutiny on it and the rest of her life.

Amy would pop back upstairs to the mezzanine bedroom alone every ten minutes or so, and I'd hear the repeated click of a lighter. Without acknowledging her absence, she'd come back down and join the group, a little more spaced out, energetic and erratic but always very sweet and full of chat. We all know Amy had a painful connection with hard drugs, it was no secret back then and is certainly no secret now. But she never, ever smoked crack or took heroin in front of me. I guess she acknowledged just how bad her addictions had gotten, and attached some shame to this, keeping the really hard drug use private. She switched between an innocent little-girl persona, and one of more dark-sided energy, but always kept it real with me.

The hours ticked by, the party got heavier. All the while we had this sense of the cameras waiting below. The people inside and paps outside – we were all chronic insomniacs, in a shadowy corner of Camden, in the dead of the night. It was autumn, freezing cold, and we had the heating on full blast. As we submerged further into the warmth of the room, we talked about the endless presence of these men on the other side of the door. And weren't they chilly?

Amy and I poked our heads out of the kitchen window and shouted down at the paps below – 'Anyone want a cuppa?' These guys who made her life hell, quite literally stalking her every move and setting up camp outside the supposed safe space of her home, were being offered refreshments at five o'clock in the morning. Gruff shouts of 'Yeah!' came up from the darkness and Amy and I put the kettle on, laughing as we waited for it to boil. We lined up eight chipped mugs and stuck some teabags and milk in, then we spat in two of the cups. Can you blame us? We grabbed some Jaffa Cakes to hand out from the cupboard. There was a never-ending supply of sweet stuff – at that time she was living on a diet almost exclusively of Lucozade, Haribo and ice lollies – there was no real food to be seen.

We headed down and handed out the tea to the blokes outside, most of them clicking their cameras with one arm and reaching out for a hot drink with the other. I was absolutely out of my tree, but we ran back inside giggling, knowing full well that we'd be causing a stir on the news desks in a few hours when the hacks got in. I suppose it was kind of camp, Amy Winehouse and Jodie Harsh, all hairspray and big make-up, handing out tea and Jaffa Cakes at 5 a.m.

I'd started to find myself in the papers often. Other than the *Evening Standard*, which took a slightly more serious tone, there were two free newspapers that reported the goings-on in the capital at this time. The *London Paper* and the *London Lite* were on newsstands from around 4 p.m., conveniently the time I'd be waking up and needing a reminder of what exactly had happened the night before. Think of them as the Instagram stories of their day.

They'd gush out of bins, and you'd trample over a waterfall of them three-deep outside Tube stations. They'd shout at you, a pick 'n' mix of sensational headlines and PR fodder in bold type. 'Where's Maddie?' 'Look at this flashmob at Victoria Station promoting a new movie!' 'How's Britney?' 'What was Amy doing at 7 a.m. this morning?' Forming the centrefold of both papers was a document of the celebrity shenanigans from the previous twenty-four hours. It was hilarious to see these pages populated by my wider circle of friends, for the most part. Peaches, Kelly, Lily, Grimmy, Amy. And, of course, I was also a regular character in these comic strips of chaos.

For the extremely famous, boundaries were an absent luxury. The paparazzi were rampant in London before phones with cameras entered the equation to mediate the night, and girls had it way, way worse. Across the pond they were upskirting Britney and Lindsay leaving clubs with no knickers on; over here it was the grubbiness of Camden and its unwashed inhabitants that was capturing the imagination of the press and public. When you're 'being papped' your senses are really shaken – the clicking sound from cameras is quite chilling, and you're temporarily blinded by flashing white light. Often when you see pictures of a celeb looking hammered, hands over their face, eyes squinting, arms flailing, it's because they just can't see where the fuck they're going, as opposed to booze distorting their features. And often, too, the paps would shout vile things to arouse a bigger reaction – 'You look rough,' 'Are you on drugs?' The only pictures that would sell were the raucous ones, and these guys were freelancers in a gig economy, right in the middle of the credit crunch. I guess they did what they had to do to get the shot.

I can't pretend I didn't love the attention and my photo in the papers – it was a dance that felt both seductive and dangerous. It certainly played to my ego. But I can't imagine how it must have been for Amy with those blokes camped on her doorstep every waking – and sleeping – hour like that. The tabloids tore her down every day. And around then the internet news cycle began to beat print media for speed, if not accuracy. Amy would head out for a pint, and her image would be everywhere before she'd even got the second round in.

As well as the pap snaps, phone tapping was rife – calls and texts were literally being listened in on. Never before had there been such a hunger for the downward spiral of a talented, young, famous girl. Mix in a dash of crippling drug addiction, and it's a recipe for disaster. The media machine could fell a starlet with one headline if it wanted to. Therefore, the irony of Amy chirpily handing out cups of tea to the big men who followed her round and tormented her was not lost on me. I was pressing my nose against the window of fame – I could smell it, and I realised how rotten it stank.

Breakfast time was creeping in. After the paparazzi were fed and watered, my night was drawing to a close. I couldn't keep up with Amy. Everyone else had left apart from Tyler, and I gave the two of them a hug and decanted into a taxi, disorientated. I was still wearing the Fendi dress Amy had given me – I'd rarely leave empty-handed. She'd also given me a Xanax in anticipation of a restless inability to fall asleep after snorting so much cocaine.

I popped the pill in my mouth as my taxi negotiated the jigsaw of backstreets around Amy's. I was coming down, weak and sensationless, and the journey up Camden Road felt like it was taking hours. Vodka was swishing in my belly and powder was buzzing in my brain as I briefly glimpsed the real world. Morning sunlight shone violently through the window, and I cursed it. I'd have avoided the illumination of daylight altogether if I could, living instead under a muted electric glow.

I crept into the flat, hoping to slip by unnoticed, but passed my roommate M.C. in the hall as she headed out to work at a modelling agency. 'You look like you've had a night of it,' she said, clocking that my eyes were like saucers. She looked sympathetic. I looked away. I could barely speak, my jaw locked and teeth chattering. I took comfort in the fact that we'd be laughing over the pictures in the evening papers later on. I sauntered about in the flat by myself, blinds shut, flicking through morning television shows, until the Xanax kicked in.

Camden was my unhealthy base, and I barely left the area unless it was for work. I ate almost exclusively at the Wagamama on Jamestown Road, and once a week I'd stroll around the big Sainsbury's to fill up my fridge with food, which would expire. Occasionally there'd be a posh dinner at Gilgamesh – the cocktails were well worth the trip up the escalators. But I craved homeliness sometimes. I'd become very good friends with the actress and designer Sadie Frost, and she was a bit of a big sister to me and Grimmy. I'd go round to her townhouse on Steele's Road, let myself in and raid her fridge. Even though Sadie had four kids living at home and loads of dogs, she loved it when the house was even more full. We'd all pile in on Sundays, hungover on her sofas, and watch the *X Factor* live shows as she nourished us back to health.

As for Amy, that fabled night at hers with the tea was at the height of a period where I'd hang out with her regularly, always at unpredictable times of the day, and in all sorts of situations. A game of pool at the Good Mixer, a gig at Proud, a wine and a line at an old man's pub . . . She was delicate, like a tiny sparrow, but so head-strong – no amount of counsel from the people around who loved her was able to straighten her out for good. I could see how bad it was getting, and there was nothing I could say or do to make a difference. We were young pleasure seekers, all in our early twenties, and with that came naivety to the consequences of our behaviour. I always gravitated towards the brighter corner of the room, the folk with good vibes, and that's where Amy could be found, too.

Beyond the beehive, bruises and broken bottles, there was a lost girl. Her closest friends and family desperately tried to intervene, but she was an addict through and through, with a ready supply of money and power. She would go to the Caribbean to get away from the claustrophobic suffocation of London, of Camden, of the paparazzi on Prowse Place, and we'd Skype and sing songs to each other in the middle of the night. I really loved her.

She moved to a bigger, more private, gated house on Camden Square, and an injunction was put in place that made it illegal for paps to camp on her doorstep. There, she achieved long periods of sobriety, and the late-night stream of visitors and hangers-on stopped. Only her very best friends saw her, and we'd fallen out of touch aside from the odd text or call. I remember one of the last Skype calls I had with her: she was in Saint Lucia, no beehive or eye-liner in sight, and played me a new song on her guitar. Something felt lighter about her, she was glowing, and she seemed to be in her happy place. A hot island, surrounded by musical instruments, stripped of the artificial 'drag', and stripped of the crutches she'd become so dependent on in London. In contrast, I was moving further into a darker relationship with drink and drugs, slowly losing the carefree sense of fun I'd moved to London with.

During my time spent in Camden, great fires ripped through the Hawley Arms and the world-famous market. On two occasions, flames spat fifty feet into the North London sky. They could have been accidents, could have been arson, could have been inside jobs. Who knows? But both the market and the Hawley Arms still stand. Camden Town is resilient, but its inhabitants were not always quite so hardy.

10

BUNGALOW 8
PUNK

hroughout 2008, I was in the papers every day. I'd fall out of club doors and kamikaze on to Louboutin-scuffed red carpets. Drag was not yet a mainstream fixture, and it may have looked as though I was the only one doing it if you weren't familiar with the underground culture of the club scene, in which it was thriving.

Most of the press referred to me as 'he', which is indeed my preferred pronoun out of drag, but after I'd spent several hours in make-up, an 's' on the front of that would have more rewarded my efforts. I enjoyed playing the role of pop art pseudo-celebrity at a time when print media was enjoying its last hurrah. The whole concept of Jodie Harsh felt like something that had been cooked up in the silver-walled lab of the Factory decades earlier in New York. But in general, I had the goodwill of the press on my side – after all, I was doing blow with most of them.

I'm a realist, and London costs a lot of money to live in. DJing in backstreet discos was unstable, and quite frankly, my rent wouldn't pay itself. A club night is what I did best, and I found a creative partner in my performance artist friend Scottee. After all, what is a party if not performance art? AntiSocial, the event where I first DJ'd, had begun to wind down, so we jumped into the hole it left at Bar Music Hall, and conceptualised the night 'For3ign'. The '3' gave it an edge. Our combined forces would make this new club night a sensation.

'Girl, we need a press stunt, a way to get the night in the papers so everyone's talking about us,' emailed Scottee. By now, I had insisted that all my work-related correspondence should take place in my Googlemail account. I'd joke that I was a professional emailer 90 per cent of the time, and a creative the remaining 10 per cent, as if it were some high-powered flex. 'I am keen to explore options for this idea,' I replied. 'Best regards, JH.'

We fixed a date and locked a venue – the 'hip' St Martins Lane Hotel, which donated a huge suite to us in return for some press mentions, orchestrated by Purple PR, who really turned the cogs inside the rumbling machine of London culture. We secured a drink sponsor and booked handsome waiters to hold trays of espresso Martinis by the front door – Scottee and I were much more entertaining when viewed through beer goggles. We invited every major media publication in town – hacks from the red tops and editors from the broadsheets, and journalists from magazines that sat on every shelf. RSVPs surged in, the senders bemused as to what we were up to. We produced this mysterious event with the meticulous precision of a couple planning for their wedding. However, once the guests arrived, there would be no script.

'I suppose we can just sit around chatting and they can listen to us rambling on,' suggested Scottee, well versed in the oeuvre of performance art. 'Just prank-call some of your celeb mates and get them to spill some gossip.' And that we did. Cloaked in dressing gowns, we bounced around the posh suite as journalists from *Vogue* and the *Guardian* and the *Daily Mirror* came by at their allotted times, and day-drank with us on the bed. We ignored their presence entirely, as if they were spectators at an immersive theatre show. I led several of them into the bathroom, and wordlessly racked myself columns of cocaine, which I'd funnelled into a little box labelled 'Fake Blow', which was a lie.

The event was an exercise in self-indulgence, and in the twilight of the noughties, a real sign of the times. By nightfall, Scottee and I were plastered, his clown make-up smudged, my purpled fringe asymmetrical. Each journalist was handed a flyer for For3ign as they exited, stumbling after several espresso Martinis, perhaps even more bemused than when they'd arrived.

As part of our deal, we got to keep the suite for the night. This could have been an opportunity to indulge in an evening of self-care and zen in hyper-luxury surroundings, but St Martins Lane Hotel felt less like a place to crash out at that time, more of an entire resort of temptations under cover of the blackness of night. We ordered room service up from its Asia de Cuba restaurant, which went untasted, and before long a midnight feast of fun beckoned us down into the hotel's basement. The elevator delivered us – still in our dressing gowns – to the sterile lobby, where our decorum would be left for later collection. We passed gawping tourists who had never seen anyone like us before. We skated across the shiny floor in our white hotel slippers, dodging oversized chess pieces that made us look like Borrowers. We were two heat-seeking missiles heading to unleash an indulgence explosion in Bungalow 8, and there I hit the fuck-it button with force.

We descended the dark stairway into the pleasure cellar, and the doof doof doof of a bass was palpable, humming closer and closer. The waxy odour of fresh paint was present, as it always was in there. The thick carpet felt like liquid under the fluffy soles of our slippers. The walls were painted with horizontal black-and-white stripes, like a Joseph carrier bag, and debauchery seeped through them.

Bungalow 8's lowest depth was a confined, corridor-like oblivion that I spent so many wasted hours in. This place would suck you in like a black hole – or a black-and-white-striped hole – at first appearing innocuous, then becoming the veiled threat of an acid trip as time slipped by.

It must have been almost midnight as we slurped through the densely packed room. We squeezed past a claustrophobic's worst nightmare – a stationary crush of perspiring people – turbocharging towards our spot behind the DJ enclave. Famous arses met squidgy banquettes and zebra pouffes. It was a motley gathering of failed rehab attempts and, of course, the spawn of rock royalty – a stark contrast to my self-generated brand of notoriety.

We were deep in an era obsessed with gossip, and this lot had a knack of generating it each time they left the house. Everyone wore dark colours, as if in mourning for their sobriety. I clocked a TV presenter I'd huffed up a few lines with at a house party a few weeks back – he'd pocketed the wrinkled, rolled-up note afterwards and done a runner. 'Oi, you owe me a tenner,' I bleated, without irony. I chatted to the DJ Seb Chew. He was orchestrating a medley of funk, soul and rock and roll. All the while, I was sure to keep one isolated eye coasting the parameter of the room, lizard-like. There was Noel Fielding, and over there was Har Mar Superstar. Everyone was out!

Daniel Lismore shuffled in, gilded with layers of gold and burgundy textures as if a religious effigy. His face was painted clown white, and one arm was cased in knight's armour. You'd hear him jangling before he even walked through the door. He was such a part of London's eventide furniture that you could see a Lismore-shaped mark on the floor when he was absent from a bash.

Mark Ronson arrived with a bag of records – he'd been playing at a DKNY fragrance launch on Bond Street. Then Winehouse joined the romp, in skinny jeans and ballet shoes. It was becoming quite the party. Amy took me by the hand and led the group into the empty office out the back, before proceeding to give someone we didn't know a haircut. It's in that moment that I first experienced 'eyeballing' – when shots were poured through the eye socket in an attempt to intoxicate with haste. I considered my carefully applied make-up and passed. The manager Chris walked in to kick us out of the office. After some resistance, Scottee and I were bribed by the flattery of drinks tickets – our love language, our currency. We headed to the bar to exchange them for a round of Skinny Bitches – a triple measure of vodka topped off with a splash of Diet Coke. Fancy cocktails always seemed to take too long to make when I was parched.

For a moment – which probably felt like years back then but was, I don't know, six months or so – Bungalow 8 was the central headquarters of the London showbiz scene. Its head girl, Amy Sacco, had shipped the concept over from New York. She was a nightlife legend, and one of the most well-connected people in entertainment. She had listened sharply to what London needed – a space to replace the Blue Bar, Met Bar and Light Bar of other West End hotels – and merged some Manhattan grit into the centre of town. Amy was the perfect host, and always kept a suite reserved upstairs for those who couldn't quite make it through the front door in one piece in front of the loitering photographers.

Bungalow was like our clubhouse. Sometimes we'd stumble in on a Friday and it would be sparsely populated, and sometimes we'd hit it on a Tuesday, and it'd be bumper to bumper. The spontaneity was all part of the fun, the not knowing what you were about to walk into. Once I ended up there on a Sunday and it was brimming with people in black bow ties. 'Why is it so busy in here?' I asked some sleazy-looking old guy at the bar. 'It's Harvey Weinstein's BAFTA party,' he sniggered. 'Who the fuck is Harvey Weinstein?' I asked, puzzled. 'Me,' the man said, as I carried on through.

I came up for air, and a cigarette, as the streets roared with post-theatre hubbub. The smoking ban had added an extra layer of narrative to an evening's plot line, and many friendships were made as we congregated away from the speakers and under the plumes of Marlboro Lights. All the coolest people smoked back then, and a blackening of the lung still felt so chic. I said hi to the female arms dealer I kept bumping into everywhere I went that year. As my jaw swung like a barn door, she showed me the brand-new handset that had recently entered the telecommunications market, called an iPhone. I hadn't held one in real life before. She brought a lighter to my second cigarette, and as my lip gloss stained the butt, she introduced the concept of apps. I blew fumes out of my nose like a cunty dragon. 'This is so major, babe, I need one, like, now!' I exclaimed, still unaware of her name, unaware of how unaffordable an iPhone was to me. I flicked my ash in time with the sentences I was speaking, emphasising each pause in breath, before heading back down into Bungalow to perform my grand display of inebriation. MGMT's 'Time to Pretend' cocooned the room in its intoxicating melody.

From that point on, self-control was beyond me, and the rest of the night became a blur, a small collection of photographic flashes. I'll remember it in short form, because it still stings: I saw a fist heading towards my face, heard the crack of a bone as it impacted my nose, and tasted a mouthful of coppery blood as I flew backwards, cartoonishly. Potentially, I provoked the punch, but I was legless by this time – *it wasn't my fault.* Scottee had headed up to the room to sleep, Daniel Lismore had headed over to Punk, Amy Winehouse had headed to Camden. I'd stayed for the roly-poly of a final vodka, just for a little push out the door. After stumbling around Bungalow like an extra in a zombie movie, I ascended the stripy stairway, its walls distorting into a Magic Eye picture, blood gushing down my bathrobe. Through the revolving hotel entrance, burly shouting and heavy-duty camera clicking serenaded my departure. The street was strobing like a hectic dance floor, cameras pushed right up against my bloodied and bruised face, recording my broken nose and the tears streaming down my cheeks. Cars honked as the photographers hurled into the street to get their shot. In the bustle, I'd lost a hotel slipper. I hailed a black taxi, its orange light flicked off, and I remember little else. Cinderella had left the ball.

I awoke in absolute decay the following afternoon, my face sticky on a red-splattered pillow, a comedown of biblical proportions. Everything felt upside down, and everything throbbed in pain. *Punched in the face at Bungalow 8?* I was so humiliated that Dignitas felt like a viable solution. I grabbed the hand mirror by the side of the bed, which I often used to chop out lullaby lines on, and I assessed the damage. My face was scarlet – caked in blood and shame. I looked like the devil.

I skimmed through pictures on my digital camera, trying to uncover evidence of my nose-shattering attacker. My mobile rang, and I snapped back into reality. Daniel Lismore on the line: 'Good morning, darling, how was the rest of your night?' 'Soo good!' I lied, wincing as I felt the cartilage in my nose shake with each syllable I uttered. Lismore would hustle me out of my slumber most mornings – or afternoons – for a forensic examination of the previous evening's activities. We'd debrief: who was out, what they were wearing, who were they kissing? As I'd swirl Alka-Seltzer into cups of ice-cold water, Daniel would be my news bulletin. I loved to hear rumour and scandal – every little anecdote would deflect from the soreness in my head as the threat of a comedown crept closer. I never sought to stir the pot, per se, but when the gossip ladle was handed to me, it was hard to resist a taste.

'Well, I'm pretty sure my nose is broken, but I'm not sure who did it,' I confessed. 'I just remember a fist flying at my face.' Daniel went silent, and I knew this gap in chatter meant concern. 'Do you think you're pushing the partying a bit hard?' he asked. This triggered me enough to wind the call down, joking about appreciating the free rhinoplasty.

The truth was, I was now worried about myself: I couldn't say no to a drink or a line. Booze was my gateway to cocaine, and I believed I needed their lubrication to enable confidence and a big personality. Moderation was a foreign word to me. When I drank, I couldn't stop, and that always led to coke, like a vicious cycle I couldn't break. When I got to that place of numbness, my head understood little other than where the next line was coming from. I could become a ravenous monster under the influence, and even my best friends would walk on eggshells around me. Some had made their excuses and left Planet Harsh altogether. I could be a liability, doing things like trying to sleep with people's boyfriends. I was turning into an unpredictable nightmare.

———

I was still in touch with my dad, albeit very loosely. Occasionally he'd be in London for work and would double up with a visit to his only son, giving little to no advance warning. I'd draw my eyebrows on with a MAC pencil, pull a baseball cap down low, and plunge into a well-rehearsed routine of responding to mundane questions from a parent who was emotionally disengaged from his child's life. 'I'm in the West End, are you around?' he texted one afternoon when I had a particularly pinching case of 'wine flu', summoning me for a grilling. I'd been out late – surprise, surprise – and ended up at a party in a room at the May Fair Hotel, which had become a hub for the in-crowd. The management was offering party-scene movers and shakers cheaper rate rooms at £100 per night in a bid to boost its newspaper presence. There were always a few paps loitering outside. Peaches Geldof had actually moved in.

'What are you doing for money, then?' Dad probed suspiciously over a rancid Costa coffee on Oxford Street. 'I'm working on some club projects, a bit of creative direction, that sort of thing,' I answered through gritted teeth, avoiding eye contact. I knew that if he found out about my life dressed in drag, it would be the final nail in the coffin for our relationship. He'd recently remarried, and his new wife knew all about me, promising my sister she'd keep Jodie a secret.

'Clubs? That sounds like a made-up job to me,' he grimaced. 'All you lot have weird jobs.' 'What do you mean by "all you lot"?' I grizzled defensively. 'You poofs.' At this, I zoned out, stopped registering words. I tried to get through the rest of the bitter-tasting coffee without returning emotionally to that evening when, aged fifteen years old, I'd been dragged out of the closet, challenged. I've always been avoidant of conflict and drama – and my dad was the ultimate psychological trigger. I couldn't understand how my mum put up with him for so many years, nor how he managed to maintain a relationship with my sister.

We failed to connect. When we reunited like this, I scarcely recognised him or my childhood. But, truth be told, I scarcely recognised myself by this point.

———

For forty-eight hours, I thought I was best friends with Rihanna. We'd bumped into each other at the K West Hotel in Shepherds Bush, which was the music industry's bed and breakfast – all the major labels would put their acts up there as their offices were local. We called it the K Hole, because you'd stumble into it on a whim and rarely remain conscious for long. Its nondescript bar would become raucous late at night – you'd always find Kate Nash or a Kasabian downing drinks with their entourage. For a while, my social life became a holding pattern of hotel lobbies, circling the St Martins Lane, the May Fair and the K West.

West London proper was never really my territory like Soho, Camden and Shoreditch were, but I'd make the occasional trip over for a big event. The city seemed to take on new colours and shapes in these less explored metropolitan areas. One BRIT Awards I went to – the one where Amy performed 'Valerie' with Mark Ronson – ended up becoming a tour around every open watering hole of every postcode starting with a W. I was pals with a new singer called Adele who was tipped for big things, and we spent the evening playing hide and seek with the moon. Our final destination was YOYO, a basement club night in the stark shadow of the brutalist

Trellick Tower in Ladbroke Grove. It was Notting Hill, but without the posh accent. Mark, still in his blue suit from the stage, stopped his DJ set so Rihanna could sing 'Happy Birthday' to me. Glorious and surreal brushes with the world's most famous and photogenic faces were becoming common occurrences.

From a musical icon to a fashion icon: Kate Moss was well known for turning any situation into an important event just by being there. The first night we ever met was at a baby shower for the casting director Jess Hallett. I'd been lolling around town at some bashes – a mock house party for the launch of a new Sony Walkman with drag legend Jonny Woo hosting karaoke in the kitchen, and the opening of an H&M flagship store with a performance from a barefooted singer called Florence. My party antennae picked up the buzz of the baby shower, and I was beckoned over to Claridge's hotel. The sound of thrashing guitars and banging drums bleeding from the suite suggested this wasn't going to be all macarons and storks, and as I banged on the door, and Kate answered, that was confirmed.

'Jodie bloody Harsh,' she exclaimed in a cloud of smoke, her arms up, ready for an embrace. 'Finally!' I replied. 'Fucking finally!' We'd been in many of the same rooms but hadn't had a moment to properly speak before. Humans are hardwired with the desire to dance, and that's where we found our common ground that night, dancing on a silk-textured carpet in a suite on the top floor of Claridge's.

While they were moving house, Kate and her boyfriend were staying temporarily with Davinia Taylor and her then-husband Dave Gardner, David Beckham's manager. The three of us bundled into a taxi and were pounced on by the paps who were thrusting their cameras up to the windows, turning the cab into a strobe-lit disco. The eternal majorness of Kate was unquestionable – she was in every campaign and on so many *Vogue* covers. We arrived at the huge townhouse, where the afters turned out to be a cup of tea and a flurry of mutual compliments. Fun and laughter was her manifesto, and on that we connected. A friendship blossomed.

———

London had become a non-stop party shop, and I binged on it. Rarely would a morning go by without the heavy thud of invitations dropping through my door. They were like love letters from PR companies, promising the best time ever. In the noughties, everything became a 'pop-up' – a restaurant, a shop, a gallery space. I was a social tourist, spoilt for choice. If there was a party, I attended it, and if there was a line, I snorted it. If we strutted into a showbiz function that felt flat, we'd hit and run, swerve around the corner and crash another one.

A benefit for a fashionable disease? *I'm there.* A banquet in a ballroom for a doomed magazine? *Hurrah!* A party to celebrate an aging addict's memoir? *You bet.* A roller disco in the Renaissance Rooms to launch a limited-edition bottle of vodka? *Are you doing cars?* The opening of the Ice Bar? *Sign me up, before it melts away.* Any excuse to drink myself silly as brands pretended the economy wasn't crumbling around us. The city was alive with the sound of velvet ropes unclicking and there'd be more events and products to launch than Addison Lees to get the celebrities to them. I arrived at Sony Ericsson's Spring Fling on a tractor. Anything for attention.

These events would start at 7 p.m. as the city exhaled after a long day of work. You knew you were in the right place as you pulled up, because of the paparazzi camped outside. I'd arrive with a big crew one hour in – any later than that would be rude, and it allowed a grace period for the vibe to get going. Once inside, our tactics were well choreographed – a clockwise circuit to acclimatise, then an anticlockwise lap to catch anyone we'd missed. 'Nice to see you!' I'd say to the familiar faces I couldn't quite place. 'Nice to meet you' ran the risk of awkwardness, in case we'd crossed paths the week before. We'd find some seating to use as a base of operations and would hog that space until we were ready to leave. A good party should feel like it has a beginning, a middle and an ending. But some events were so dull, we'd press the eject button before the opening credits finished rolling.

I'd developed an insatiable appetite for the kiss of a camera. There was a group of old-guard snappers who'd be trusted to roam inside these events, like Dave Benett and Richard Young. These were the friendly pros that the superstars would stop and pose for – and chat to.

I never went to a single event out of drag, after realising early on that the notion of celebrity surveillance was weird. My masquerade became a useful tool. I'd pass people I knew from the scene in the street, and they'd have no idea it was me. I enjoyed it – somehow it felt like a superpower, a force field.

When I saw my picture in magazines and newspapers, it felt like an achievement to thrust drag, and therefore queerness, into the face of Middle England – people eating their cornflakes. I certainly hadn't started drag thinking everyone would be comfortable with it – even those closest to me. It felt somewhat punk to be a brazen, rollicking drag queen running around London with some of the world's most famous people. But it didn't feel like it was really me. It felt like a charade. I felt like an imposter.

At this point, I went out every weeknight, apart from Fridays, when there didn't tend to be events on, as they'd miss the daily London press. I judged a voguing ball at the Royal Opera House alongside Beth Ditto – the final contestant got to the end of the runway, squatted, and pissed. Genius! I was invited to a party at Harvey Nichols, this time for Billionaire Boys Club, and you bet they let me in this time. Kingsley was my plus-one that night, and we hung out with Pharrell Williams behind the DJ booth. There was an extravagant, budget-less party for MTV at Sin, which I hosted with Le Gateau Chocolat. I saw Dita Von Teese ride a giant spinning lipstick for MAC Cosmetics and went to the opening of a fridge door, literally, for Smeg. I walked in a surprise fashion show at an Agent Provocateur party in lingerie as Kate, Sadie and Daisy Lowe cheered me on – Fran Cutler was carried out as the finale like Liz Taylor in *Cleopatra*. There was one week where Florence and the Machine seemed to play at a store launch every single night. And you could barely reach for a canapé on a Tuesday without hitting a Scottish guy in plastic nu rave specs singing his synth-pop tunes. He was called Calvin Harris, and he introduced me to a girl who worked with his manager at the time, and she took charge of my DJ bookings.

I started to DJ at a lot of corporate events, wooed by the purvey-ors of 'lifestyle' with big annual budgets to spend. Sometimes I'd play at something fabulous in a beautifully curated venue, and other times I'd be playing at, I don't know, a Phones 4u store. Everything blurred into one. It felt like I was selling shit to cunts, and the pay was fabulous.

I'd spend all day burning CDs and scribbling weird titles in black marker pen – 'fun house', 'slutty pop', 'commercial shit', 'harder stuff'. But the craft of mixing two records together seamlessly remained unlearned by many of the other celebrity faces that were booked for these parties, and their knowledge of music seemed anecdotal. I was determined to be taken seriously. I was not a novelty DJ.

The DJ holds the fate of the party in their hands. I was au fait with a vast array of genres, and stayed on top of every new release via a company called Your Army that posted promo CDs to DJs with little questionnaires asking for feedback on the tunes. I could command a fee of £150 for a club DJ set, but my agent helped me make much more for brands with deep marketing budgets. I balanced the two worlds, playing for corporate cash Monday to Thursday, and in sweaty raves at the weekend. I worked myself to the bone, constantly dodging the threat of being broke in a city no one can afford to live in. Even my friends who were millionaires could barely afford to be in London. It's all relative, I suppose. Somehow, everyone hustled and made it work.

There came a time where if you didn't have a Jodie Harsh DJ moment at your party, you hadn't launched your product right. You couldn't miss me as you walked into the festivities – a sparkly dress, thick lips filled with Restylane, and of course the blonde beehive hair, which by now an haute coiffure called Charlie Le Mindu was manicuring on a weekly basis. His buzz was high wattage, and all the fashion mags were talking about his hair theatre.

Some of my outfits looked as though I was doing a dare, and inspiration came from varied cultural touchpoints, such as Bet Lynch, *Showgirls* and the Care Bears. I became a muse to the shoe designer Terry de Havilland, and he'd send me boxes of snakeskin wedges, which I'd clomp around in so hard that the tongues would flap about; I'd have to get Kingsley to stick them back together with his glue gun. My handbags were covered in garish designer monograms and were usually fake. A glance inside one would reveal a bounty of bad health and addiction – a ten-deck of cigarettes, a wrap of cocaine, a diamanté-encrusted Sony Ericsson C901 (gifted!), a couple of rolled-up notes, a Valium and a few loose Airwaves gums, caked in flecks of tobacco.

———

There was a place we went with an inconspicuous doorway that sat in the gutters of Soho, steps from the busy thoroughfare of Oxford Street, and it was called Punk. The room was narrow, packed with curios, and drenched in a red-light-district glow. Sometimes you'd find huge amounts of jollification in there, and at other times it was an embassy of London's worst people. Whenever I went, I'd barely set foot in the main club at all, instead spending hours in the kitchen out the back tooting with London's great, good and awful. That's where *everything* happened.

Smash and Grab was Punk's Thursday-night fiesta, organised by DJ/chaos-carousers Queens of Noize, who knew everyone. They were part of the Kate, Sadie, Fran crew, and one of the duo, Mairead Nash, was the manager of Florence Welch, who was really breaking through at this point, along with her Machine. If you weren't going down to Smash and Grab every Thursday, you were kind of knocked out of the loop. At least one freshly famous musician from the cover of the *NME* could be found frolicking around – Ladyhawke, Mystery Jets, Kele from Bloc Party, and so on. Beth

Ditto would be dancing on a table along with her make-up artist Andrew Gallimore and hairdresser Lyndell Mansfield, who had a bright-pink mop of curls atop her head and was always the most fun person in the room. Henry Holland would be down most weeks, never far away from his best friend Agyness Deyn who by now had become the emblem of late-noughties Britain. There was so much media heat on her, she could melt chrome. She was lovely, and really had that thing, that *je ne sais quoi* that defines an era, the thing that only one star at a time is allowed.

One Wednesday I celebrated the birth of a new Nokia phone at Punk. An American singer who was beginning to bubble called Lady Gaga played a DJ set. Paris Hilton took selfies, before we even started calling them that. Gaga invited me to a show she was doing at the London Astoria that weekend and asked me if I could bring some club kids down to help fill it up. I declined – it still felt too triggering to return to that place, all those years later. She seemed like the real deal, hyper-engaged with everyone she spoke to, and obviously belonged in the great pantheon of megastars. Two weeks later, her song was number one.

The day after the phone party, I ignored exhaustion and went out yet again. After a cocktail soirée to celebrate the opening of a handbag at the Mulberry store, I crashed into Punk for the second time in twenty-four hours. Beforehand, I'd gone home, thinking I was going to call it a night. But cocaine doesn't work like that – it keeps you wanting more, pushing back any hopes of the session diminishing. After a scrub and a shower which returned me back to my male layer, I was restless, and did something quite unprecedented for me. I went out as J.

I jumped on the night bus – the first time I'd been on board one for what felt like several hundred years – and hopped off at Tottenham Court Road. I walked round to Smash and Grab like a stray dog, whispered into the ear of the girl who did the door – 'it's Jodie Harsh' – and descended into the deep cavity as the perpetual drone of A-Trak's remix of Yeah Yeah Yeahs' 'Heads Will Roll' punched my eardrums. With my senses heightened, I fought through aimless figures scattered across the dance floor. Without my heels, a brigade of peroxide blondes, a repetition of headscarves and fascinators, and a barrier of floppy fringes towered high above me. I didn't know where I was going; I couldn't see. The usual hoopla ensued all around – the dressing-up box, the tombola, Grimmy on the decks and Scottee in a bath of baked beans – but it looked different without my eyelashes glued on. People were dancing, snogging, being silly with their friends, while I felt naked and exposed, and regretted letting my mask slip. I locked eyes with Alexa Chung, who didn't recognise me, and looked away. In that moment I knew that if I was to have fun, and flourish, and feel free, it had to be under the cloak-and-dagger of my drag. I escaped to the disabled toilet, locked the door tightly and hid. I sat there for a good twenty minutes. I recognised I was starting to overdose on the world of showbiz. I was losing my sanity and my way.

———

It was February 2009, and one of those days that barely seems to get light before the sun disappears at 4 p.m. London had been considering spring all afternoon, but at the last minute opted for winter with violent lashings of evening rain. I'd been invited to attend the *Elle* Style Awards, one of the hottest tickets of the social calendar. As

I pulled into the line of cars outside Big Sky Studios, I caught tantalising hints of sparkly Julien Macdonald dresses sheltering under dripping umbrellas. A red military jacket with metal adornments and gold, gem-encrusted trousers somehow seemed appropriate for my own attire. Photographers were stacked on bleachers by the media boards, and a pack of paparazzi buzzed around the car drop-off point, jockeying for the best vantage point as stars stepped out of cars, their cameras wrapped in waterproof plastic bags. A subscription to a tip-off service like Media Eye or Fashion Monitor alerted them to every happening in town, including who was attending.

I stepped out of the Mercedes that had been sent to collect me by *Elle*. My hands trembled, a symptom of imposter syndrome, which I suffered from when I was boozeless. A drinking ban had been self-enforced for the evening. I knew this was a big one. I knew I couldn't be trusted.

I was led into a hall of extraordinary scope where a drinks reception was taking place – it was 7.30 p.m., and we were being seated for dinner at 8 p.m., which really meant 8.30. I spied Pixie Geldof, Sienna Miller, Alexa Chung and Will Young. My head told me these people hated me – they didn't – and I quietened it by reaching for a pre-made mojito from the bar. It gave me brain freeze as I sucked it down. And then I grabbed another, and another, and from that moment on, I lost all control, as 'That's Not My Name' by the Ting Tings echoed around.

I quenched my thirst until I was blackout drunk. When I came to, I was pissing against a wall in a corner of the dining room close to where the waitstaff were dispensing the main course of lamb chops and pea purée. Sienna was collecting her award on stage as I stumbled back to my table bellowing 'Is ANYBODY having fun here?' The sound of hushing and tutting coming from five hundred VIPs haunted me for years. Worst of all, it was reported all over *Popbitch* the next day.

I hadn't been blacklisted just yet. Grimmy – who had graduated from being my resident DJ to becoming one of the biggest broadcasters in the country – would call me up on his Sunday-night Radio 1 show with Annie Mac for a gossip live on air. I'd write for various glossy magazines – finally using my writing degree for something. And I'd pop up on TV shows – talking heads and sofa chats, anyone who'd have me.

Mary Portas, the 'queen of shops', had a programme on television, and one episode required a drag queen to come on and style a group of older ladies. It sounded like fun, a bit of camp, and the show was garnering millions of viewers, so a great way to get my face out there. By chance, one of the viewers happened to be my dad, who was sitting on the sofa eating dinner on his lap with his wife. I'd imagine he'd have hardly been expecting the plot twist of seeing his son in drag for the first time, but there I was, in all my glory. It was my second coming out to my dad, years and years after the first time when I was fifteen. He recognised my voice, and turned to his wife, asking, 'Is that my son?' She replied, simply, 'Yes.' He went silent. From that day on, we never spoke again. I never even had a birthday card.

11

MASS
THE BATH HOUSE

t was Christmas, the season to be fucking jolly. A sad little fake tree sat in the corner of my living room. Half of its plastic branches were bent out of shape, its star was lopsided and its fairy lights had short-circuited, no longer winking to a four-to-the-floor beat. *Is a Christmas tree just a tree in drag?* I pondered, as if it was a great philosophical question.

After one particularly tempestuous forty-eight-hour night that blended into all the others, I began the process of turning back into J. I removed the wig, which instantly wiped away the etching of Jodie, like a kid's Magic Writer board resetting. I relaxed with an exhale of relief, a bright-red band of pain marking my forehead, the dent in my scalp a reminder of hours of near-migraine pressure. I placed her into a cupboard, on to a featureless polystyrene head, next to a small army of ten identical hairspray-caked wigs lined up on the shelf. 'See you tomorrow,' I promised, begrudgingly. The conveyor belt of partying was getting exhausting.

I hunched cross-legged in front of my dirty mirror. Dusty make-up collected like snakes of gunk in its grooves. I peeled off my lashes, which were hard and messy with glue. I blinked several times, my eyes adjusting back to complete vision. I untacked the small gemstones I'd tweezered into the outer corners of my sockets, which had earlier sparkled under the disco light, and now felt so small and insignificant in the honesty of dawn. My left cornea was bloodshot from an accident several weeks back in which I'd crunched the eyelid shut on to a mascara wand. I had never felt pain like it, and immediately thought I was going to be blinded. At Moorfields hospital they told me I had actually sliced the surface, but it would recover completely with time. Thankfully, my eyeball had stopped throbbing by now.

The shattering of my self-made fantasy now well underway, I unclipped a dangling earring from the left side, the side where the wig hair wasn't hiding the half of my face that I hated. My lobe relaxed back into flesh. Why wear a second earring if you can't see it? That's the illusion of show business. I unpeeled my golden leggings, one limb at a time, the pleather sticking to my skin with dry sweat. I ripped my vest off with force, it, too, soaked with perspiration and smelling like club. Free of clothing, I bided my time on the floor in nothing but black underwear, nail varnish and a face of Illamasqua and MAC pigments.

The sepia tones of a London morning lit up my bedroom, which had floor-to-ceiling glass on one side and a broken blind. I took a lump of cream into my hands and smushed it over my face, the whiteness curdling into the make-up and turning my skin into a browny-orange mess, a disregard of the concentration I'd put into painting it hours earlier. Fragments of iridescent glitter bounced back the glow of the morning sun, while swimming in the muck. As my lipstick and gloss joined the after-party, my face went an embarrassed pink. A few swipes of cotton wool revealed a tired, battered visage, and the visible fractures of a broken nose, a cracked tooth, eye bags and grey, blemished skin. Three full washes with hot water and cleanser on a flannel would be needed to purge the remnants of my disguise, but that could wait until tomorrow.

Dismantled and defaced, I stared back at a different person.

There was that egg with no eyebrows – I still shaved them off to create more physical space to experiment with make-up. 'Is this even me any more?' I asked out loud, to no one. I chuckled – it was quite a sight. 'I guess we make a good team, me and you,' I lied, giving myself a dirty look in the mirror.

———

New Year's Eve, a night of revelry for all. While I preferred spontaneous fun to obligatory celebration, it was the date that DJs could charge a premium, and I was happy to cash in. I was booked to DJ at Torture Garden, a much-fabled fetish party, which was taking over the club Mass in Brixton. A brand-new year. A brand-new decade. A brand-new me. At midnight I was to take my final sip, and then I'd ditch the booze and the coke and live a much healthier, happier and less hungover life. It was, of course, another futile promise I failed to keep.

Kingsley and I suckled on a bottle of Lambrini as our cab crossed over the spine of London, making its way south of the river, past vomiting out-of-towners and squawking flocks of dancers looking for a place to move. I was in a party-shaped mood, but adamant that I'd be entering 2010 a sober person.

We pulled up to Mass, an imposing church building just down from Brixton Tube. I'd never been to this club before – I rarely crossed the Thames at all. 'It's a real church!' Kingsley observed, as we climbed out of the cab. 'We're going to burn alive the moment we walk in!'

The characters that stood in a meandering line through the forecourt suggested society's rules of dressing didn't apply here.

Corsets, chaps, rubber, leather, and exposed buttocks and breasts. We charged to the front of the queue, a doorman's tree trunk of an arm softening as I explained I was tonight's headline DJ. I clutched my rosary, flashed the interior of my Lulu Guinness bag to the doorman, and we penetrated the house of worship without so much as a frisk.

The sights inside were undeniably blasphemous. Across the great thumping space, desires were freed and untamed. In the lobby, sins were acted out. Stilettos dug into chests, quivering men were tugged around on leads by their mistresses, fleshy parts were spanked, and the smell of latex curdled with the memory of a different kind of religious experience. In the toilet, a gentleman with a truck driver's physique entered a cubicle as his wife kept guard outside. He exited minutes later in a floral dress and lipstick, an alter ego unlocked. The wife held the handbag as luscious tresses were flicked and tweaked in the mirror, a smile forming on his face.

Industrial music enticed us into the heat. Synths spat and fast drums clattered around the cathedral of a main room as a lone flashing strobe rendered bodies aglow. It shot static images of movement – a rhythmical insanity in its cadence. Flash, flash, flash, flash. David, the promoter and high priest of this obscene revel, brought us a pair of shots, which were thick and bloody. Sambuca. We swished them back, and it burned.

After agreeing to meet in the DJ booth, Kingsley evaporated into the night. I moved slowly in the opposite direction, pushing through the insane choreography, trying to acclimatise to the unfamiliar floor plan and overcrowded humanity. I pressed flesh with perverts and freaks, and ducked under a shower of embers flying from an angle grinder being whizzed by a girl in a red corset on stage. I scooched past an entire foot being sucked. I recognised a face through a muzzle – a usually more dapper man I used to know from the Mahiki scene. He was old of money and blue of blood, and I remarked how lovely it was to see him in a nipple clamp. What a dark horse.

As scandalous as this environment sounds, it was a pretty middle-class affair. A lot of these fetish clubs we went to – Slimelight, Stunners, the WayOut Club – felt like a performance space, a stage to express yourself on as opposed to a place to cum and go. It was all about belonging. And there was truly something for everyone here – I was even batting off attention myself. As ego-boosting as it was to be the object of some clown-chaser's lust, I had a job to do.

Midnight was minutes away by the time I took to the pulpit where the DJ equipment nestled. The guy presiding before me had been edging the crowd and it was my duty to bring them to climax with some heavy hitters. His booth monitor was yanked up to skull-shattering levels. I hit the cue button and brought his track to an immediate standstill, cutting against politeness. I twisted the gain button clockwise so my music penetrated harder on the dance floor. I smashed in the Steve Angello remix of 'Sweet Dreams (Are Made of This)' as 2009 played out its final moments. The entire auditorium erupted. A countdown commenced, and I impatiently gulped down a glass of champagne that had been handed to me for the midnight crescendo.

Ten . . . nine . . . eight . . . I saw the frolic of hugging and kissing begin on the dance floor. Seven . . . six . . . five . . . I lowered the volume on the Eurythmics song. Four . . . three . . . two . . . one . . . 'Happy New Year!' Confetti rained down and mistresses kissed their gimps. I hit play on Prince's '1999' – so predictable, so ill planned. And minutes later at 12.05, even more predictably, I reached for another glass of champagne. I downed it in one second, breaking my promise. In that moment, I knew 2010 was going to be trouble.

After my DJ set, there was still a corner of time left to explore. My curiosity was piqued by word of a couple's room, which turned out to be a lewd orgy in the church's crypt. The sounds of skin slapping on skin accompanied the unforgettable vision of dozens of people trysting on holy ground. Torture Garden took sex positivity out of the bedroom and placed it in a musical environment. Hasn't clubbing always been about sex, and exhibitionism, and voyeurism?

By closing time at 5 a.m., I couldn't wrap up my adventure – the coke wouldn't let me. Kingsley had befriended a gimp and spent the night sending him off to the bar to buy us rounds of drinks. He was a cash pig who got off on being used for money – *perfect*! We took full advantage, and he was happy to oblige. His entire face and body were covered in a wet-look turquoise material, and he had little holes for his eyes and mouth. He only spoke if he was spoken to. It didn't get any better than that.

I was wired, crucified – and as the lights came up on a new year's dawn, I invited ten or so people back to mine – people I'd known for an hour. I was on the prowl for party partners with whom to continue the depravity.

In the flat, my perilous joyride got weird pretty quickly. Déjà vu. My resolution of sobriety felt almost comedic, as if it were a joke from the outset. When I had one drink, all bets were off. Eight hours later, I was sketchy and sordid. It was as if I had been spiked, but it was me that was spiking myself.

A fire-breathing performer from Torture Garden was knelt in

front of my sound system, fumbling for the aux lead. A man dressed as a First World War soldier was K-holing in the corner, the only movement coming from his eyebrows, twitching to an off-beat. A couple of creepy crawlies were foraging in my kitchen for glasses, talking in unison. A dinner plate, freshly heated in the microwave, was being passed around by the gimp on which contents of baggies were being poured. A woman called Lara who I always saw out, and always had really strong coke, was talking at me in tongues, slurring so much she needed subtitles to be understood. And me? I ignored it all as I dissolved into the sofa, under a double tranquilliser of tequila and some powder of undisclosed concoction. I didn't really know any of these people, and didn't want to be around them, but I also didn't want the party to stop. Occasionally I'd wind up finishing an afters off alone, which felt subversive at first, and then grim. By 7 a.m., my enthusiasm for this impromptu gathering was lost.

Where were my real friends, you ask? They were there – not in the living rooms and the after-parties, but most of them were still with me. 'You've stopped smiling,' warned Kris, my flatmate. 'You start your nights engaging and funny, and wind down into a conceited toddler.' That told me. I always brushed it off. I was always *fine*. I liked to keep my genuine chosen family and my fake friends quite separate, compartmentalised. My drug use was encouraged at work – nightlife being one of the only industries where it was almost mandatory, at that time. But it was stopping me from dancing, literally and metaphorically. Happy hour was almost over.

By 10 a.m., my high had truly diminished, and a person I didn't recognise from the club was on all fours searching for specks of spilled blow on the carpet. I took myself off to my bedroom – no explanations, no goodbyes. I just left these people alone in my house as they unravelled into howling insanity. I stared into my make-up mirror and asked my reflection why I got myself into messes like this, and why couldn't I just take drugs like a normal person. I felt like I belonged in the bin. Oh, and the person hunting for specks of coke that I didn't recognise? Well, that was me.

I lay like a plank in bed, listening to the sound of birds chattering, torturous to my brain, and to the buzz of my own teeth vibrating. The boom boom boom of my rapid heartbeat played a countermelody to the bassline coming from the lounge. Every molecule of my being hated the tune it was playing. Under my cold, comfortless duvet, fictitious objects appeared before my eyes and dark thoughts penetrated my mind as I came down. I lay listening for hours, praying for sleep to come, before finally slipping into dreamlessness, my heart racing at one hundred miles per hour as the rest of London ate lunch. I awoke the following evening to a skeleton staff still in the living room, still partying.

———

This charade played on throughout the first half of the year. My twenty-fifth birthday party was a standout – particularly because I barely remembered being at it. My nerves were verging on hysterical in the lead-up to the event. I blamed this on being a sensitive Pisces, but can see now it was more to do with my innate insecurities and abandonment issues.

My real birthday had been swallowed by a Tuesday, and on the following Thursday, better late than never, we descended upon the House of St Barnabas in Soho, another former place of God. A well-executed theme can be a direct route to legendary party status, and this night's was art-directed around Sofia Coppola's movie *Marie Antoinette*. I took that mood board literally by getting completely off my head.

A tapestry of friends I'd woven together over the past years showed up for me – Luke Day, Gary Card, Alice Dellal, Natalie Munro, Princess Julia, Brett Lloyd, Titus Groan, Namalee, Elgar, Thomas Knights, Mel Blatt, Laura Whitmore, Shelly Would, Miquita Oliver, Mika Doll, Pelayo, Tracy Sedino, Joshua James, Bishi, Kingsley, Jo Berryman, Rowan, Ken, Sarah Shotton, Matthew Williamson, Jaime Winstone, Scottee, and my mum and sister. Real friends, fair-weather friends, fake friends, and family. Kim Jones DJ'd – he came in from Paris for the occasion, where he'd just landed the head job at Louis Vuitton.

Simon made it – he was supposed to be in New York on a business trip that was cancelled at the last minute due to a volcanic ash cloud from Iceland covering the skies of Northern Europe which grounded all flights. It was a visible force field that prevented people travelling forwards and kept some away from home.

As I reached a quarter of a century, I was *really* getting on. I'd had my first Botox the week prior – injected with it at my dinner table at a venue in Notting Hill called the Supper Club. I was looking fresh but feeling mentally and physically worn down.

Tagged photos on Facebook showed me arriving at my party with massive Pompadour hair and ultra-emphasised, 'Pat McGrath for Dior'-inspired make-up. Many of my friends took the French Revolution theme literally, even though I hadn't enforced a strict dress code. The room was quite a spectacle.

There's a key to throwing the perfect party. Guests are usually a little nervy at first, so the most welcoming thing you can do is to stand at the entrance at the beginning of the night, helping every-one feel at ease as they walk in. It's you they've come to see, after all. But that night I hid upstairs, in the kitchen, cooking up a recipe for disaster, those habitual ingredients of coke, alcohol and ego. Later, a cake was wheeled out into the assemblage with a picture of my face in its centre, surrounded by twenty-five candles. I took the knife and stabbed it into the sponge, raspberry jam oozing out of my throat, as a cloud of smoke wafted above. It was my party, and I'd cry if I wanted to.

———

My spiral was brought to a pathetic crescendo at the Bath House the night of 24 June. I had well and truly reached the zenith of my partying by this stage. My life had become a tragicomedy. I was constantly on the corner of a bad decision, with temporary highs leading to crushing comedowns. TV appearances and DJ gigs had all but dried up, half of my real friends were out of reach, wary of my erratic behaviour, and I had begun to wither into emotional obscurity. This was my last hurrah.

We were somewhere in the no man's land of Liverpool Street. A former Turkish bath was the setting for a night called Caligula which happened every Friday. The opulent little den was originally built in 1895 as an underground haven for cleanliness and relax-ation, and over a century later, I would wind up there most weeks for the opposite kind of unwinding. Down through a graveyard, past a little church, hidden from view, away from the main thor-oughfare, the funny little Victorian building formed the portal into a very naughty vortex.

That Friday, I flexed my privileges and wriggled past the queue forming along temporary railings, past club kids and dandies and girls in pillbox hats waiting to get in. Some gasped as they clocked my wig. I air-kissed several others and moved on through in haste, then plunged beneath the paving stones.

Down the spiral staircase and into the belly of the club, I followed crumbling walls eroded by rapture, some plastered with faded erotica, some covered in cracked marble and grand mosaics, the relics of its life as an ancient spa. Enclaves were packed with oddities – physical and human. It felt like I'd gone back in time to a place where Jules Verne might have hung out. Part of the floor plan was carved up by dusty red drapes which obscured secret spaces that could only fit a few bodies at a time. I ducked into one, closing the curtain on myself to text my friend Alexis and discover her whereabouts. Undelivered – no network.

The air was gooey with the pungent memory of whisky and tobacco – I added to it by lighting up a secret cigarette – you could get away with smoking in the darkest nooks of these catacombs. My ears were caressed by an organ and high hats that signalled the arrival of Azari & III's 'Hungry for the Power', muffled by the heavy velvet, cued up by the DJ Mark Moore from within a giant golden birdcage out in the middle of the club. I blew a small ring of smoke from my lungs and heard someone steps away. 'Miss Harsh – are you in there?'

I flung my Marlboro Light to the ground and twisted it into a skid of papery ash with the sole of my shoe, as a hand I recognised pushed through the curtain, covered in chrome skull rings. The drapes flung open, and Leo Belicha catapulted into my hiding place.

Leo was a Brazilian-born conduit of illicit fun and the master of

245

the revelry at Caligula, along with his more subdued business partner, the musician and DJ Jim Warboy. He was an expert connector, and indeed very well connected – he knew Grace Jones, and you'd rarely see him without Róisín Murphy, who was the coolest woman in electronic music.

'I heard you'd snuck in, bitch. Want to do a surprise DJ set for us?' Why not, I thought – anything for the love of music, and anything for some attention while hiding in plain sight. *So* borderline introverted extrovert. I had a wallet of CDs in my bag, and I could borrow Mark's headphones. Leo's silhouette was always made up of a Jack the Ripper cloak and a witchy, wide-brimmed hat. His metal-clad hand grasped mine, and he pulled me out of the cubbyhole, through the muddle of the main room, and into the birdcage – a hot sweaty centrepiece, where all make-up would inevitably get smeared.

Even as I began to unravel mentally, playing music would always hold me together. I felt alive when I DJ'd, and I adored weaving the story of someone's night through beats, lyrics and melodies – a common language we all understood. Dance music was political at its core, a place for marginalised communities to unite, and no matter how wasted I got, that thought never left me. As my hands glided over the CDJs, twisting the knobs and pushing the dials, I looked out and took in the vista. Caligula was a festival of the extreme – on a podium to my right, a lady was squirting breast milk into a champagne glass, a look of ecstasy on her face. She handed it to a clubber, who proceeded to down it in one gulp. This was truly some Ancient Rome shit.

I keyed a mountain of cocaine up my nose in full view of the dance floor. Cameras in phones were so primitive and grainy at that time that they were rarely used, so my depravity went unrecorded.

I raged, off my face, pounding the buttons, hanging off the night's host Andre J., who counterbalanced my vibe with a blast of positive energy, and Alexis, who had arrived finally and climbed up into the birdcage. Alexis was a stylist, so she was always wearing something loud and fabulous. I danced around with her as my face contorted and my nose bled until someone from the crowd offered me a tissue.

'Royal T' by the Crookers soundtracked the hooliganism in front of me, and I mixed it into 'Shoes' by Tiga, and that into 'Happy House' by the Juan MacLean. A DJ called David Guetta, who used to come over from Paris to play at Discotec at the End, DTPM and other parties I used to work at, was finally making waves on the radio, and he had a tune out called 'Memories'. I played that, but it was a misstep – too commercial for this crowd. 'Coma Cat' by Tensnake quickly reignited the party. I guzzled Jack Daniel's from the bottle – my payment in kind for the impromptu set – and liquid spilled from my mouth to the mixer. Gradually, all sense of time left my body as my music glued people together. I can't remember what else I played.

Eventually I climbed out of the birdcage, hacking into the drudge of the dance floor. I squelched through, knocking people aside, walking away mid-sentences, ignoring invitations to air-kiss. Hurricane Harsh had hit yet again, and it was sucking the energy out of the room.

Near 4 a.m. we were spat out of the place. We lurked around the bend, then Alexis, who was pharmaceutical-free but put up with my usage, headed to Moorgate to catch the night bus home. The sky was a dusty shade of marmalade, and the moon was pregnant, but I saw only a dirty darkness. Cocaine by now was feeling much less profound than it once did. Its magical quality had long since depleted, leaving me needing more and more and more to get the same high.

Alone, I went everywhere else that night. I went to Heaven but the gates were closed. I went to Bungalow 8 but they were kicking people out, too. I went to a sketchy after-hours club under the pavement called Public Life, which used to be a toilet, and I went to several unnamed corner shops until one would serve me a bottle of cheap vodka. A joyless city murmured around me.

In bed, a symphony of voices joined the conversation in my head, preventing any possibility of sleep. I was worried about having a heart attack – there'd be no one there to save me. God, was I dying? This was no way to live. I finally managed to block out the white noise, and everything cut to blackout.

Church bells outside my window announced the top of a new hour, 2 p.m. The morning after was already nibbling away at the afternoon. The sun spilled through a crack in the half-mended blinds creating shards of light, and I could see dust particles swimming around within them. I remained fermenting in bed, polluted, unable to move. I traced the route of my night through branded napkins and matchbooks that were stuffed into my handbag, and Addison Lee receipts in my email inbox.

Since I'd hit my mid-twenties, my hangovers were generally set to one hundred, but this was a whole new nadir. I lacked the Viking gene that allowed some of my friends to power through, carrying on with their lives as if they hadn't spent the last twenty-four hours in a spiral of self-sabotage. I looked feral. I felt crap. I consistently felt The Fear. In the narrative arc of my life, I believe we call this rock bottom.

I somehow regained enough stamina to reach into the drawer in which I stuffed half-empty, crushed boxes of paracetamol. I popped a couple of white pills from their blisters and necked them down with the lubrication of two-day-old water, ignoring its musty film. A failed attempt to override my hangover left me with no choice but to roll over like a groaning corpse and return to my crumpled grave of slumber.

I woke again at 3 p.m. in a moment of pure clarity. I bolted upright, winded. I knew in that moment that I could never drink again, that this had to be the last time it happened. There was no devastating earthquake, no intervention, no ambulance, no police cell. I was just battered by my relentless lifestyle, with a career and personal life in a sad little pile on the floor. I was sick and tired of being sick and tired, and it had to stop now, or I would end up dead.

With rubbery legs, I waded through my bedroom, which looked like a crime scene. Clothes paved the floor like an archaeological dig site – an excavation required to find a matching shoe. I stopped, just for a second, at the spot where I did my make-up, and looked at the reflection of myself, trapped inside a distorted funhouse mirror.

My flatmate Kris was in the living room as I entered. He was used to this routine of next-day self-flagellation by now, but I told him, with absolute conviction, that I was never drinking or drugging again. I told him with so much certainty, that this time he believed me.

Later that afternoon, I sat at the kitchen table. The XX played out quietly from my stereo, beckoning me further into the mud of a comedown. I stared at my phone – my emotional rebound ricocheting – thinking about who I should call. My friend Fat Tony, the DJ – who I'd danced to so many times since my nights out in

London began – picked up first. He was now clean and sober, and I wanted to know how he did it. I wanted it for myself.

'I'm at the football, who's this? Hello? I can't fuckin' hear ya!' he screamed into the phone. I hung up, panicked. I texted: *It's Jodie Harsh. I need some help.*

He called me back, and hours later we were having dinner, me slumped over the table in tears, him serving me matter-of-fact advice on the next steps I needed to take to sort this drug and drink problem out.

The nine years since this story started at the Astoria had gone by in a blazing flash. The city I was so enthralled by had discarded me like a broken toy in the attic. I'd finally merged with the shadows of clubland and I needed to take radical action to prevent myself disappearing entirely.

The music had been lowered, and the lights were up. The party was finally over.

On Saturday 25 June 2010, halfway through my twenties, I vowed to never have a drink or drug again. And I kept my promise.

12

RECOVERY

On Monday, I sat on a hard plastic chair, tucked into the back of a nondescript room in a medical centre. Fraught with fear, I was stone-cold sober, with emotions heightened from Friday's comedown. I avoided eye contact with every person that walked in and fixed my gaze upon the clock on the wall that counted down the seconds to 6.30 p.m., when my first twelve-step meeting would begin. A kettle grumbled next to cups of dusty coffee granules, awaiting their water. A plate of crumbling Party Rings was scavenged as people entered. The smell of roll-ups and Marlboro Lights wafted through the open windows, because even though it was a place of health, it was June. Every time a chair leg screeched on the floor, I jumped out of my skin. These nerves felt even more intense than the ones I'd get before a DJ set, or the gut-wrench before a birthday, or the anxiety before a club night. I felt the distance that comes with being a stranger in a new place, particularly when sober.

Everyone introduced themselves with their first name and their reason for being present. I kept my eyes on a row of posters advertising antenatal classes and help groups for overeaters, chewing the skin around my fingers, turning it pink. When it was my go, I could barely make a sound. After a tense interlude, I managed to croak out, 'I'm J, and I'm an addict,' and a chorus of voices projected, 'Hi, J,' back, and I started to cry. As this was going on, a white mug was being passed around, with 'It works if you work it, so work it, you're worth it!' printed in bold letters. *Sounds like a hair advert,* I mused through my tears. Pound coins were being dropped in, creating a slow, percussive jingle against the ceramic.

This was a very different kind of party. But a scan of the room, as I would do at a club, gave me some recognisable faces – an adult movie star who used to be famous on the scene, a PR who'd booked me for an event once, a trans girl who used to hang out with the Ruby crew, who always had great coke. There were professional-looking people, smart in their work clothes, as if they'd wandered in after taking a wrong turning on their way home from the office. I sat there next to Fat Tony, feeling proverbially naked and exposed, wondering if people knew it was me out of drag. The narrator in my head gave me one hundred reasons to get up and leave, but my legs were jelly and refusing to go. I was certain everyone in that room was judging my presence. I was completely undone.

Some dogma was read from laminated cards. 'What is an addict?' 'How it works.' I shuddered at the warning of jails, institutions and death. There was so much to take in, so many confusing words. But then I heard guts being spilled and war stories not unlike my own wreckage, and joined in the communal 'well done' as a man disclosed he was two years clean today. I took on Tony's advice to listen out for similarities, not differences. I sat there and absorbed a tale of experience, strength and hope from a man who was teetering over the edge, holding on for dear life by the skin of his twelve steps. His condensed story was all very 'live, laugh, toaster bath'. Across the hour, people shared back for two minutes each, many with irony and humour. I identified with so much, and realised I could belong there, in a new type of club.

As the final moments of the meeting arrived, we clapped for

people celebrating multiple years and multiple months sober, and then the secretary asked if it was anyone's first time attending a meeting. The entire room *did* then look in my direction, and I went beetroot. Sweat oozed from my forehead which was exposed without the comfort blanket of my wig. Tony pushed me up, literally, and I collected a little white key ring. White for surrender. It was not unlike the drinks tickets from Bungalow 8, but was marked with the words 'Just for Today', rather than 'One Drink'.

The meeting closed. 'Welcome home,' said the person to my right, as our bodies wound into a hug. The unfamiliar intimacy jolted me. I recognised the supernatural magic of that room, but like all good magic tricks, I couldn't yet understand how it worked. I understood that if those people could talk about being two, three, four years sober, then perhaps I could do it too. I walked back out through the sliding doors of the health centre smiling, ready for more, ready to feel, ready to learn. 'Keep coming back,' said a person I didn't know.

After that first meeting, a few of us went to Balans at 34 Old Compton Street. Despite it being refurbished and under a different name, it would always be the Old Compton Cafe to me. I recalled our mornings here as teenagers, in between Heaven and Trade, buzzing off our tits. I remembered that it used to never close. Now, here I was, on the right side of midnight, knotted together with a group of recovering addicts, ordering a plate of Thai chicken noodles, swapping stories and words of encouragement. It was the same, but it wasn't. I developed connections with people that night that felt so much deeper than the wordless conversations through the mist of the dance floor.

Someone Tony knew had just relapsed, and there was genuine

concern around the table. I was invited to more meetings and told where the best ones were in London's geography. People gave me their number and asked me to call them if I felt shaky or just wanted to talk. They were nice to me without expectations of getting anything in return. There was fellowship.

'Back in the day you'd be able to bribe the waiter here for an alcoholic drink and they'd serve it in a teacup!' I revealed, as if I was a wise old owl. 'Oh, darlin',' Tony swiped back. 'I used to live above this place in the nineties and you'd be able to buy *anything* downstairs then.'

Fat Tony was as well known for his barbed wit as he was for his DJ sets – you wouldn't want to get in the way of his acidic tongue and bespoke insults. With our matching dark sense of humour, we laughed and laughed, sometimes at other people's expense, but always with good hearts. 'Clean' was a dirty word on the club scene until Tony came out as a proudly sober addict, and he was a pillar of the recovery community. The first time I properly spoke to him – off his nut, at the Egg – I had him pegged for a scary person, but a few years later, he was the one who looked after me and looked out for me when I needed it the most. It's partly down to him that I'm around today.

I arrived home that night in a pink cloud of optimism. There was no membership, no entrance fee, and everyone was welcome. It felt like I'd been moving at one hundred miles per hour for the best part of a decade, and I'd crashed the car into a wall. It was time to be still for a moment and deal with my emotional whiplash, one day at a time.

I'd really done it all. I'd snorted everyone under the table, drunk the bar dry, even done gak off a movie star's tits. I'd *really* done it. For just about long enough, I'd experimented with pushing limits – and it seemed, in the end, I just wasn't very good at handling the party compared to other people. And I'd really tried – I'd put a lot of time and effort into it. I thought about how many festering hangovers I'd crammed into those ten years, strung out on the sofa, wasting my life away. I thought about the bubble I'd lived in, and how all bubbles burst eventually. I thought about the obnoxious behaviour, and I thought about the blackouts. London had swallowed up so many boys like me before, and I refused to be another tragic story. The broken light bulbs around my mirror had to be repaired, the residue of my recklessness wiped clean. There was no going back.

With an overdrawn bank account and a phone that would rarely ring, the thought of asking to move back home with my mum or sister crossed my mind. But I snapped out of that quickly – leaving London was not an option: I would simply have to coexist with its vices. Since those early days travelling up from Canterbury on the train, Soho had always been my nexus. I'd dreamed of its utopian pastures, then it became my safe space, then my promenade, then a fruitful land in which I invented a new life. And now, I zigged and zagged across it with a different gang of misfits. We were the walking wounded, the partied-out, dipping into church halls and back rooms and coffee shops. They told me to get to ninety meetings in ninety days, and as the calendar pages turned through summer, the majority of my early sobriety was spent in Soho.

Such a dark horse, our Soho. As I danced there throughout my era of excess, little did I know the area was also a tightly packed warren of recovery. Through the grid of unbecoming alleyways and streets, past all the places I used to go, breathing in the unmistakable fragrance of eau de urine, I discovered these stark rooms of motley crews bonded by the understanding of trauma. Vodka was replaced by tea, cocaine replaced by Hobnobs, and private leather booths were replaced by hard plastic chairs in a circle. Every day, I'd tap my Oyster card on the Central Line to Tottenham Court Road, walk down Old Compton Street, the thrumming heart of Soho, and disappear into one of its veins – Greek Street, Dean Street or Frith Street. They were the pathways to quiet, nourishing rooms in the middle of a deranged part of town, and it's there that I would go to rebuild myself.

My drinking sprees were replaced by double meeting days, and rather than DJing I took on commitment roles like being in charge of laying the key rings out, greeting newcomers at the door or making the tea and coffee. I formed a new ensemble, and they all wanted the same thing as me – to be clean and serene. Drama and spectacle followed me into meetings too – within the first few weeks I'd witnessed a seizure and a punch-up.

NA and AA were interchangeable for me – narcotics and alcohol were my ugly twin sisters, one rarely seen without the other. Their mirrored programmes began to provide me with a toolbox: ways of coping and new ways of looking at things. If I felt the urge to push the fuck-it button, I was to roll the tape forward and remember where a drink or a drug took me. It taught me to trap any intrusive thoughts that might lead to a bad decision.

———

Back in the day, Soho was a boggy marsh, before being utilised as rich farmland. In 1536, it became a royal park and deer-hunting ground for King Henry VIII. Its town planning really began in 1660. Politicians such as Sir Edward Wardour and builders like

Richard Frith began to buy up and develop the area – namechecking themselves and the Bishop of London, Dean Henry Compton, in the streets they built. The post-Great Fire building boom saw mansions cropping up all over Soho Fields, but shabbiness was always part of its appeal. As the city around it grew, the parish remained small and low, like a countryside village, an irregular map of alleys and squares. These streets became home to immigrants, and its rich cultural diversity took shape as French, Greeks and Italians moved in. Artists and the old-school media players adopted the district as a fashionable quarter – Charles Dickens was *obsessed*. Although Soho weathered plague and various other diseases over the centuries, it was an outbreak of cholera in 1854 that finally pushed the wealthier residents to Mayfair in the west, as Soho morphed into a niche destination for night-time entertainment. After the First World War, the popularisation of cocaine and jazz music led to a huge boom for the area. Theatre, drinking and dancing took over the square mile, and along with those came the sex, and sex work. And then, in the 1980s and 1990s, the clubs and the gays moved in, completing its transformation into an adults-only resort. This urban transmutation had a gravitational pull felt by creatives, weirdos, thespians and queers, and indeed me. Soho lifted many eyebrows, lifted many penises, and without a doubt lifted the spirits of all who danced in her. There was nowhere else like it in the world.

As I worked on my personal rebuild, the Soho around me was also undergoing its own rejuvenation. What once felt like a refuge for the fast and the dubious was beginning to feel like any other British town centre. Landlords got greedy and rents started to soar. An infestation of Prets and Leons replaced the brothels, and candy-pink Simmons Bars replaced dives. In an optimistic surge after the bleakness of the recession, the sleaze was being pushed out by the fun police, and its inhabitants were being priced out by fat cats.

In my sobriety, I saw Soho by daylight for what felt like the first time, and its texture felt different. Its rough edges seemed sanded down. Meandering through the squished-in squares and cobbled lanes, I strolled past sexless glass buildings. After evening meetings at St Anne's Church, I fought through hordes of tourists queuing to see *Jersey Boys* on Old Compton Street. I wandered past La Bodega Negra, the restaurant's exterior covered in neon sex-shop signs, a camp pastiche of the Soho that was slipping away. Myriad queer bars – the gay town halls that once spread across this rainbow terrain – were shuttering, as if money men were bleaching the sleaziest neighbourhood in the Western world to make it a family-friendly theme park. But Bar Italia remained untouched, and still served the best panini in town at 3 a.m. Garlic and Shots stayed. The Groucho members' club was still a raucous fail-safe any time of the day thanks to its manager Bernie, the Prince of Soho.

In truth, Soho will never sit still in peaceful harmony – the sound of diggers and drills and the sight of cranes rising above the rooftops were as much a part of its landscape as the pulsing neon signs and vomit on the street. This part of the city is always going to be incomplete, ever-expanding, an ongoing project, just as I was. I guess us humans always want our home to remain the same, without realising that, just like us, the landscape must move on, too.

———

Plugging into meetings gave me the mental nourishment I needed, and before long I was able to study my emotions like an X-ray. I began to raise my hand and share what was going on inside my head. Through sizzles of embarrassment and vulnerability, I swept up my ongoing emotional debris under strip lights, in full view. Being a stranger felt liberating. Tony led many of the meetings I went to, and they were often chaotic and fun – not unlike a night out, to be honest. I loved my new life.

Getting sober gave me a second to breathe. The last nine years had been about survival: running away to London, navigating club life, doing drag, working my arse off – it was *all* just about survival. I needed to take a beat.

Before long, I was told I had to get myself a sponsor, which is another recovering addict who helps guide you through the programme. I asked a lady called Susie who I had heard share eloquently in a meeting, and she was the first of several who would help me untangle some of my issues. There were twelve steps in the recovery programme, which was where the real paradigm shift is meant to happen.

Step one was easy at first – I had admitted I was powerless when I first walked into the room. My brain was wired to a different circuit board than other people who could drink reasonably. I was never one to have a glass of wine with dinner and then be able to call it a night. I rebutted the word 'addict' as it sounded so harsh, but went along with it.

For steps two and three, we talked about God. It is not a religious programme, and God's name can be replaced by 'universe' or 'energy', but I was unable to accept something or someone I couldn't even see was holding the reins. I had enough authority-figure complexes going on to hand any control over, but I faked it, anyway.

Step four was where things got interesting. I began the excavation of my past by listing the fears, anger and resentments I had towards everyone of significance to me. I carried my ring binder around for a year, dragging my heels, bleeding honestly over the pages, and when I finally finished the cathartic inventory of my life, I felt amazing. I wrote about my dad, and Mr Bailey, and all the cunts I'd dealt with in clubland. I wrote about being jealous of Kingsley because he was better looking than me, and of all the friends I perceived to be more successful than me. I even let rip on that bitch who didn't let us into that party at Harvey Nics – as petty as it might sound to hold on to a small detail like that.

I was on an epic self-fact-finding mission, summoning the ghosts of my past, painting a true picture of my faults and having to sit with them. I won't go into it all here – that's between me, myself and I – but the consequence of this reckoning was that the past no longer defined me. I let it all go. I even forgave my dad – our fractured relationship was his loss and, as the parent, his responsibility to fix. The steps enabled me to rid myself of some of my resentments towards him, after I'd walked with them through the years like a phantom limb.

In step eight, I made a list of the people I might have harmed emotionally. Admitting my faults forced me to shed the ego I'd been overdosing on. I shrivelled with embarrassment as I owned up to kissing people who weren't single, bad-mouthing my best friends, stealing money from the till at the End. 'I've heard worse,' said Susie. 'A lot worse.'

In step nine, I reached out, where appropriate, and apologised. All the expensive therapy, hypnosis, juice cleanses and colonics didn't flush things I was carrying out of my system like this did. Although mortifying at times, this purge of toxic sludge helped right some wrongs, and it helped me form empathy and forgiveness for my old self.

We continued through the autopsy of my psyche. In an emotional roll call, depression and anxiety raised their hands. I needed to strip back Jodie for a moment and see what was lurking under J's bonnet. I remembered that he's my friend, and I cared about him. He needed to be coloured back in – not treated as a watered-down version of my work persona. Both J and Jodie made up the sum of me, but one had been given more attention over the past few years. Drink and drugs were just a symptom of this, a scab covering up the toxic relationship I had with myself – it was only when I stopped using them that I realised how bad they were for me. I had problems a bottle or a packet could not fix.

———

As my third month approached, I made a phone call to Susie. 'I think I'll just do this for a year, then I should be all right,' I announced. Completely delusional, of course. I thought this soap opera just required a commercial break and a bit of a recast. My desire to use drink and drugs had faded so quickly that I thought I might be able to have that one glass of wine with dinner now. 'Listen to what you're saying,' she responded. 'You've come so far already, and now you want to throw it away. You haven't done all this work to go back to being trashed in a nightclub.' She was right; my life had begun to turn around in twelve weeks, but it could just as rapidly go back to the depths it had been in before I went to meetings. I collected my red ninety-day key ring, and stopped sleepwalking. I threw myself head first into the programme. I took newcomers under my wing, remembering what it was like to be at my first meeting. And if an unruly thought did drop into my mind – if 'just one drink' felt like a good idea for a split second – I'd feel my stomach flip and harness that understanding of powerlessness from step one.

In twelve-step meetings, someone from the group would be asked to speak for fifteen minutes on their experience, strength and hope, and that was called 'doing a chair'. No script, no template – just an anecdotal TED Talk on why you're sober, how you got sober, and what you do to stay sober. Eventually I was asked to do a chair for the first time. I'd met the most famous people in the world, walked into some big rooms, and DJ'd some pretty amazing stages, but being asked to chat about the real me to thirty people in the back of a health centre threw me into a massive spiral. I was petrified.

'Just share from the heart – you'll be great,' Tony reassured me. 'You've got a story to tell.' I thought about myself intoxicated, standing alone on a packed dance floor, and about how far I'd already come since then. The most memorable chairs I'd witnessed had been confident and hilarious – two personality traits I felt I'd lost, momentarily. I felt I had to deliver an Amy Schumer stand-up routine with an expert recital of the twelve steps. 'Take that pressure off,' said Tony. 'It's not about the crowd, it's about you.'

I sat in the centre of the room, next to the table with all the different-coloured clean-time key rings. My posture was folded up like a croissant. I thought I was going to throw up. As people started to walk in, I kept my eyes firmly on the exit. Was it too late to do a runner? It was, and doing this talk was all part of the service I should provide to the programme in return for its helping me. I threw on a cloak of make-believe confidence.

Tony handed over the microphone, introducing me as Jodie by mistake, which felt jarring for a second but helped break the ice, and I began to stammer through a treasury of misadventure. I marinated on my life in digestible mouthfuls – my first drink, my move to London, my journey as a pisshead DJ. I laughed about my final drunken night out at Caligula – I said it was like the collapse of Ancient Rome, but with better hair, a historically rooted joke that didn't really land. *Tough crowd,* I thought. I spoke about my reputation being in the gutter, my dwindling desirability, and how I had escaped with my own teeth and at least some of my sanity intact. 'The problem with this city is you're never more than six feet away from some coke.' 'Or a cokehead!' bellowed a heckler. I signed off with, 'I guess I put the fun into dysfunctional,' in a delivery I'd rehearsed for a week, as fellow addicts raised their hands to share back.

If that makes it sound relatively easy, it wasn't all smooth sailing. I even swapped out my vices – smoked twice the number of cigarettes, ate whole bags of Haribo at bedtime, and guzzled so much coffee I felt like I was on speed. I was a recovering addict – but there were caveats.

If you burn the candle at both ends, the bit in the middle – your life – is going to melt into pieces. And if you're allergic to drugs and alcohol, with that addict gene, then you're like me, and I hope you take that big first step of facing your demons. It's not easy, and even though I was still young when I got sober, I wish I'd discovered the salve even sooner. 'You weren't that bad,' friends would say, unaware of my private pain.

I could blame so many people and so many reasons for being how I was, but the culprit in the centre of the chaos was me, and only me. And I am not judgemental of those in my orbit who drink and take drugs. If you do party and it doesn't affect you negatively – thank you! Quite frankly, in my industry, we need people like you.

Most of the time I was rigorous with my recovery – doing my step work, showing up to share, helping with service, being of use. I sat with, and helped, people much worse off than me – people who were homeless, or on the very last of their nine lives, or beaten up both physically and mentally. My problems felt trivial in comparison. Recovery isn't for everyone – at certain points I thought it wasn't for me. There were weeks where my willingness to commit was minimalistic at best. I'd skip meetings and forget to call my sponsor. I thought I could outsmart the fellowship, but I soon came running back when I realised I couldn't go it alone.

Along the way, I lost friends, new and old, to drink and drugs. Some people would walk in one day, all smiles and laughter, and the following day I'd hear they had relapsed, or worse. One friend who was in the events business and had a decade of recovery under his belt caved to the worst degree. He ended up killing his mother in a deep crystal meth psychosis, before turning himself in to the police. He later hanged himself in prison. Drugs and mental health really can take you there. I held on to every lesson, good and bad, and stayed clean and sober, one day at a time.

———

After four months, my social battery began to recharge, and I was itching to get back out to the physical dimension of nightlife. I was gagging for it, in fact – one more evening at home would have felt too virtuous. I hit some sober raves with friends in recovery, but they felt tame and boring, and no one was dancing. I was glad that they existed, but I missed the whirlwind of carnage a proper nightclub offered up. I also missed being in drag, and the queer superpowers it gave me. I was adamant I should be back in dark, sweaty rooms, engaging with the night, only this time without altering my brain chemistry. I was convinced the universe had some interesting stage direction mapped out for me. And I listened to it.

'Do you think I should change my name?' I asked my friend Alexis on the phone. 'My stock has plummeted. I should just be someone else.' I was considering a rebrand, a fresh start, a new project. Alexis gave it to me straight. 'You could do, but can you be arsed? Just change your behaviour.' In truth, I really couldn't be arsed. The whole Jodie Harsh thing was instantly recognisable, and I'd put in my ten thousand hours – I was almost an expert at playing her. I was going to stay for the extended version.

London can be an empty town when you've pissed off most of your friends and the phone's stopped ringing. You're replaceable, and you're disposable. But there was life in Jodie yet – I decided to rebuild my career from scratch. In a burst of hustle, I awoke from my prolonged disco nap and emailed the promoters of G-A-Y.

A decade before, G-A-Y, and its home, the Astoria, had an elastic pull on me. A long time had passed since I was that little fugitive in a crop top, sneaking into the city I was seduced by, intoxicated by the things it taught me. It felt like anything could happen at any time back then. I'd only set foot in G-A-Y twice since I was barred as a whippersnapper – to see Madonna emerge from a gigantic disco ball, and to support Amy as she launched *Back to Black* there, a night that was cut short by her leaving the stage to puke one song into the set. Well, it appeared that G-A-Y was my heel back in the door to a regular pay cheque. During the construction of a high-speed railway line that was to be built right through the Astoria's dance floor, the team behind G-A-Y had acquired ownership of Heaven and moved the night over there. On Fridays, they had a spare room to fill, up in the lofty Star Bar. I knew those four walls so well.

The club night was hardly a destination for musical connoisseurship, but I pitched hard to bring my flavour to it. I would lean into my house-music lineage and DJ for three hours – a long time for me. I'd be down there every Friday. The show was back on the road. The party was far from over.

Once, I felt I had to be drunk to DJ. Now, newly liberated from liquor and chemicals, I had to focus on the intoxication of club culture instead. This was my real reason for returning to the dance floor – my passion for it. But being the 'life of the party' was a difficult reputation to live up to, and now I had to do it without the crutches of a glass of vodka and the sniff of a line. Challenge accepted.

As important as it had been to separate from Jodie for a while to focus on my recovery, it was *so* good to return to her – I'd missed that part of myself. I stood there, in the empty room, deep under the platforms of Charing Cross Station, and ruminated for a moment. I remembered the friendships that formed there, and fleeting bursts of intimacy. I daydreamed of dancing right in the middle of that floor until closing time.

The house lights dipped suddenly, and I jolted back into work mode. I hit play on the CDJs: 'The Weekend', by Michael Gray, which summarised my returning enthusiasm for the dance floor. The stealthy security guards bobbed their heads – always a good indication of a banger. The sonic textures on the loud sound system thwarted my eardrums, and my heart began to thrum in sync with the kick drum.

Just as the doors were about to open, I suddenly felt hypersensitive without the sedation of booze. I wasn't used to playing opening sets, but caught in my mid-career lull, I knew I had to eat humble pie. There's a real skill in warming up a room, and I admired anyone who could do it well, because I'd never cracked it. The superhero costume of drag helped. It had always been my armour.

The initial trickle of attendees flopped through. Starting with a void in front of me, and seeing it gradually fill up with strangers felt like watching a movie. People I didn't know thrilled all around, and without a numbing agent, I felt their energies. I was reminded of the poetry of nightclubbing. I harnessed the art of the moment and slowly built a vibe from the ground up using just sonics, hoping to enhance someone's weekend. That communal feeling, that collaboration between clubber and DJ, felt more visceral than ever.

From the slightly raised booth, I was voyeuristic to unfolding plot lines. Being detached, rather than in the core of the party, felt new, but OK. I clocked a young guy – he must have been at least eighteen, because Heaven had become much tighter on ID checks – who wandered in shortly after we opened. He was wearing an outfit that would have been painstakingly questioned in the lead-up to his night out, and he skirted the circumference awkwardly. He appeared to be alone. Our eyes locked for a moment, and he smiled, and I smiled back, recognising my younger self.

At twenty-five, I was a veteran, but for some, the clubbing story was just starting. I wondered where I would be now if I hadn't followed through with those vows of adolescence, hadn't hurtled into

London every weekend. Discovering I had a safe space and finding my tribe had brought me home. Nightclubs had been my avenue down which to stomp bravely, express myself freely, and ultimately grow up, and I think they probably saved my life. When the room was full, the kid had disappeared into the anonymity of the crowd, on his 'choose your own adventure' journey. I hope he chose wisely.

DJing for G-A-Y at Heaven saw me through the first year of my sobriety, and created a base layer of income that allowed me to eat and live. Other gigs appeared on the horizon, and the rhythm of work was back in my blood. I drank so much Red Bull that year, I'd often think I'd been spiked. A couple of times, I reached for the wrong drink by accident, and a whiff of whisky threw me into a spin. But it wasn't appealing. I knew I couldn't go back. I held on to how miraculous it was that I was able to see a new chapter through a sober lens without temptation, and I was relieved to be able to be there, operating in the club world I felt so much passion for.

I hit play on Jodie Harsh: the remix. We were back out dancing.

13

DIU
SHADOW LOUNGE
MADAME JOJO'S

n the centre of the stage, under a little spotlight, I belted out my rendition of 'If I Only Had a Brain'. My straw wig was teased to perfection, my choreography was on point, and my make-up warmed under the glare. I was in heaven: the little boy who was told he was gay in the playground before he knew what the word meant, finally the centre of attention. As I held my final note, I tossed a shoulder and winked at the audience as applause erupted. That felt delicious. I caught my mum beaming at me from the front row.

When I look back at the pictures, I don't see the Scarecrow. I see a limp-wristed kid who was told off for lisping by his father. I see his first time in drag, his first time being noticed for a creative flair. His first time being the star of the show.

Years later, I was still in Oz. Some things would get broken, and some people would get lost along the way, but I was still dancing down the Yellow Brick Road.

———

I was back blazing through Soho's ill-lit underworld – I had missed its dirt and danger. A reliable Addison Lee dropped me at the cross-roads of Old Compton Street, Wardour Street and Brewer Street, still a minuscule precinct of densely packed, naughty recreation. Where vaudeville theatre and peep shows once flourished before my time, the Shadow Lounge, Madame Jojo's, the Village, Freedom and Escape stood proudly.

My heels felt sharp and musical clacking on the pavement. I shook my head to offers of 'cocaine, cocaine' from shifty dealers, and pushed through a cloud of weed smoke. As I tried to cross the road outside Prowler, I was caught in the impassable procession of the Hare Krishnas. The old Raymond Revue Bar sign was illuminated above my head, that vestige of a Soho gone but not forgotten. It seemed to be taking its last blinking breaths. Thieves still infected the bustle of Brewer Street – I dodged a hand that reached for my iPhone as I stepped up to the door. A near miss, thanks to my streetwise reflexes. You always had to keep your wits about you in Soho. It seemed like this district of debauchery hadn't completely cleaned up its act just yet.

I met my friend Munroe Bergdorf under the silver rhinestones of the Madame Jojo's sign. Cloistered beside the sordid magic of Walker's Court and a greasy noodle bar that opened late for the well-oiled, it was an iconic spot that had hosted burlesque, drag and live-music nights since the 1950s. The club was a refuge for anyone who refused to conform. Back when I was drinking, I'd often find myself shaking free of a blackout at the anarchic White Heat. Every Tuesday it was packed to the brim. It's where I first saw Bloc Party, Grimes and the Horrors perform live. I remember Bob Geldof bursting through to drag his daughter Peaches out of there – it was the night before her GCSEs.

By 2010, I'd be more likely to rock up on Wednesdays to their 'Trannyshack' fete. Back then, words like that would be volleyed about with reckless abandon. You certainly wouldn't want to name a party that any more.

Munroe was hosting the door and beckoned for me to jump past the queue of queens in regalia, trans women, and a few good-time gay boys. She yanked me in for a hug and a quick-fire-round catch-up – she was by now a close friend, and one who had never known me to be drunk or high. She was brilliant fun, and a reliable confidante on the other end of the phone. I hated when people didn't pick up a call – I'm old-school like that. Munroe and I would talk on speakerphone most nights while we were getting ready – she was moving from a job in PR into the nightlife world, where she felt more embraced as a trans woman.

At the same time, I was starting over in clubland, and reshaping my life from the ground up. Abstinence gave me the opportunity to be more socially selective and allowed me to cultivate genuine relationships with people. I had built a wall up – physically, through drag, as well as metaphorically. But now I let it down selectively, for good folk, aware of the importance of the real ones in among the transient friendships you had to keep making in clubland. But thinking about it, most of the people I knew and loved, I had met at night.

Madame Jojo's was a palatial dream of kitsch – all brass railings and raspberry velvet. It felt like an artefact from a Soho that had already departed before I arrived, something from a James Bond set, or the Kit Kat Club in *Cabaret*. The neighbourhood had once boasted myriad basements and boltholes where one could dance and misbehave, and now it was down to the last few.

I tottered through the swell, mwah-mwahing empty air kisses to painted faces I recognised but names I didn't know. I slipped into the dressing room, which felt carnivalesque. A vision of half-made-up, half-naked performers in tucking panties greeted me, as did the festering fumes of a drag queen garment rail. Lady Lloyd was fiddling, preparing to take over the DJ decks from Tasty, her pert bottom hanging out of something Westwood and threadbare. I saw Genie D in the corner – she was a cockney drag queen of perhaps eighty years, with a solo tooth, and a 'hit' single called 'Spider On Me 'Ed'.

Then a few paces across the flickering lights of Brewer Street brought us to Shadow Lounge. This place was Soho's idea of plush. Inside, magnolia was out and aubergine tones filled every inch. Shadow was born in the ribcage of an old porno cinema, and started its club life as a fabulous sink of salacious antics. I first went there in the days when it was in direct competition with Sweet Suite, a time when I was barely old enough to step over the threshold of a nightclub. A decade later, we called it the Shallow Lounge, and this particular Wednesday night it was modestly populated. I clocked a hen party in pink cowboy hats on the light-up dance floor and a pair of reality TV contestants rollicking around the once-infamous stripper pole. The DJ was crashing 'Firework' by Katy Perry into 'Levels' by Avicii in an empty room of terrible acoustics, and he looked over it.

Me and a couple of pals I'd scooped up across the road sat in a cordoned-off VIP booth, the exact spot where I used to buy my coke from a discreet waiter. A middle-aged woman in a trilby and pinstripe jacket chewed my ear off about the club scene not being the same any more. 'I used to go to Trade back in the day, you know, back when it was still good,' she declared through cracked, dry lipstick, as a little clump of white powder tumbled out of her nostril, landing on her lap. A male companion, who was all tits and teeth in a very deep V-neck knitted jumper, chimed in. 'Yeah, London's over, babe, it's shit now. I'm moving to Manchester.' I laughed awkwardly as I started to stand up. I couldn't bear people moaning about the good old days. You know what was good about those times? You were young. Things change.

'Babe, where are you going? You're fab,' one of them cried in a shrill voice. I couldn't tell which. My social battery was low, and I'd deported myself from the VIP booth. Since I quit self-medicating, my tolerance for drunk, meaningless chit-chat was pretty much down to zero.

The sonic trail of 'We Found Love' led us to the exit. We thought about where else might be open at this time on a weeknight within the limits of Soho and stalked across to the other side of its boundary, leaving the tacky dancing of the Shadow Lounge to sprawl beneath the street. We slunk through the passage of clip joints and video shops round the back of Shadow and galloped down Old Compton. We migrated alongside the animals that come out when the sun goes down. In the exact spot Henry VIII stalked his trophy deer, we hunted down our next club.

We cut past Ronnie Scott's, and looped around to Trisha's. This institution was a mainstay for the media set, and a migraine of a speakeasy – all mismatched furniture and forgotten nooks. Trisha herself was in there – she was a bastion of old-school Soho and poured drinks for the literary agents, off-duty jazz singers and winding-down West End dancers.

I nursed a Sprite. It was 1 a.m., and I was sober and tired. I did something completely alien to the old, derelict me – I called it a night. I thought about my past behaviours, and how this would just be the beginning in a great scheme, a long-form adventure, and the thought made my chakras tighten up. I stepped out on to Greek Street, hailed a hackney carriage, and headed home to sleep.

Nocturnal wanderlust had taken hold again – sobriety happily intact – and I was back out almost every night, restoring my social register. My night-vision goggles were firmly back on, and I had my sights set on a new club night. My friend Mark had a car – a rarity in this town, or at least in my social circle – and we drove around from party to party, scoping out the scene for research purposes. There were more venues around then, so much breathing space for parties to survive and thrive. I spent a whole month underground in subterranean other-worlds, plotting and planning my next move.

I yearned for that familiar feeling of being the central figure of the fiesta, curating the line-ups, playing host. A shoal of people dancing together within four walls represented everything I stood for and believed in – liberation of the dance floor, the creation of a space for marginalised people, the nourishment of community. I was good at providing that, and after being knocked down, I felt it was my duty to get back in the ring and provide it once again. I had my reservations, of course – I used to be in among it all, getting fucked up, and I'd bucked the order of things by getting sober. Could I still deliver that good time? Did I still have that disco energy? Could fragments of my career as a club promoter be salvaged?

There was no question that this club night had to be mine, and only mine. I was still working through some authority issues – a learned response from some of my past relationships – so I couldn't share ownership with anyone else: no business partners for me. I got word of a little venue marooned down the arse-end of Greek Street that was empty on Thursdays, and cold-called to see if they'd hire it out to me on a weekly basis. Within a day, I was in Diu for a meeting.

The floor plan was a Soho dream. Passing through a little

vestibule and down some stairs, making a sharp right, took you to a rich matrix of wine-cellar-like rooms with curved ceilings. It was dense with sneaky private spaces. I loved how your eyes couldn't take in the whole club in one sweep. Little hidden corners piqued my curiosity and I imagined secret liaisons occurring within them. The walls were gold, and tiny twinkling stars were encased in the ceiling. Multiple rooms were carved out in a circular pattern, and I liked the idea of a return to more intimate settings like the clubs I'd read about from the eighties. Squeezing everyone into tiny spaces could get things going a bit faster, like a pressure cooker. I told the owners to give me ten weeks to create an impact. It took three.

A bankrupt Britain was emerging from the doldrums, and, with my body resuscitated by the rhythm of the cultural heartbeat, I could sense what was needed: a sweatbox with a grumbling sound system and a bad smell that never lifted. I called the night Room Service.

I gathered my source material – the clubs of a New York long gone – the Saint, Paradise Garage, the Tunnel. And, just like I did with Circus, and For3ign, I assembled my cast. A collective of DJs like Fat Tony, Severino, Smokin Jo, and my flatmate Kris, who I could trust to curate a hypnotic orchestration of house music from opening time until 3 a.m. I put together a family of hosts, the most popular girls in town like Munroe and Johanna Londinium, and some fabulous club kids like La Pequena and Smiley Vyrus, who could summon their squads down on a guest list. I set a lighting colour palette with the venue's technician – reds, yellows and purples only – green and blue made people look older than their years. I held auditions for a team of go-go boys, who'd shake their butts in little thongs. I felt like Robin Williams in *The Birdcage*. I was back to being a social benefactor.

The hot-pink logo was plastered all over the streets and the opening night came in a flurry of excitement. 'Jodie Harsh is back in Soho!' cried the free club rags, despite the fact I had never really left its frayed edges. Most of my favourite NA meetings were at the walk-in NHS health centre on Frith Street, about twelve steps around the corner from the entrance of Diu.

We ran into problems immediately. The music wasn't loud enough, for a start – I accepted the lack of a Funktion-One system, but I expected a little more of a thud. As DJ Steve Pitron cued up his first track on opening night, it sounded tinny and light, and it was obvious that a room full of bodies would absorb what little sound there was. You could hear everybody's conversations on the dance floor. I dived over to the booth, which was the size of a plane's cockpit, and found it was redlining at full volume. From the floor, through no fault of his own, it sounded as if Steve was playing on a kitchen radio.

It stank in there – the cafe next door virtually pumped garlic through the air vents, but we made it much worse. I can smell it like it was yesterday – simmering, steroid-injected meat. Mix together the pong of armpit and mephedrone, and the festive aromas of poppers and urinal cubes, and you've got the stench that hung in the air of Room Service. It really assailed the nostrils as you oozed through.

The club was so over the council-enforced capacity of three hundred people that the constant flow of movement between rooms I had envisioned became impossible. I slid through gaps in the gridlock, having half-conversations with clubbers, barely completing sentences. Small talk had never been a strength of mine. And those little crannies that I saw and thought anything could happen in? Well, it did. I must have marched into at least five mini-orgies in blind spots on one lap of the club. I was concerned for the venue's licence and broke them up. 'Behave yourselves, boys!' I barked, like some bawdy soap opera pub landlady.

By midnight, I was convinced we were the hottest club on the planet, literally. It was so uncomfortably humid that liquid cascaded down the walls and trickled into the DJ equipment. Infinity mirrors, intended to give the illusion of a much bigger space, failed in their mission. They became great Niagara Falls of perspiration. Make-up dribbled in the corners of my eyes and the sweat on my upper lip mingled into my red pout. I licked the saltiness, took a deep breath, and sloshed through the vapour. I'd draw comparisons with the Battle of the Somme, if it were appropriate. The main bar was three-deep, so I assumed we were making bank. The venue denied they'd turned the air conditioning off to keep the tills ringing – I was dubious. And then there was the very real threat of someone fainting at any moment, which added suspense to the night.

Glamorous Monique, the LA icon with augmented lips and 38 FFF boobs, was crowd-surfing atop a daisy chain of muscle Marys. George Michael was huddled among a swarm of party boys at the corner table – I said hi and took a mental picture of that tableau. Fabulous! Lindsay Lohan was there – she would have been thrown out for smoking on the dance floor if it weren't for Daniel Lismore negotiating with security. Oh, it was good to be back.

The notion of a 'gay club' seems like an anachronism these days, but from that first night, it was clear our communion was Gay with a capital G. Room Service was a whole buffet of testosterone with a sprinkle of club freak mixed in. It felt like a new market for me, but I had that ability to transform from scene to scene, the only constant in my career being my wig. The display of flesh in sex-sodden Soho was nothing new, but by 1 a.m., every vest and T-shirt in the room was tucked into a back pocket. 'It's definitely one for the TOTO crowd; that's our demographic,' I explained to Munroe the day after on the phone. 'What does that even mean?' she asked. I could hear her preparing to eye-roll. 'Tops Off, Tits Out!' I said. 'I'm going, bye,' she retorted, and hung up, laughing.

Some naysayers grumbled that the crowd was too male-heavy, but we always encouraged girls along for the ride, and we loved having our female and non-binary family down at Room Service. Deep in that temple of flesh, there was a real sexual charge in the room, so it was great fun to see non-male faces sandwiched in between slabs of hairy abs, as if trying to escape. That first night, it was clear the party was all about shared bodies and shared experience, soundtracked by great house music, and I felt confident in sticking to that mission statement. If my dance floor inspired beautiful moments of togetherness and the exchange of bodily fluids, the roll of the dice had succeeded.

As I'd proved my worth to the club owners at the first party, they installed an expensive set of gigantic speakers. I was poised for week two. 'I was born to be on that weekly party treadmill,' I convinced Susie, my sponsor, who was concerned that spending so much time in clubs again might play havoc with my head.

Lo and behold, I was struck by my traditional curse of the difficult second night. Only 150 people showed up. It was not enough to cover my costs, and not quite enough to pack out the space, but still a hundred more than were dancing in the Shadow Lounge that night. I knew, because I'd sent a spy over.

By week three, we were back to our usual programming. It was rammed. Now that things were set up, I could confidently walk into the party at twelve thirty, avoiding the awkward first two hours as the club filled up. I wanted to pull up on Greek Street in an Uber Exec, duck past the iPad-wielding door host and wade into a peak-time bowl of demented soup.

I texted Jasmine, my trusted assistant, when I was on my way down in the cab. 'How is it?'

'Bonkers. Stampede outside.'

'Perfect. Hot?'

'Sweltering. Just warning.'

'HMMMM. Any PWK?'

The acronym stood for People We Know, meaning, were there any scene faces I needed to double-kiss hello to, was there anyone famous in the house, and were any of my real friends there yet . . . ? I picked up the phrase from a friend who ran a members' club, and used it before every party I threw. So useful.

Hysterical scenes greeted me and I made a beeline for the Laser Room at the back, finding the atmosphere to be already loopy. Heat radiated from the walls like a hammam. I'd opted for the poor choice of insulated Jeremy Scott ski trousers with wings attached to the hips. I resigned myself to a night of drench, and every conversation was based around shared suffering. We never did get that air-con fully sorted . . .

We took our music very seriously at Room Service. I'd rushed in to a Julio Bashmore track – a bootleg remix of '212' by Azealia Banks began pushing through it aggressively. Boys were snogging – I was happy to create a space where encounters between complete strangers could freely occur on neutral ground. Someone told me there was a blowjob happening beneath the DJ booth, and I believed them. Queens were hanging from the low ceiling as if they were checking for asbestos. This was the mad energy that gave me life.

At one point that night, the fog machine got stuck on full pelt. We were using a tutti-frutti-scented liquid – it didn't smell as organic as one might have hoped – and it was too thick for the mechanism. It must have tripped out the wiring, because we couldn't turn it off, and only the manager, who was nowhere to be found, knew where it was plugged in. The entire venue filled up as if we'd started a bonfire on the dance floor, and you couldn't see your hand in front of your face. Gym bunnies were tripping out and spluttering, shrouded in greyish quicksand, only making out the occasional blurry pop of a disco light. The smog seemed to carry the stench of poppers along with it, so everybody got a bit dizzy. Stuff like that happened all the time there.

A few of the queens from a new American show called *RuPaul's Drag Race* were there. I was big into the idea of drag bursting out into the mainstream, and not just designated to an abstract underground. The art form shoves queerness down people's throats, which is only a good thing for the cause. It had been in the backstreets and the edge of society, and now it was re-emerging on to TV, bigger than ever. I knew the world would catch up eventually. Diva explosion: detonated.

Out on to Greek Street with Scottee for a moment of respite from the mugginess and a half-time Marlboro Light – I still hadn't kicked that habit. It felt like a plague pit of crime out there. The stretch of Greek Street that became the Room Service smoking area was littered with silver nitrous oxide canisters. It was so loud and raucous out there that it was nigh-on impossible to hear a conversation while smoking. Young bandits hung around to pickpocket weaving guests as they departed, a famous Soho dealer was selling dope to passers-by from his wheelchair, and there was a foul-smelling hot-dog stand that would pull up at peak time – honestly, all the signs of a great party. Everyone's jaws were gurning, and there was the familiar presence of a barefoot dishevelled girl who used to run backwards and forwards shouting at everyone in tongues. Rumour had it she'd served time for slicing a punter's nipple off, unprovoked. She was terrifying, but at the same time a mascot of the old Soho I loved. I once made the mistake of asking if she needed any help, which seemed to encourage some kind of demonic exorcism, and the bouncers had to jump in and protect me.

I lit up a second cigarette in succession. 'Oh, here she comes, the walking bed sheet,' bitched Scottee, announcing the inevitable arrival of Daniel Lismore, who'd parted the crowd like Moses. He was trailed by a line of disciples in drag who almost tripped over his flowing hair, and as he got closer, I noticed a pair of black eyes. Attacks on queer people were increasing at a frightening rate, even in Soho. 'What the fuck happened?' I gasped, at first unsure if it was some ironic make-up look. 'I was with Kelly Osbourne and Steve Strange,' Daniel began, getting the key points in at the top of the story. 'Some guy spat at me, thinking I was vulnerable because I had balloon tits and stripper heels on.' They should have known better, I thought. 'I told him off, then he retaliated by punching me to the floor. Luckily my balloon breasts saved me.' The police had been called by a passer-by, and they'd let his attacker go, instead questioning lovely Daniel as his face dripped with blood.

I had friends who carried cans of mace for peace of mind. Being shouted at and abused on the street was part of the invisible contract you had to sign when you were 'different'.

Room Service was a funny old environment to be a sober person in, but I've always done things unconventionally. I seethed with jealousy as a pair of boys I used to bump and grind with disappeared into the toilet together, a four-legged beast spied under the cubicle door. A quick flash of *Could I? Should I?* No – I fast-forwarded the tape and reminded myself of my strong step one.

'Why aren't you drinking? Want a line?' asked some party goblin leaning into the booth, as I sat with Fat Tony downing Red Bulls as he DJ'd. 'We don't do drugs – fuck off!' growled Tony, dipping the booth monitor, as I cackled.

By this point, months into my recovery, booze and drugs were much less triggering. What really got me going was being HALT – Hungry, Angry, Lonely, Tired. Any of those four things turned me into a demon. Unable to anaesthetise sensations with chemicals, I was left to fester in my feelings. That's why I needed the programme, the people and its tools – I had to learn to deal with real life.

I got sober at the right time. There was a more aggressive hedonism taking over London's queer scenes. GHB and crystal meth were dark and rife in clubs, continuing to destroy lives. Now the city was in the grip of mephedrone, which was basically weedkiller. It gave you the alertness of coke, the spaced-out feeling of ecstasy and the horniness of GHB. It burned your nose like hell, but it was dirt cheap, and everyone seemed to love it.

The 'chill-out' scene was booming – where people would get together at designated homes to escape into the depths of sex and stimulation. I often wondered if this culture evolved due to the tide of HIV and AIDS that decimated our elders before the time we came along. We were still told we'd get sick and die if we loved who we wanted to love. I wondered if Section 28 and the erasure of gay identity at school had left permanent scars. I wondered, too, if there were myriad pockets of trauma from dads like mine, wishing their kids weren't quite so different, and telling them. What effect would that have on a generation?

I felt lucky to escape this scene by some serendipitous timing, but I heard horror stories. There was one boy, called Kevin, who had just moved to London from a little village in the north. He loved Room Service and came every Thursday in a brand-new top. I'd always have a chat with him and give him a drinks ticket – buying a new T-shirt for a party every week was an expensive habit. He couldn't have been older than twenty-one and I loved having him there. He was good energy, always smiling. On New Year's Day, he was at a chill-out, where he had a GHB-induced fit. The other people at the party – who weren't his friends – plonked him down on the sofa to recover, then left to go to a circuit party. When they returned twelve hours later, he was still in the same position on the sofa, dead. Sadly, there were a lot of boys like Kevin in London.

———

Six months into Room Service, business was booming at the department of commerce and drama. I got paid my bar percentage and door money in cash, and I'd sit in the office counting it at 3 a.m., heels off, rubbing the soles of my feet and wincing as my ingrown toenails were freed from their entrapment.

I've always thought of the raving industry as very respectable, and important for the country's economy, therefore I always paid every penny of tax I owed. The last thing I wanted was an embarrassing cat-and-mouse chase with HMRC. Since my initial foray into club work, I'd heard horror stories of club promoters and DJs fucking each other over, sending flyers to the Inland Revenue to show where they'd been playing, resulting in huge investigations and fines. No, sir, not for me – I declared it all. Club folk who don't pay what they owe are a perennial gripe of mine – the only things you can't escape on the dance floor of life are death and taxes.

Before Room Service, I'd been bent double for cash, borrowing money from my mum and racking up big credit-card bills that I'd only paid the monthly minimum on. Cheques would bounce until I moved money over from different accounts, as if I was playing the stock market. Now, thanks to the club, I was solvent, and then some.

When I'd get home from Soho in the first light of Friday, I'd sit in the middle of my bedroom and lay out my profit into stacks of £100, covering every available surface. I felt like Scarface. Money made me feel valued. My flatmate walked in one time and wondered what the hell was happening, as I perched cross-legged in the middle of thousands of pounds, my face full of make-up and my wig set down next to me. I looked like some rich circus clown. I guess seeing all that cash reminded me of freedom and made me feel successful. But my bank balance never fed me the same way that throwing a great party or performing a great DJ set ever did. That was real wealth to me.

In the aftermath of my recovery, it wasn't all success, success, success. My career also needed time to recuperate. I set up a Friday-night party at Moonlighting a few doors down Greek Street, as a sort of overspill for Room Service – after all, not everyone could make it out on a weeknight. I truly brought my B game, and it was barely even a one-hit wonder. Clubland could be cut-throat. There were a few rushed half-hearted projects like that. They taught me to focus on one project at a time – greediness ate up my creativity.

Around the same time, it seemed Diu was suffering money troubles – I think Room Service was the only night bringing in any profit. At 9 p.m. one Thursday, an hour before our doors were due to open, the bailiffs came knocking. Disco lights were pulled down, the smoke machine was finally unplugged, and the DJ equipment was lifted out and stacked into a van. We'd booked the New York-based DJ Honey Dijon to play that night, who I was a massive fan of, and it was set to be a major moment for us. At the eleventh hour – literally at 11 p.m. – we were rescued with a set of CDJs and a mixer from a bar called Circa down the road, where Munroe DJ'd. We were back on, temporarily. That's community.

———

Deep into summer 2011, and London was undergoing unrest. Riots in the streets meant shopfronts were being pilfered and the news was full of looting and arson. There were false rumours of captive animals being let out of the cages at London Zoo – lions and giraffes were allegedly roaming the streets as if the city was a game reserve. Much was exaggerated by the media, but it was impossible to deny the city had reached its tipping point as austerity measures kicked in.

Every other venue in Soho seemed to be boarded up or sold to a big chain. Our venue shuttered up, and Room Service relocated across the street to a different club. It never brought the magic that Diu did. I was slowly giving up on preserving the old Soho and looked further east. All good things move on, and the best parties have always thrived on uncertainty and precarity.

Shortly after celebrating one year clean and sober, I received a call from my mum. 'Turn on the news,' she said. 'Your friend Amy Winehouse has died.' I was confused – as far as I knew, Amy had cleaned up her life. I opened Twitter, and saw it was true. The world was shocked, and, as we mourned her, everyone in her orbit secretly wondered if we could have done more.

London was a city in a permanent state of change, fragile yet resilient. The same could be said about me, as I continually worked on myself, while keeping the party going. I refused to fall over on the dance floor, even though decadence was the easiest way to go down. Gradually, a lot of my favourite clubs were obliterated or built over, but collective memories couldn't be erased. Night-time venues were regarded as frivolous by most people. They weren't real culture. They were noisy, smelly places, full of trouble and danger. But not to me, and not to my friends. To us, they were essential.

AFTER-PARTY

Bethnal Green
Working Men's Club

t was the end of the night at Bethnal Green Working Men's Club. I'd dropped into a party that unified so many people in what had otherwise become a fragmented club scene: Sink the Pink. The night was a high-voltage shock of DIY fun and, in 2012, it felt like it was the very centre of London. At the same time, London felt like it was the very centre of the world. I still loved this city, and most of the time, it loved me back.

Backstage, no one wanted to go home. They *were* home.

Glyn, the night's co-founder, was doing a handstand while his business partner Amy held the fort. Jake Shears was deep in conversation with camp queen Ginger Johnson, who was in a wedding dress like Kate, Britain's new Duchess of Cambridge. Louie Banks was taking photos. The DJ Joshua James was talking about hi-NRG with John Sizzle. Jonny Woo was lighting a firecracker from his bottom. Steph was collecting glasses – she was old-school, and had been at the venue since anyone could remember. Jonbers Blonde had been swinging from the rafters, and Sam Smith was helping her down. Bryan Adams was there, somewhere, randomly. Jacqui Potato was, of course, laying an egg. There was no rhyme or reason to any of it, and it was brilliant. Oh yes, and the Vengaboys were in the house, after performing on the Sink the Pink stage.

Since I'd walked into the Astoria more than a decade before, and shot like a rocket into orbit in front of the Vengaboys, I like to think I'd helped sprinkle London's skies with some stardust, even if

I did plummet back down to earth like a burned-out shell several times. Here I was, two years sober, still shining, still hungry for it.

I walked out through the emptied main room, past the wood-panelled bar and the twinkling heart that framed the stage. My ears were ringing, and I could still feel the energy of the crowd vibrating in the walls, the ghosts of joy. It seemed small in there without the comforting dimensions of club life. It looked so much bigger when it was packed with bodies. It must have been a mirage.

I thought about all the people who had loved that club over the years. It had been there since 1887. Like me, this place had lived many different lives.

A notification told me my Uber was outside, finally – the Olympics were turning this city into a bloody nightmare to get around. I crunched across the carpet, kicking away discarded cans and tinsel.

Squeezing through a gap in the door, I was out of the haze, and back into reality. I had an early start the day after – in a studio, of all places. I'd been starting to learn how to make music. It was a new way to channel my energy, and tell my stories. The change in tempo felt exciting, and scary. And after the studio, I had a DJ set, somewhere outside of London. I couldn't stand still in one place for too long any more.

It had been a fun night. Very fun. But was it the best night of my life? Nah, no way. I still don't think I've had that yet.

I turned back to look at the venue, its crumbling brick facade. The sun was rising behind it, painting the sky a burnt orange. *This place will probably be gone soon,* I thought, *just like all the others.*

That's the thing with London. They can bulldoze this city to the fucking ground if they want. But they can't stop us dancing – we'll just find another floor to do it on. As long as there are freaks and lovers and music, there will be clubs.

And as long as there are clubs, as long as there's a party, I'll be there.

In Memory of Those Who Went Home Early

When you live a life on the edge, sadly you must expect a few comrades to call it an early night. Here are the friends and family who slipped out the back door after this story ended.

Dad

While I was in the final stages of writing this book, my dad died, very suddenly, of a heart attack. I'm a believer in letting go of anger, and the moment I heard he was gone, I dropped any negativity I held against him. I had a brilliant, creatively nurturing childhood with my father – my love of music, performing and writing all came from him. We'd listen to Motown and blues and read books every night, without fail. I'll continue to remember that stage of our lives together fondly. After we fell out for the second time, neither of us reached out to reconnect. I wrote him a letter several years ago, but I didn't end up posting it.

Simon

Simon was a teacher and a mentor as well as a dear friend. To me, he personified Soho, and London. He helped shape my tastes, my opinions and my humour. He became family, and he's another piece of my London puzzle gone. My memories of him are tinged with happy tears.

Amy

We all remember that fateful day when Amy was found dead by a bodyguard in her home. I'd just turned one year sober when I heard the tragic news. I'd been imagining the newspaper headlines for a while, and then it happened – the Queen of Camden and the voice of a generation had left the stage.

Mary

My brilliant grandmother. She *loved* seeing me glammed up in my 'uniform'. She taught me to be fearless and be myself no matter the consequences. I miss her letters, her yummy food, her ability to talk to animals, and her healing hands. I was lucky to know her.

Kingsley

Just after I handed in my first draft of *You Had to Be There*, Kingsley passed away. He was so loved by so many people – *everyone* knew Kings. For a long time, we came as a pair. I'll cherish our decade of best friendship that stretched the duration of the years covered in this book. He's an angel now, flying high, dancing to Janet Jackson's 'Together Again', helping style my wigs, making me laugh.

Tomas

I had a roaring time with Tomas and his milieu. The first years of my London life were spent surging through dance floors and in and out of apartments until dawn with the most fun, rule-breaking crowd one could ever meet. Tomas, and his legendary ten-inch penis, will be missed by thousands.

———

IN MEMORY OF THOSE WHO WENT HOME EARLY

There are others in my world and in this book who left before the music stopped. Alexander McQueen, Lyndell Mansfield, Annabelle Neilson, Simon Hobart, Pete Burns, Sarah Harding, Judy Blame, Matt Irwin, Richard Nicoll, Peaches Geldof and many others. London, and the dance floor, is less fun without them.

Life is precious. Dance while you can.

In Memory of the Places We Danced

As I wrote this book, I ruminated on a clubbing landscape that had become almost unrecognisable. While I changed as a person, so did London nightlife. I'm not usually the retrospective type, but the realisation that most of these venues had been bulldozed, even if just metaphorically, brought me great sadness.

No clubs? No culture. In the last twenty years the mass extinction of nocturnal spaces has increased at an alarming rate. Apart from the lucky few, most venues are vulnerable to greed, re-appropriation and redevelopment, as well as moral outrage and media panic. The government's lack of intervention and support – despite music and nightlife being such a ginormous sector and bringing the UK money and prestige in exports – continues to baffle me. The cost of living crisis, Brexit and the Covid pandemic added further to the obliteration in more recent times.

But, like people, discos are not built to last. These windowless rooms we dance in are temporary pulses of pleasure – it's important that, like people, we value them while they're still here.

The London Astoria

The place my party journey began. Crossrail brought on its timely eclipse, and the last G-A-Y night here was in July 2008. The concrete pillars in the belly of Tottenham Court Road Underground Station hold up the ghosts of my past. It's a grave of memories – my first dance, my first kiss, my first drug. Everything in this town reincarnates as something else – that's just the London way – and this one is a fast train to Shenfield.

Turnmills

Oh, those early Sunday mornings thrashing around this corner of Clerkenwell. The former stable's lease came up for renewal in 2008 and the owner pushed for a lucrative office redevelopment. The global economy derailed the process for several years as it sat empty, but nowadays people sit tapping away at their computers on the former dance floor. Outside its meeting rooms, blue plaques mark the names of legendary DJs who spun there.

Pacha

Bizarrely housed within a bus terminus, the Ibiza superbrand's London outpost was refurbished in 2013. The DJ booth was repositioned, and a new room was created, but it failed to keep the flame alive, and it shuttered in 2014. Pacha took over the West End's Café de Paris in 2021 under their Lío umbrella, which uses a cabaret restaurant concept as opposed to a traditional dance club.

Sweet Suite

This one didn't last long at all. After a short-lived splash, the venue took on many guises, including the gay club LoProfile. It ceased operating as a disco in 2013 and the ground floor became a Vapiano pizza restaurant before that, too, closed. The guts of the club, where all the dancing happened, remain a mystery.

Ghetto

Like its next-door neighbour the Astoria, Crossrail buried this venue for ever. If you travel down the escalator into the Elizabeth Line at Tottenham Court Road Station, you're cutting right through the heart of Ghetto's dance floor. Say hi to the ghosts for me.

The End

After years of being the best club in London (I think that's actually official), the End changed hands and was retitled the Den. Its rather on-the-nose renaming should have served as a warning – the new club failed to emulate what had come before, and it closed in 2009. The last time I walked past, it was still boarded up.

Plastic People

This compact sweatbox was full of life and became a Petri dish for so many talented artists. After twenty years of operation, its perfectly calibrated sound system was ripped out and a swansong night was held in January 2015. It's now the Sunset Bar, and holds the latest licence in the area, which isn't saying much.

Boujis

The press reported that a major brawl resulted in the local council placing Boujis in a 'last-chance saloon' status. Then, a small punch-up in 2016 shut it down for good. The young royals' favourite club became a Five Guys burger bar, but the Boujis club lore didn't end there – some of the original team assembled B London around the corner.

Too2Much

The Raymond Revue became Too2Much became Soho Revue Bar became the Box. Lines continue to form down that dirty little alleyway, and debauched delights titillate inside, just as they ever did. I'm glad the Box is keeping the spirit of the area alive – it's still Soho, still sleazy, just a little more expensive.

Madame Jojo's

Once owned by porn and property baron Paul Raymond, Jojo's and her drag queens were forced out in 2014. Bouncers allegedly pulled out baseball bats hidden in bin liners to attack a group of assailants throwing glass bottles. Amid hard-fought, albeit fruitless fights to save Soho and its spaces, she ceased to glitter and twinkle. It was never previously a site of violence, so hopefully this mildly blemished reputation won't stop her from reopening one day in a new frock.

Aquarium

One of London's last remaining twenty-four-hour-licence venues suffered a similar fate to Madame Jojo's. A man was hospitalised for head injuries after being hit by a champagne bottle, and the council said, 'no more'. She thrummed for years and years, infecting all who swam in her with athlete's foot. It's currently NQ64, a games arcade bar, and is open until 2 a.m. at the weekends.

Mahiki

The venue changed hands, the tiki theme was removed, and the treasure chests were retired. Now called Tabu, it's an Asian-themed disco that might evoke the feeling of being in a backstreet of Seoul.

Movida

Nestled in next to the Palladium Theatre, this pleasure cellar has changed its outfit many times since I threw my twenty-third birthday party there, including Toy Room and Inca. It still operates as a nightclub today.

The Grill Room

Once a haunt of Oscar Wilde, this jewellery box of a room within Hotel Café Royal is no longer a raucous nightspot, but it is the backdrop for award-winning afternoon teas. The dancing powder has been swapped out for icing sugar!

The Cross

The famous doors closed for the final time on 1 January 2008 as work began on Europe's largest urban regeneration project. It's funny to see an area that was once so stark and sketchy become so gentrified. The Cross is now the Tom Dixon flagship store, in the heart of Coal Drops Yard.

Canvas

Bagley's, which became Canvas in its later years, always felt like a dystopian corner of an abandoned amusement park, but it was a real vanguard of the nightlife scene. No records have been played in the Victorian warehouse for years – it's now the main heart of University of the Arts London. The cobbles leading up to it – so much of a death trap in heels – remain.

Punk

Punk vanished without warning – no big crescendo, no farewell party. Today the site is occupied by a massive branch of Zara. My nights hanging out in its engine room will never be forgotten. Soho is a poorer place without it.

Bungalow 8

The black-and-white-striped walls in this subterranean bunker were a backdrop for every celebrity in the late noughties, but they've been painted over now. At one point Bungalow lost its liquor licence, and the place stayed open as a dry venue, a sort of celebrity Prohibition-era spot. It's still glitzy and dimly lit, operating as the Blind Spot bar underneath the St Martins Lane Hotel.

Mass

Rumour has it, the landlords of St Matthew's Church declared Mass's lease forfeit. Bailiffs attended at dawn to change the locks and post notices informing the club had been repossessed. The church still operates as a place of worship upstairs – I'd imagine the congregation weren't the biggest fans of hosting Torture Garden parties in their crypt.

Boombox

A club night rather than a venue, but a worthy mention as a huge part of noughties London club ecology. It was open for precisely one year – and the star of Boombox combusted as quickly as it was born, on New Year's Eve 2007. Its home, Hoxton Bar and Grill, still operates as a restaurant and drinking den.

The Bath House

This little gem of a building is still there, pretty much exactly as I left it. Now available exclusively for private hire, the Victorian spa has been scrubbed up and the birdcage dismantled, but it's thankfully one of the few London clubs mentioned in these pages that remains open.

The Shadow Lounge

After a refurbishment that saw it wrapped in LED-screen walls, Shadow fell victim to Soho's curse of clubs and the sweaty press of dancing bodies was no more. It lay dormant for a while before becoming a strip club.

Diu

I loved this little candy jar of a club, but after eighteen months my Room Service night began to stagnate. We'd heard whispers of a venue sale and decided to move across the street to another venue. Diu rebranded, then shut down, and the area around it was redeveloped into posh restaurants to coincide with the Soho spruce-up no one asked for. It's now the Little Scarlet Door, a house-party-themed bar.

———

Thankfully, at the time of writing, Heaven, Fabric, Ministry of Sound, the Scala, KOKO and the Hawley Arms still provide spaces of love and escapism for London. But one thing's for sure: these sanctuaries can be ripped away in a heartbeat.

The Guest List

Firstly – a massive thanks to you, the reader, for coming out for a dance with me. What a night! I've previously been the least retrospective person imaginable, and notoriously (almost laughably) private, but presenting my life to you in words has been beyond cathartic.

Thank you to Harriet, my literary agent at CAA, who approached me with the idea of writing about my youth. I initially resisted, but she convinced me to get a few chapters down, and before long this book was off and running. I loved writing it so much, and hopefully it won't be my last – so thank you, Harriet, for encouraging me to put finger to key (and finally use my writing degree!). A big thanks to Chris, my DJ agent at CAA, for connecting the dots and putting me on some of the most incredible stages around the world. What an adventure we're on!

Thank you Hannah Knowles at Faber for absolutely everything. I couldn't think of a better home to publish my memoir and editor to guide my storytelling. Thank you to everyone else at Faber who has been instrumental in this book's birth, especially Hannah Turner (publicity), Hannah Marshall (marketing), Rachael Williamson (project editor), Sara Cheraghlou (editorial assistant), Robbie Porter (designer), Pedro Nelson (production controller), and freelancers Sam Matthews (copy-editing) and Jodi Gray (proofreading). What a dream team!

Thank you to everyone I work with at Lucky Management, CAA,

Cherry Create, Listen Up, Feel It, Plugged In and Outrise. I'm so lucky to have such amazing people to support my mad ideas.

Thank you especially to my manager, Billy, for encouraging me to tell my story. He knew I could do this before I did.

Thank you to my early readers – friends who'd get emails with paragraphs of the material with subject lines like 'thoughts????????' and 'what the hell am I doing . . .' – notably David and Tash, Karen, Yann, Bestley, Kane, Dylan, Connor, Clayton, Tom, Jake, Russell and my amazing assistant Sert.

Thank you, Thomas Knights, for unearthing the cover photo (taken in Soho, somewhere around the 2010 mark). And thank you to Sarah Knights for the help tracking it down on a hard drive when Thomas was in LA – lifesaver!

Thank you to the friends who jogged my memory and filled in any factual gaps with texts, calls and late-night phone calls: Amy Sacco, Cozette, Jonny Hooley, Jasmine Blatt, Munroe Bergdorf, Tegan, Finn, Dean Piper, Daniel Lismore, Henry Conway, Fred Nash, Sadie Frost, Caiden, Heather, Jonjo Jury, Glyn Fussell, Luke Blackall, Hanna Hanra, Princess Julia, Rhyannon, Rich McGinnis, Dan Oliver, Scottee, Daniel Winterfeldt, Jaime Winstone. 'What was that awful person called again?' . . . 'Remember that little club down that alleyway?' etc., etc.

Thank you to Andro for reading the whole book out loud to me, from start to finish. It was an invaluable step before I made my final tweaks.

Thank you to my family for the eternal support, especially my mum and sister – I hope you don't find this book too gnarly. I'm fine! Thank you to my dad, too – he was an incredible parent while I was growing up, and even though I say I have no regrets in life, I do feel immense sadness that we stopped seeing eye to eye. I'm writing these acknowledgements the day after your memorial service, and I hope you're up there watching over me with pride.

I holed myself up a few times at Margate House to write some of the chapters – thank you to Will and your team for letting me stay, my home away from home. Kent for ever!

Thank you to everyone on this crazy journey – even if you're not mentioned in these pages, you helped shape me along the way. Thank you to people from my past who I'm no longer in touch with – they say life is too short for falling out, but sometimes, like seasons, friendships move on and change. You're still part of me and I hope I'm part of you.

Thank you to the writers and musicians I love. There are only twenty-six letters in the alphabet and eight notes in an octave but they've formed a lifetime of pleasure, escapism, inspiration and education. I am, first and foremost, a fan.

Thank you to those who work hard in London clubland to keep the dance going – and to absolutely everyone across the global industries of sound and socialising. These are lean times in nightlife, and your service is appreciated. Thank you to those of you who go out, support clubs, pay to get in and spend money behind the bar. Club culture needs you – without the people, there's no party.

Thank you for being there.